MASTERS AND STUDENTS

MASTERS
AND
STUDENTS

Jesuit Mission Ethnography in
Seventeenth-Century
New France

MICAH TRUE

McGill-Queen's University Press
Montreal & Kingston · London · Ithaca

ISBN 978-0-7735-4512-0 (cloth)
ISBN 978-0-7735-4513-7 (paper)
ISBN 978-0-7735-8199-9 (ePDF)
ISBN 978-0-7735-8200-2 (ePUB)

Legal deposit first quarter 2015
Bibliothèque nationale du Québec

Printed in Canada on acid-free paper that is 100% ancient forest free (100% post-consumer recycled), processed chlorine free

This book has been published with the help of a grant from the Canadian Federation for the Humanities and Social Sciences, through the Awards to Scholarly Publications Program, using funds provided by the Social Sciences and Humanities Research Council of Canada.

McGill-Queen's University Press acknowledges the support of the Canada Council for the Arts for our publishing program. We also acknowledge the financial support of the Government of Canada through the Canada Book Fund for our publishing activities.

LIBRARY AND ARCHIVES CANADA CATALOGUING IN PUBLICATION

True, Micah, 1981–, author
Masters and students : Jesuit mission ethnography in seventeenth-century New France / Micah True.

Includes bibliographical references and index.
Issued in print and electronic formats.
ISBN 978-0-7735-4512-0 (bound). – ISBN 978-0-7735-4513-7 (pbk.). –
ISBN 978-0-7735-8199-9 (ePDF). – ISBN 978-0-7735-8200-2 (ePUB)

1. Jesuits – Missions – Canada – History – 17th century.   2. Indians of North America – Missions – Canada – History – 17th century.   3. Indians of North America – Canada – History – 17th century.   4. Canada – History – To 1663 (New France).   I. Title.

FC315.T78 2015   266'.2714   C2014-906588-4
                                        C2014-906589-2

Set in 11/14 Adobe Garamond Pro
Book design & typesetting by Garet Markvoort, zijn digital

For Kim Dao

CONTENTS

ILLUSTRATIONS

ACKNOWLEDGMENTS

I am deeply indebted to Professor Michèle Longino of Duke University, who provided constant support and clear-eyed advice from the inception of this project through its final stages. She gave freely of her time and expertise, and as a result I am sure that this book is immeasurably better than it otherwise might have been. I am grateful for her generosity and friendship, and I could not have asked for a better mentor. I also wish to thank the other faculty members at Duke University who engaged with my work: David Bell, Roberto Dainotto, Laurent Dubois, Alice Kaplan, Walter Mignolo, Helen Solterer, and Orin Starn. Each gave valuable input at crucial moments in the project's development. Several of them made startlingly perceptive comments about early versions of this material that haunted me for years, and left clear marks on the finished book. Professors Luca Codignola of the University of Genoa, Vincent Grégoire of Berry College, Sara Melzer of UCLA, John Steckley of Humber College, and the anonymous referees commissioned by the press also graciously provided useful guidance, and I thank them for their interest in my work. I am also grateful to my friend John Lytle, who helped me muddle my way through a few lines of Latin that I needed to decipher for chapter six, and to John E. Bishop, who provided some useful feedback on an early draft of chapter five. Brenna Heitzman and her mother Barbara Heitzman first introduced me to Maria Doria Russell's novel *The Sparrow*, which led my thinking down a path that proved most fruitful. I am sincerely thankful for the helpful comments of my fellow graduate students at Duke University, and my colleagues at Tulane University and the University of Alberta who graciously listened to or read various versions of this material, and to the audiences at conferences in North America and Europe who did the same. This book is richer for the input of fine and generous scholars too numerous to list here. Any deficiencies, of course, remain my sole responsibility.

A number of institutions graciously provided financial support at various stages of this project, for which I am most grateful. This book has been published with the help of a grant from the Federation for the Humanities and Social Sciences, through the Awards to Scholarly Publications Program, using funds provided by the Social Sciences and Humanities Research Council of Canada. At Duke University, the Graduate School, the Department of Romance Studies, the John Hope Franklin Humanities Institute, and the Center for Canadian Studies funded my research and travel to conferences at early stages of this project, as did the Faculty of Arts at the University of Alberta once the project began to reach final form. A preliminary version of parts of chapter two appeared as "*Maistre et Escolier*: Amerindian Languages and Seventeenth Century French Missionary Politics in the *Jesuit Relations* from New France," *Seventeenth-Century French Studies* 31, no. 1 (2009): 60–71 (http://www.maneyonline.com/sfs). A preliminary version of chapter six, much revised and expanded here, appeared as "Travel Writing, Ethnography, and the Colony-Centric Voyage of the *Jesuit Relations* from New France," *American Review of Canadian Studies* 42, no. 1 (2012): 103–17 (Taylor & Francis Ltd, http://www.tandf.co.uk/journals). I thank both publishers for permission to reuse this material. The team at McGill-Queen's University Press – and especially Kyla Madden – has my deepest gratitude. Their professionalism in ushering this book into print was a breath of fresh air, and I was impressed at every step with their courtesy and skill.

Finally, I wish to thank members of my family who consistently supported this work and showed interest in it: Shelley Mc Laughlin-True, Tom and Nick True, and Giang, June, and Phong Dao. More than anyone else, my spouse, Kim Dao, deserves my sincere thanks for her support and patience during the nearly nine years that I spent working on this project. This book is dedicated to her. Last but not least, I am grateful to my sweet and exuberant daughter Alex, for providing comic relief during the final stages of this project.

PREFACE

The questions that this book takes up were on my mind long before I had even heard of the seventeenth-century Jesuit *Relations* from New France. My hometown, Haines, Alaska, was founded in the nineteenth century by Presbyterian missionaries who promptly set to work transforming the lives of the Tlingits who had occupied that corner of Southeast Alaska for centuries. At the same time as missionaries were actively suppressing Tlingit customs, European and American anthropologists were striving to preserve them in writing. Their accounts of their time among the Tlingits sometimes now serve as guides for modern members of that group who are seeking to relearn their ancestors' way of life, a phenomenon that apparently is not unique to Alaska Natives.[1] I vividly remember reading, while in college, an article in Haines' weekly newspaper that chronicled a local Tlingit woman's effort to persuade the University of Washington Press to reprint *The Tlingit Indians*, a book based on the unfinished nineteenth-century manuscript of ethnographer George Thornton Emmons. Her interest in seeing the book reprinted stemmed from a desire to preserve traditional cultural knowledge, she told the *Chilkat Valley News*: "A lot of our elders are passing on, and there's interest in the community to rekindle our heritage. We want to learn, and this book is such an accurate history. There are so many people who want this book."[2] I was fascinated by the fact that the woman's effort to access the knowledge of her own ancestors necessarily involved relying on the perceptions of an outside observer. Did Emmons' particular point of view, I wondered, have a discernible impact on the observations he recorded? What about the pressures no doubt exerted by his intended audience, presumably other anthropologists, or perhaps general-interest readers who had little previous knowledge of Alaska Native life? And what would reliance on his work mean for modern Tlingits? Would it produce a renaissance of their culture, or would the renewed cultural practices actually be something new, a version of nineteenth-century customs that reflected how they were perceived, shaped, and recorded by Emmons for the edification of a non-Tlingit audience?

In retrospect, I can see that my encounter with that article in the *Chilkat Valley News* was the beginning of my interest in textual representations of Otherness, and although I eventually found myself studying texts that were the products of intercultural encounters in very different historical contexts – the Mediterranean Sea and New France, primarily in the seventeenth century – the fundamental questions that I ask still are not much different from those that occurred to me while reading the newspaper many years ago. At its most basic level, this is a study of the fraught process of writing about unfamiliar cultures. It asks how we make sense of the unknown, in dialogue both with its representatives and with readers whose worldview more closely matches our own. Although I focus here on a relatively narrow topic – Jesuit missionary writings from seventeenth-century New France – I gesture at questions that might fruitfully be applied in any number of contexts.

A few preliminary remarks are in order. First, this book reflects the uncomfortable choices that await anyone who wishes to study the seventeenth-century Jesuit *Relations* from New France and to publish scholarship about them in English. Reuben Gold Thwaites' century-old edition of the texts remains the standard, despite the clear superiority of the more recent edition by the late Jesuit priest Lucien Campeau. Unlike many others who recently have studied the *Relations* or drawn on them as a source of historical information, I have opted to base my research and analysis on Campeau's *Monumenta Novae Franciae*. This choice, however, is complicated by two factors. First, the *Relations* appear in Campeau's edition in French only, whereas Thwaites' edition offers facing-page English translations of the texts, a feature that surely accounts in part for the continued popularity of the older edition. Because I am writing here in English, I have made use of Thwaites' translations in the chapters following these preliminary remarks. Although popular and widely cited, Thwaites' translations also, unfortunately, are often inaccurate. My own corrections to those translations, based on Campeau's text, are indicated in brackets and explained in endnotes, when necessary. In the rare cases where Thwaites' *Jesuit Relations* does not include a translation for a passage under examination, the translation offered is my own. Although circumstance forces me to draw on Thwaites for translations, I encourage the reader to consider Campeau the better starting point for any study of the *Relations*. It is for this reason that I have included in endnotes Campeau's text, in the original French, of all passages from the *Relations* cited here, instead of being content with Thwaites' translations alone. By giving Campeau's edition a prominent place in this book, I hope to avoid contributing to the continued primacy of the Thwaites edition, even if I must still rely on it for translations.

A second factor complicating my preference for the Campeau edition is the fact that it only includes the *Relations* published up to 1661, leaving the final decade of the published series unaccounted for. This is due to Campeau's death in 2003, and the failure so far of his Jesuit colleagues to finish his work. When I cite the *Relations* published after 1661, then, I reluctantly cite the Thwaites edition only. Fortunately, due to the nature of the published series itself, I refer only rarely to texts published after that date. The bulk of the missionaries' descriptions of the unfamiliar cultures of the New World were published in the 1630s and 1640s, when the Jesuits were grappling most intensely with their efforts to get to know their Amerindian would-be converts. The texts from the 1660s are largely given over to accounts of the violent clashes with the Iroquois that rocked New France during that decade, making them less significant to this study of Jesuit mission ethnography than the earlier texts in the series. Despite its weaknesses, which occasionally force recourse to the Thwaites edition, I endorse the Campeau edition as the soundest option to use when conducting research, for reasons that I and others have set out more fully elsewhere.[3] In keeping with the practice of other works that have drawn on these editions, Campeau's *Monumenta Novae Franciae* is abbreviated as MNF, and the initials JR are used to designate Thwaites' *Jesuit Relations and Allied Documents*.

It was recently pointed out to me that the common scholarly practice of referring to the Jesuits' seventeenth-century texts as the "*Jesuit Relations*" – which I myself often have done in my published work – improperly conflates the missionaries' reports with the popular Thwaites edition. The texts were not originally published under the title *Jesuit Relations*, but only came to be referred to that way after the appearance of Thwaites' work. To distinguish the texts themselves from one popular edition thereof, I use *Jesuit Relations*, with both words italicized, only to refer to Thwaites' edition. Otherwise, I refer to the texts as the Jesuit *Relations*, with only the second word italicized, since the French term *Relation* was the title under which the texts were published in the seventeenth century.

My use of the word "ethnography" to describe accounts of Amerindian cultures penned by Jesuit missionaries long before the emergence of anthropology as an academic discipline will no doubt aggravate some readers. It is an anachronism, but one that I employ purposefully and thoughtfully. Although sometimes taken to be a hallmark of shoddy scholarship, anachronisms also "provide a retrospective lens, enabling us to see more clearly what was less evident at any earlier time."[4] The Jesuit missionaries who wrote the *Relations*, and their counterparts in Europe who edited and published them, surely did not think of their texts as ethnographies, and especially not in a way that directly reflects the theories and standards of the modern academic discipline of cultural anthropology. And yet, the texts' enduring popularity is largely due to the fact that they contain rich data on poorly known groups, the fruit of experience of and presence among those groups. In this, they certainly resemble more modern ethnographic texts, and their frequent use as a source of data for modern ethnohistories suggests a certain kinship to ethnography regardless of whether the label is applied explicitly. Specifically framing the texts as ethnographic writing – and more precisely as *mission* ethnography – makes explicit a relationship that often is presumed, bringing into relief the ways in which the texts both resemble and differ from that particular form of writing. Casting my subject as Jesuit mission ethnography allows me both to explore the particular nature of ethnographic writing carried out by priests in a specific historical context, and to reflect on the relationship of that project to modern forms of writing about unfamiliar cultures, for which the Jesuit *Relations* are so often used as a source of data.

Finally, a brief word is in order about the names used here to designate the various indigenous groups with which the Jesuits were in contact. The names "Huron," "Montagnais," "Algonquin," and "Iroquois" are labels imposed on Amerindian groups from outside, by the Europeans who first encountered them during the colonial period. Increasingly, the name "Huron" is being replaced in ethnohistorical scholarship with "Wendat," the name that group used, and still uses, to designate itself.

Similarly, "Innu" is sometimes now preferred in place of "Montagnais," and "Nadouek" has been proposed as a more appropriate alternative to "Iroquois."[5] Although my first instinct was to embrace the more culturally sensitive terms that are increasingly used by modern scholars and by some Amerindian groups themselves, I ultimately decided to adopt the designations employed in the *Relations*. Using the names that Europeans gave to Amerindian groups reinforces one of the central premises of this book: descriptions in the *Relations* of various groups are not scientific specimens, but representations that reflect how the missionary authors of the *Relations* understood the groups with which they interacted. Those perceptions do not always correspond to modern understandings of the makeup of Iroquoian and Algonquian groups, or to how those groups perceive themselves. Using terms such as "Huron," "Montagnais," and "Algonquin" to refer to the groups that the Jesuits wrote about emphasizes the mediatory role that long-dead European observers play between Amerindian cultures and the modern scholars who seek to understand them. This book, after all, examines not those groups themselves, but rather Jesuit portrayals of them. Adopting the currently preferred terms would risk obscuring or downplaying the degree to which the ethnographic information in the *Relations* was shaped by the texts' authors and audience, as well as by the encounter on the ground in New France between Jesuits and Amerindians, a counter-productive move in a book that aims precisely to explore those processes. Names such as "Wendat" and "Innu" appear here in only the rarest of instances, when used by a quoted source or when used to designate a modern member of those groups who has expressed a preference.

One case in which this book is not consistent in its preference for the names used by the Jesuits is the generic term used for all of the Native groups encountered and described by the missionaries: Amerindian. The term the Jesuits most often used, "*sauvage*," has unpleasant connotations in its English translation – "savage" – that were not necessarily present in the original French, but are nonetheless best avoided altogether. Many common alternatives – such as "Native American," "American Indian," and "First Nations" – call to mind relationships with the modern national governments of Canada and the United States that did not exist at the time of contact. Employing these terms in the context of colonial interactions that occurred on both sides of the present border would make little sense, and would risk superimposing over my analysis of the texts a political dimension that simply was not operative in seventeenth-century New France. "Amerindian," as a modern scholarly invention, has its own shortcomings, but is nonetheless more palatable than the alternatives.[6]

MASTERS AND STUDENTS

CHAPTER ONE

Introduction: Jesuit Mission Ethnography

It was predictable, in hindsight. Everything about the history of the Society of Jesus bespoke deft and efficient action, exploration and research. During what Europeans were pleased to call the Age of Discovery, Jesuit priests were never more than a year or two behind the men who made initial contact with previously unknown peoples; indeed, Jesuits were often the vanguard of exploration. The United Nations required years to come to a decision that the Society of Jesus reached in ten days. In New York, diplomats debated long and hard … whether and why human resources should be expended in an attempt to contact the world that would become known as Rakhat when there were so many pressing needs on Earth. In Rome, the questions were not whether or why but how soon the mission could be attempted and whom to send.

– Mary Doria Russell, *The Sparrow*[1]

It is with a reference to the long history of Jesuit exploration and contact with previously unknown cultures around the world that Mary Doria Russell begins her science fiction novel *The Sparrow*, set in the mid-twenty-first century, about a Society of Jesus mission to a newly discovered planet. Russell's story follows Puerto Rican priest Emilio Sandoz and a small band of colleagues and friends as they depart Earth for the fictional planet of Rakhat in Alpha Centauri, the solar system closest to our own sun. After Sandoz's friend Jimmy Quinn, an astronomer, discovers music emanating from the distant solar system and deduces the existence of sentient beings there, Sandoz and his companions immediately begin to contemplate a voyage to the far-off planet. Perhaps not surprisingly, given that the group is composed of both Jesuits and laypeople, the question of the proposed expedition's aims is soon raised. "Do you mean a mission or do you mean a mission? Are we talking science or religion?" asks a skeptical member of the group. "Yes," comes Sandoz's non-sequitur reply.[2]

In our own age of space exploration and espionage thrillers, the word "mission" often designates a dangerous and distant attempt to obtain information for the benefit of the home left behind. And yet the term also applies to the movement of information in the opposite direction in relation to the home, as those on religious missions fan out across the globe not primarily to learn about another culture, but rather to teach their own particular worldview.[3] Although these examples may suggest a fairly clear distinction between scientific and religious missions, Russell's novel reminds us that in at least some contexts – a mission by priests to locate extraterrestrial life, for example – the very concept involves the circulation of information in more than one direction. Because of the unfamiliar nature of Rakhat at the beginning of Russell's novel, any religious mission there would unavoidably also be a journey of discovery. Sandoz and his colleagues would not be able to preach Christianity to the people they encountered without first learning about their languages, cultures, and pre-existing beliefs, whether the accumulation of knowledge was identified as an end in itself or would be a mere by-product of close contact with potential converts. The fictional missionary's playful acknowledgment of the multiple meanings of the word "mission" summarizes this book's point of view on a real Jesuit mission, one of many throughout the world during the period that corresponded to Europe's colonization of the Americas.[4] The seventeenth-century Jesuit mission in New France, from which Russell herself drew inspiration, is treated here as simultaneously two different *kinds* of mission, an enterprise that served both to extract information from a distant and poorly understood place and to furnish Europe's religious knowledge to the inhabitants of that place.

Regardless of how scholars have theorized the process of observing and then writing about unfamiliar cultures in colonial encounters, the texts produced by Jesuit missionaries in New France often are thought of as an effort to move information in one direction – eastward, toward Europe. And that is indeed one important aspect of what the mission accomplished. Upon their arrival in New France in 1632, the priests focused their attention on Algonquian-speaking groups, including the Montagnais who inhabited the area east of the St. Maurice River, up to Sept-Îles, and the Algonquin who resided to the west of the river, in the Ottawa Valley and surrounding area. After a few years, they expanded their efforts to include the Huron, the five Iroquoian nations that inhabited the land between Georgian Bay and Lake Simcoe in modern-day Ontario. The Jesuits also eventually were successful in expanding their reach to the five member groups of the Iroquois League, which were divided among smaller communities throughout what is today upstate New York. It was not until 1667 that all five Iroquois groups were finally at peace with the French, and the Iroquois – enemies of the Jesuits' Algonquian and Huron allies – mostly appear in the Jesuits' texts as a shadowy menace that threatened at any moment to attack and kill the missionaries and their would-be converts alike. Ties were established with individual groups at various times from the early 1650s on, but the situation was never stable.[5] Their long stints living among and interacting with various Amerindian groups have made the Jesuit missionaries famous among ethnohistorians of North America, no doubt due to the extensive written observations of the languages, customs, and beliefs of the continent's Amerindian inhabitants that were the fruits of their experiences. Although the Jesuits' proto-ethnographic work usually is recognized to be biased, naïve, or otherwise problematic, their accounts of Amerindian cultures undeniably reflect an effort to extract from a distant and poorly known place information for the benefit of the home left behind.

Without invalidating the role that the Jesuit missionaries played in transferring to Europe and to posterity information about Amerindian cultures, this book seeks to account for other aspects of their project that may have bearing on the ethnographic qualities of their texts. Not only did Jesuit priests famously furnish lessons to European readers and to posterity about the inhabitants of the New World in the pages of their texts, for example, they also heeded questions and instructions from their readers and superiors that arrived in letters and other forms of feedback with the ships that landed in the colony each spring. And it is important to remember that the Society of Jesus has had, since its very creation in 1534, a profoundly pedagogical orientation, operating colleges across Europe and throughout the world, a history that informs the argument about Jesuit mission ethnography in each of the following chapters. This instructional mission, laid out in the sixteenth-century *Ratio Studiorum* and the *Constitutions* of the Society itself, was of course not abandoned when the Society's members began travelling to exotic destinations such as China, South America, and India, and collecting detailed information about the peoples they found there. Jesuit missionaries sought to teach their own particular worldview to would-be converts, even as they received lessons on indigenous languages and cultures from Amerindian "masters." At every turn, then, the missionaries found themselves simultaneously masters and students, by turns powerful and weak, knowledgeable and ignorant. This book analyzes passages of ethnographic interest in the Jesuit texts in light of the authors' position between Europe and the New World, learning from and attempting to persuade the inhabitants of both places. The Jesuits' two simultaneous missions – seeking information and also disseminating it – provide the framework that this book uses to reflect on the nature of Jesuit ethnographic writing, and to assess how some of the data collected by the priests has been put to work in the service of ethnohistorical studies of the Amerindian groups that the missionaries encountered in New France.

Such contextualization of mission ethnography is sorely needed, a situation that Russell's novel can help to illustrate. Despite its playful recognition of the various implications of the word "mission," the tale largely mirrors conventional perceptions of the Jesuits' New France mission that focus on the fruits of its observational labours, the lessons about Amerindian groups that missionaries furnished to Europe and continue to furnish to modern scholars. Sandoz and his companions arrive on the planet years before any other organization – governmental or religious – is able to plan a voyage of its own, and the priest, a linguist by training, immediately begins an intensive effort to learn the languages of Rakhat's inhabitants. Other members of the expedition undertake detailed studies of the two intelligent species that are discovered on the fictional planet, as well as its flora, fauna, and atmospheric characteristics. Although the adventure ends in tragedy, with Sandoz returning to Earth alone after the death of his team, physically disfigured and emotionally shattered due to mistreatment suffered while held prisoner on the faraway planet, it is a resounding success from a research standpoint. Russell's imaginary mission produces reams of information that add up to the sum of Earthlings' knowledge about the planet and its inhabitants. Sandoz, previously agnostic despite his status as a priest, undergoes a belated spiritual awakening when confronted with the beauty of the unfamiliar planet and its inhabitants. But neither the priest nor any of his colleagues quite get around to preaching Christianity to their extraterrestrial acquaintances. Instead, they focus on gathering linguistic, anatomical, and botanical data and writing articles intended for submission to learned journals back on Earth.

Russell's portrait of Jesuit missionary work among extraterrestrials mirrors the emphasis that scholars have placed on the role of the Jesuit *Relations* in collecting information and then disseminating it among readers who had stayed at home in France. Students of colonial encounter and Amerindian cultures at the time of contact are practically unanimous in their assessment that the reports produced by Jesuits are the richest source of information on the Amerindian cultures of eastern Canada as they existed in the early to mid-seventeenth century. Indeed, it would be difficult to overestimate the influence that such texts have had on attempts to reconstruct the cultures of the Iroquoian and Algonquian groups of eastern Canada as they existed at the time of contact with French colonists. In a comment typical of social scientists who draw information from the Jesuits' texts, historian Allan Greer remarked in his 2000 introduction to the *Relations* that they "constitute the most important set of documentary materials on the seventeenth-century encounter of Europeans and Native North Americans."[6] Indeed, even Georges Sioui, a Huron-Wendat historian who seeks to restore an Amerindian voice to the discussion, and who maintains that the missionaries' written descriptions were meant to undercut Huron culture and justify the colonial project, finds it necessary to draw information from the Jesuit texts.[7] And reliance on the missionary accounts as a source of information certainly is not new. They were one of the major sources for Joseph-François Lafitau's 1724 *Moeurs des Sauvages Amériquains Comparés aux Moeurs des Premiers Temps*, a work that is often cited as one of the earliest works of comparative ethnology.[8] Although the value of the texts as the premier source of information on the cultures that the Jesuits encountered in seventeenth-century New France is perhaps beyond dispute, this book will show that closer attention to the various ways in which the authors were both transmitting and receiving lessons as they composed their observations can add much to scholarly understandings of Jesuit mission ethnography, and can in some cases correct the record.

Although Russell depicts Jesuit missionizing in a way more consistent with its importance to modern academic anthropology and linguistics than with the society's efforts to convert non-Christian peoples, her novel nonetheless brings to light unique aspects of the Jesuit mission project that are easily pushed to the background when the texts penned by priests in the New World are read primarily as a source of data. By placing her fictional Jesuit mission in the context of a first encounter with extraterrestrial life, Russell reminds us that Jesuit missions often were conducted in largely or completely uncharted territory, in places that took weeks or months to access and among peoples whose very existence had been unknown only a short time before. For modern anthropology, in contrast, the existence of culturally different and remotely located non-Christians is no longer news, and modern means of travel and staying in touch with the home left behind surely make even the most adventurous ethnographic fieldwork less daunting than what Jesuits – in seventeenth-century New France or on the fictional planet of Rakhat – had to confront. Like blasting off for an unknown planet in our own time, crossing the Atlantic must have required of seventeenth-century missionaries audacity, courage, and faith that go beyond what is required of modern anthropologists in their fieldwork. This perhaps explains why Russell, an anthropologist by training, stocks her tale with direct allusions to the Jesuits' historical ventures into the unknown "for the greater glory of God," including the New France mission. Indeed, it was precisely the example of New France Jesuit missionaries such as Isaac Jogues, Paul Le Jeune, Jean de Brébeuf, and others that led Russell to make her fictional explorers Jesuits instead of Franciscans, Protestants, secular adventurers, or diplomats.[9] By reminding modern readers, for whom the concept of first contact is now perhaps easiest to imagine in the context of future space travel, of the daring required in such a confrontation with Otherness, Russell's novel invites the reader to consider the exact nature of a religious mission made under such circumstances.

In seeking an account of Jesuit mission ethnography that goes beyond the lessons about Amerindian cultures that New France missionaries furnished to Europe and to posterity, this book draws primarily on the famed Jesuit *Relations*, reports from the New France mission that were published annually in France between 1632 and 1673.[10] Similar Jesuit texts that were published in 1616 and 1627 and works by contemporaries such as Gabriel Sagard, Samuel de Champlain, Marie de l'Incarnation, and others also are considered. The *Relations* are part of a long letter-writing tradition of the Society of Jesus, but are also unique within the body of Jesuit mission reports from around the world due to the unparalleled regularity and longevity of the annual series. From the earliest beginnings of the order in the sixteenth century, members were required to write weekly letters to Ignatius Loyola. The Society's founder himself explained his reasons for requiring regular correspondence in the *Constitutions*, a collection of rules and instructions for members: "Still another very special help will be found in the exchange of letters between the subjects and the superiors, through which they learn about one another frequently and hear the news and reports which come from the various regions. The superiors, especially the general and the provincials, will take charge of this, by providing an arrangement through which each region can learn from the others whatever promotes mutual consolation and edification in our Lord."[11] In 1565, the growing Society reduced the requirement to a single report per year, submitted by the leaders of each province to headquarters in Rome, and circulated among the far-flung Jesuits. Passing the reports to outside readers was, in these early years, expressly forbidden.[12] By the time the New France Jesuits began writing their annual reports, however, a tradition of publishing such texts had developed in the order's missions elsewhere in the world. Even a rapid perusal of Auguste Carayon's 1846 historical bibliography of Jesuit writings reveals that annual or nearly annual *relations* were published for Spanish and Portuguese Jesuit missions in Japan, India, and elsewhere at various times in the sixteenth and seventeenth centuries.[13]

It is clear that the Jesuit texts with which this book is primarily concerned were intended for publication, and designed to captivate readers in order to attract material and political support for the mission. Jesuit missions around the world were expected to support themselves by attracting "gifts of land, goods, and money from churches and individuals, from the state, and from converts in the field," making the task of appealing to readers in texts like the *Relations* crucial for the success of any evangelical effort.[14] Accordingly, the Jesuits' New France texts, in contrast to the generally less compelling narratives composed by English visitors to the New World, were filled with skilfully written and vivid descriptions of Amerindian cultures. This perhaps explains why Henry David Thoreau turned to the *Relations* and other French accounts of encounter, and not texts written in English, when he wanted to read about life in the North American wilderness.[15] As will become clear at various points in this book, the necessity of pleasing readers and convincing potential supporters of the mission of its value ensured that more was at work in the Jesuits' writing strategies than a care to accurately report their findings on the subject of Amerindian cultures.

The available evidence suggests that the Jesuits' efforts to appeal to readers by writing exciting and well-crafted narratives were a great success in France. At just *vingt sols* a copy, they were among the most modestly priced offerings of Sébastien Cramoisy, who published all but the 1637 instalment, and it seems that sales were brisk.[16] The many editions and reprintings that Cramoisy produced of most of the *Relations* may be taken as a measure of their popularity. In addition to the multiple legal editions of the *Relations*, pirated versions were produced in Lille and Avignon, suggesting that the texts were in high demand in seventeenth-century France.[17] And the texts themselves contain indications that the authors believed their words were reaching a wide audience. In 1636, missionary Jean de Brébeuf reported having heard that "old France is burning with ardent desires for the New." In mission superior Paul Le Jeune's eyes, France was "on fire" for the mission, and the *Relations* were read by "a large part of France."[18]

And yet, the very title emblazoned on the frontispiece of each of the texts – *Relation* – hints that they had a purpose that was broader than merely exciting French readers and supporters with tales of distant cultures and events. According to Antoine Furetière's 1690 *Dictionnaire Universel*, the term "relation" referred in seventeenth-century France to "the account of some adventure, story, battle ... especially said of the adventures of travelers, of the observations that they make during their voyages."[19] Although Furetière's definition seems to designate the genre as a vessel for transporting information from the exotic destination to the home left behind, more than one scholar has observed that the term can also imply an operation more complicated than a unidirectional transfer of knowledge. Sara Melzer, writing not only of the Jesuits' accounts but also of other, similar seventeenth-century texts, suggested that "[t]he *relations de voyage* were *relational*, in the religious sense of *religare*, with a Latin root meaning to fasten or tie together."[20] Georges Van Den Abbeele made a similar point, suggesting that such texts served to allow readers to vicariously experience the voyage for themselves, and especially to replicate the traveller's experience of comparing the home and the exotic destination. According to Van Den Abbeele, "The 'relation' (from *refero*, to bring back) itself acts as a voyage that brings back what was lost in the voyage. It institutes an economy of the voyage. If it acts as a voyage it is because *qua re*lation it repeats the voyage by recounting the itinerary in chronological order at the same time *qua* re*lation* (from *latus*, borne or transported) it displaces the topography into a topic of discourse."[21] *Relations* – and the Jesuit *Relations* from New France chief among them – do not, it turns out, serve only to illuminate one place for the benefit or amusement of another, but also to bind the two places together textually. This hidden meaning encoded in the title of the texts aligns well with what has already been said here about the Jesuits' simultaneous and overlapping missions, and invites precisely the kind of analysis of the texts that has been proposed so far in this chapter.

Over the course of the forty years in which they were published, the *Relations* were signed by eight priests: Paul Le Jeune, Jean de Brébeuf, François-Joseph Le Mercier, Jérôme Lalemant, Barthélemy Vimont, Paul Ragueneau, Jean de Quen, and Claude d'Ablon. Studies have sometimes been dedicated to the work of particular Jesuits, especially the longtime mission superior Paul Le Jeune,[22] but this book treats the series holistically. This decision to avoid focusing closely on the individual priests who wrote the *Relations* no doubt comes at the price of failure to account for the theological, personal, and political differences that are known to have existed between them. As Luca Codignola has pointed out, for example, "the plentiful sources of the Society of Jesus have revealed that, even within an order usually deemed monolithic in the extreme, there were differences and jealousies. Barthélemi Vimont, who had problems with fellow Jesuit Paul Ragueneau, was recalled in 1659. Ragueneau himself then returned to France, together with Joseph-Antoine Poncet de la Rivière, because they had been engaged in political controversy. We do not know the reason for the sudden departure from Canada of Amable de Frérat,

...ho spent only one winter in the colony, but we know that Nicolas Adam was reputed to be 'the worst possible choice for the Canadian mission.'"[23] Despite what might be lost in glossing over the differences between individual authors or contributors, this choice is appropriate in a study of the ethnographic qualities of the texts because the influence of the *Relations* in that domain has not been limited to any one of the authors, but instead is generally attributed to the series as a whole. Indeed, the texts are packaged, in their modern scholarly editions, in ways that encourage scholars to perceive them that way. Regardless of which edition one prefers, the texts are bound in massive, multi-volume collections that give scant attention to individual authors. And at least in the case of the Thwaites edition, individual texts often are split between two volumes, as if the integrity of the individual text were less important than that of the series as a whole.[24]

The conception of the texts as a single product also is licensed by the way authorship apparently was understood from the beginning of the Jesuits' project in New France. The author listed on the frontispiece of each instalment was not always the same person who melded the individual reports of various priests into the *Relation*. Instead, the texts usually bore the name of the New France superior, who theoretically oversaw the editing process in New France, although exceptions abound. The 1641 *Relation*, for example, was attributed to Barthélemy Vimont, superior of the New France mission since 1639, but actually was composed by Le Jeune and Jérôme Lalemant. The *Relations* for 1652 and 1653 were composed in Paris by Le Jeune, then procurer for the mission, the first on the basis of notes sent to him by Ragueneau, and the second to replace Ragueneau's *Relation*, which had been lost in transit. And it seems that Le Jeune repeated the bizarre task of ghostwriting reports on events in New France from his position in Paris several more times over the years.[25] As the above examples suggest, the role of author was, in the New France mission, more a bureaucratic position than an individual feat of writing, and the name that appeared on the frontispiece of each *Relation* was not necessarily that of the person most responsible for its contents. Most of the texts were attributed to the mission superior, suggesting that the order wanted its annual reports to appear to come from the most authoritative voice possible, its leader in New France, and to maintain the appearance that each text was first and foremost a high-level official communiqué.[26]

The author function was, for the Jesuits, more a matter of preserving the semi-illusory image of the *Relations* as official, internal correspondence between important order officials than of giving credit where it was due.

Even in years when the mission superior himself assembled the *Relation*, he was not the only significant contributor to its contents. The process that yielded the published texts, which is examined in more detail in chapter six, reinforces this book's premise that the texts reflect not just news sent from New France to France, but a more complicated exchange of ideas in which multiple parties were implicated. Far from personal narratives dashed off for private purposes, each *Relation* was carefully composed and revised, and then worked over by multiple people before reaching the public. Lawrence Wroth offers a good description of the process undergone by the first-person narratives of individual missionaries in the Canadian wilderness: "Such reports in the form of letters or journals, coming fresh from the field of action and composed under circumstances of the greatest difficulty, provided the raw material only of the printed Relation." Even this "raw material," as Wroth calls it, can be understood to have been authored collaboratively, since missionaries would not be able to describe Amerindian life without having first learned about it from their New World interlocutors. And the lessons that those interlocutors offered were, in turn, filtered through a Jesuit quill before reaching the mission superior. Composed under often-difficult circumstances, such reports surely were not sufficiently polished to be sent immediately to France for printing. Indeed, as Wroth put it, "[i]nto them went much that was impolitic or at best unessential to the purposes of the published series … The Canadian superior, therefore, edited the original reports, removing portions here, altering the language there, and welding the several pieces before him into a concise and comprehensive story of the year's mission in Canada before sending to the French provincial in Paris the composite Relation thus formed." The provincial, in turn, "with current European conditions in mind, gave it a final editing."[27] Although this book, for the sake of convenience, sometimes attributes individual *Relations* or passages therein to the person credited on the frontispiece of each text, the reader should bear in mind that "author" of the *Relations* was as much a bureaucratic role as a literary function. Attribution of a particular passage to any one missionary does not mean that he was solely – or even primarily – responsible for its form or contents. It can be said that multiple parties, from Amerindian interlocutors to typesetters in Paris, had a hand in producing the contents and form of the texts, despite the fact that the *Relations* often appear at least superficially to be thrilling narratives of firsthand contact with perplexing, violent, and otherwise unfamiliar people who lived far from Europe.

The popularity that the Jesuit *Relations* enjoyed in their own time has been no less pronounced since the advent of anthropology as an academic discipline, which in its early days took as its immediate and urgent task the collection of all available information on indigenous groups that were presumed to be disappearing. James Clifford traces this development to Bronislaw Malinowski, author of the 1922 classic *Argonauts of the Western Pacific* and perhaps the archetype of the professional anthropologist that emerged in the early twentieth century. According to Clifford, "Malinowksi gives us the image of the 'new anthropologist' – squatting by the campfire; looking, listening, and questioning; recording and interpreting Trobriand life."[28] The previously distinct tasks of fieldwork – until then often conducted by amateurs – and armchair theorizing were now melded into a single profession, the authority of which rested both on its practitioners' personal, direct experience of other cultures and on their interpretive skill. Similarly, the American brand of anthropology initiated by Franz Boas and cemented in place by his large generation of students emphasized intensive fieldwork conducted by university-educated scholars. In what is sometimes now called "salvage anthropology," professional practitioners sought to thoroughly document cultures whose decline and eventual disappearance seemed inevitable to early-twentieth-century observers. As George Marcus and Michael Fischer described the project of "salvage anthropology" in their 1988 book *Anthropology as Cultural Critique*, "The ethnographer would capture in writing the authenticity of changing cultures, so they could be entered into the record for the great comparative project of anthropology, which was to support the Western goal of social and economic progress."[29]

In this context, the Jesuit *Relations* were considered a highly valuable source of information that otherwise would be difficult to obtain, and scholars quickly elevated the priests to the status of precocious early fore-

runners of cultural anthropology. Francis Parkman, for example, emphasized both the scholarly qualifications and firsthand experience of the
Jesuits in his well-known book, appealing to the dominant modes of
ethnographic authority in the nascent academic field. Wrote Parkman
of the *Relations*, "Though the productions of men of scholastic training, they are simple and often crude in style, as might be expected of
narratives hastily written in Indian lodges or rude mission-houses in the
forest, amid annoyances and interruptions of all kinds. In respect to the
value of their contents, they are exceedingly unequal. Modest records
of marvellous adventures and sacrifices, and vivid pictures of forest-life,
alternate with prolix and monotonous details of the conversion of individual savages, and the praiseworthy deportment of some exemplary
neophyte. With regard to the condition and character of the primitive
inhabitants of North America, it is impossible to exaggerate their value
as an authority."[30] Much like Malinowski and the earliest generations of
professional anthropologists, the Jesuits were, in Parkman's estimation,
men whose erudition and personal experiences rendered credible their
written accounts of Amerindian cultures. And Parkman's relative disdain
for the "monotonous" religious aspects of the texts confirms that the real
interest of the *Relations* was, for him, their proto-ethnographic contents.
Writing in the middle of the twentieth century, Elisabeth Tooker similarly suggested in her classic ethnography of the Huron that the authors of her seventeenth-century sources, the Jesuit *Relations* chief among
them, possessed both of the qualities that distinguished the new anthropologist from nineteenth-century amateur fieldworkers and armchair
ethnologists: field experience and interpretive skill. Wrote Tooker, "the
period of intensive Jesuit missionizing in Huronia, 1634–1650, produced
the most extensive collection of material on the Huron … In the *Jesuit
Relations*, the Jesuits applied their almost intuitive devotion to scholarship to the study of the Huron, as in other writings they applied it to
Western culture." In introducing Gabriel Sagard, a Recollet Franciscan
missionary and her second major source, Tooker went so far as to call
him a "participant-observer," applying what has been called "the classic
formula for ethnographic work" to the seventeenth-century priest. All
that was left to do for the modern scholar, Tooker suggested, was to omit
"the obvious biases of the writer" and type up the missionaries' material
into a modern monograph.[31]

Cultural anthropology's inward-turned gaze in recent decades has produced a more critical attitude in some quarters toward cultural descriptions penned by missionaries, explorers, and other colonial amateur ethnographers. Instead of a set of discrete facts to be dutifully collected, culture has often come to be seen, in the words of James Clifford, as "always relational, an inscription of communicative processes that exist, historically, *between* subjects in relations of power."[32] Accordingly, the personal experience and interpretive skill of the fieldworker and writer – though certainly still important – have lost ground to "discursive paradigms of dialogue and polyphony" as authorization for the ethnographic account.[33] In the movement led by Clifford, George Marcus, and their contemporaries, accounting for the position of the ethnographer in relation to the ethnographic subject became preferable to posing the writer as a detached, privileged observer. This shift also has affected how anthropologists understand the colonial observers on whose texts they sometimes rely, and whose work was not informed by any sophisticated theory of ethnography nor any pretense of neutrality.[34] Whether complicated by the writers' cultural baggage or by a failure to credit Amerindians with influence and agency of their own, texts produced by European colonists and explorers that once were considered gold mines of ethnographic data now are generally recognized also to reflect the interaction of multiple cultures, agendas, languages, and voices.

To go along with these new understandings of intercultural contact, cultural anthropology has developed new understandings of the ethnographic texts that it produces, recognizing the interpretative possibilities afforded by the process of translating experience into text. Ethnography is not, after all, like lepidoptery, in which specimens are collected and preserved for later study. Written ethnographic accounts, whether in the form of rudimentary field notes or a finished monograph, are not morsels of the target culture, but versions of that culture furnished by interlocutors with agendas of their own, and filtered through the beliefs, language, and culture of the ethnographer. Regardless of how (or whether) individual anthropologists have chosen to confront this challenge, the problem has been made clear in recent decades. As Clifford wrote, "ethnography is, from beginning to end, enmeshed in writing. This writing includes, minimally, a translation of experience into textual form. The process is complicated by the action of multiple subjectivities and political constraints beyond the control of the writer."[35]

In the wake of these developments in anthropological thought, even scholars who use the Jesuit *Relations* primarily to extract data about Amerindian cultures and French Canada's earliest years now recognize that the Jesuit authors had particular concerns and assumptions that may have coloured their perceptions. As former professors in Europe's Jesuit colleges, the priests were, after all, master rhetoricians, adept at framing the information in their reports in ways that favoured their own ends. Denys Delâge, for example, characterized the texts this way: "Such 'relations' were generally addressed to a devout French public, and the narrators were also actors in these accounts. As missionaries, their aim was to convert the peoples whom they were observing to Christianity. The individual narrator therefore assumed the stance of a judgmental spectator vis-à-vis these societies, which he posited as pagan. From such a perspective, the narrator obviously cannot give a 'neutral' ethnographic account of the habits and customs of the American peoples."[36] The Jesuits, as Delâge and many other scholars now insist, created *representations* of Amerindian cultures, filtered through the biases, beliefs, language, and culture of the missionary writers and editors. Despite their increased awareness of the factors that complicate any effort to describe a foreign culture in writing, many modern ethnohistorians frequently still end up implying or asserting that Jesuit biases are easy to detect and filter out, as will become clear at various points in the following chapters.

Some scholars, such as anthropologist Carole Blackburn, have come to treat such factors as a fertile site for analysis in their attempts to account for how cultural knowledge was produced in dialogue with Amerindian groups in the colonial New World, rather than as biases to be identified and then somehow mitigated. Instead of taking at face value signs of the Jesuits' experience in New France and scholarly attention to detail, Blackburn proposes a much more nuanced vision of the production of knowledge in and on New France, with which this book has much in common. Blackburn's aim is "to cast the critical lens of ethnography on the Jesuits in a way that not only pursues the various meanings in their *Relations* but also examines the ways in which they struggled with Native people over the creation of meaning in New France."[37] Her approach downplays the outdated notion of the scholarly Jesuit proto-ethnographer relying on experience and interpretive prowess, and instead seeks to understand colonial interactions as a process of reciprocal influence between the Jesuits and their Amerindian interlocutors. Other social scientists similarly focus on what the *Relations* and texts like them can tell us about how Europeans and Amerindians influenced each other in colonial America. Sociologist Karen Anderson's book *Chain Her by One Foot* uses the texts not as a simple source of data on Amerindian groups, but instead to study how relationships of power within those groups – particularly gender relations – were altered through the influence of Europeans. In other words, she uses the texts not to study the lessons furnished to the Old World about the New, but rather to observe how French social norms were implanted in New France.[38] Historian Richard White's *The Middle Ground*, to cite just one more example, emphasizes a process of mutual accommodation and invention that took place in Amerindian-European contact, what he terms a "middle ground" upon which each group moved toward the other instead of rejecting or adopting unfamiliar cultures wholesale. Such studies are, perhaps not surprisingly, attentive to issues of language – to *how* the Jesuits described Amerindian groups and their relationships with Europeans instead of merely *what* they described.[39]

Others, including both historians and scholars of literature, have read the *Relations* and texts like them to see what might be gleaned from them about intellectual conditions in Europe, instead of to understand the phenomenon of colonial encounter or to mine them for data as if they were ethnographies in the Malinowskian mold. Anthony Pagden's *The Fall of Natural Man*, which focuses on the Hispanic New World, is a classic study in this vein. Scholars of literature have, perhaps not surprisingly, long shared this interest in reading the accounts of adventurers and travellers as textual representations of Otherness that might say as much about Europe as about an exotic, distant place and the people who lived there. Gilbert Chinard summarized one of the questions that motivates such studies in his influential 1913 book: "They were read, it cannot be doubted; now we are left to ask ourselves what one found in them, and what influence these picturesque *relations* and descriptions of savage customs could exercise on contemporary readers and on the movement of ideas."[40] In this spirit, the *Relations* recently have been used to illuminate seventeenth-century French politics, economic ideas, literary debates, lexicography, philosophy, and religion in studies that seek to understand how new information from a distant place may have influenced European concerns. French literature scholar Sara Melzer, for example, has argued that the Jesuit *Relations* and other, similar texts "provide us with a powerful lever to pry open the official view of *le grand siècle* which has dominated our field."[41] In such readings, the *Relations* have as much to tell us about the relationship between Worlds Old and New as about Amerindian groups or the ways in which they made meaning in dialogue with European visitors.

The *Relations* also have been a major source of examples for those who study the poetics of the *relation* or *récit de voyage*, a genre that took France by storm in the seventeenth century, with approximately 1,500 examples published during that period, testifying to their bona fides as texts that are now, in at least some quarters, found to be as interesting for their language and formal characteristics as for their ethnographic contents.[42] The relationship of the Jesuit *Relations* to this genre will be examined in more depth in chapter six, but for now, it is sufficient to remark, as Gordon Sayre has pointed out, that it was often distinct during the colonial period from the more developed portraits of Amerindian cultures that preceded the academic discipline of anthropology, and the two forms of writing claimed authority in different ways. Wrote Sayre, "Exploration literature promised both wealth and news: new places, strange people, and new things. It recorded European penetration into the 'virgin wilderness' of the New World and depended rhetorically on primacy, novelty, and particularity, though frequently the new adventures were to places known from (even copied from) previous voyagers' accounts, and occasionally new places were imagined. By contrast, the ethnographic genre was a discourse that suppressed novelty and was reluctant to be disrupted by new data that did not fit the paradigm." Despite the seemingly contradictory goals of the two kinds of writing, they often, as Sayre notes, appeared together in hybrid texts, of which the Jesuit *Relations* from New France are certainly prime examples. Texts such as the *Relations* that function both as thrilling accounts of foreign travel and as detailed descriptions of Amerindian life are caught in the tension between two seemingly contradictory claims to authority: the firsthand, experience-based accounts of novelty on which the credibility of travel writing depended, and the claim of universal truths to which the authors of sustained portraits of

Amerindian cultures appealed in suppressing and explaining away new information that might have cast doubt on the Old World's existing knowledge.[43]

The ways in which the *Relations* balance these two seemingly conflicting textual projects – simultaneously exposing and obscuring differences between Amerindian cultures and the more familiar examples of Europe – is, in a broad sense, the subject of this book. Although both ethnohistorical and literary perspectives on the *Relations* have produced fine works of scholarship that are worthy contributions to evolving understandings of colonial America, the Amerindian groups that lived there, and the impact of both on Europe, much work remains to be done. Social scientists now often bring to bear on the *Relations* nuanced understandings either of how knowledge was produced in dialogue in New France or of how it reflects the European intellectual context of the time, but generally stop short of examining those two aspects of mission ethnography at the same time. Scholars of literature, on the other hand, have been keenly attuned to the various ways in which the texts made meaning in France and functioned as a genre, but have not fully accounted for the aspect of the texts that is the primary source of their longstanding popularity among ethnohistorians: the apparent precocious ethnographic skill and rigour that the Jesuits deployed in their interactions with Amerindian groups, and the richly detailed descriptions of those cultures that were the result. This book attempts to bridge the gap, and to prod forward both ethnohistorical and literary conceptions of the texts, by better accounting for the Jesuits' position between European and Amerindian cultures, drawing lessons from and simultaneously attempting to make a convincing argument to each. By focusing closely on descriptions of Amerindian customs, practices, and beliefs, this book explores how the ethnographic "facts" recorded in the *Relations* were distinctly shaped by the particular nature of the Jesuit approach to their mission – in both senses of the word.[44]

The remainder of this book tells the story of Jesuit mission ethnography in New France, from the arrival of the missionaries in the New World through the process of interacting with Amerindian groups and producing the *Relations*. This is not a chronological account of the Jesuit mission, but it does examine the missionaries' fundamental tasks in the order in which they were carried out. First, the priests arrived in New

France and learned to communicate in Amerindian languages. Then, they set about preaching Christianity while also learning about Amerindian beliefs and cultural practices. And finally, they wrote accounts of their work for the benefit and amusement of readers in France, rhetorically framing Amerindian cultures in ways that responded to European intellectual and political conditions and suggested that their conversion to Christianity was both possible and imminent. Each of these steps here is examined not only in light of Jesuit activities in the New World, but also in the context of the ideas, controversies, and anxieties that would have been on the minds of the readers for whom the Jesuits were writing in the first place. In other words, this book traces various aspects of the Jesuits' role as masters with regard to their European readers – the ways in which the missionaries collected specific lessons about Amerindian cultures and then rhetorically framed them in the annual *Relations*. In doing so, each chapter focuses on an aspect of Amerindian cultures of which the Jesuits are reputed to have been precocious anthropological students, with the exception of chapter six, which examines instead the lessons that the missionary authors received from France at the same time as they were sending lessons of their own to the Old Country. In every chapter of this book, then, we see the Jesuit missionaries as both masters and students with regard to their European and Amerindian interlocutors, from the preliminary steps of the mission through the publication of the *Relations*.

The first chapter following this introduction examines the political circumstances surrounding the Jesuits' ascent to the status of sole spiritual stewards of New France in 1632 in relation to their own characterizations of their efforts to learn the languages of Amerindian potential converts. In the wake of a temporary British takeover of the colony in 1629, French missionaries (including both Jesuits and Franciscan Recollets) were expelled. When the colony returned to French hands shortly thereafter, a low-simmering struggle over access to the area ensued, with the Jesuits eventually emerging victorious, at the expense of the Recollets who had also hoped to resume their work there. The Jesuits' rivals and former collaborators continued for years to lobby French authorities for the right to return to take up what they perceived to be their rightful place in the mission, necessitating Jesuit defence of their position. Chapter two argues that Jesuit descriptions of their efforts to learn the Amerindian languages of New France constituted not only an account of their preliminary interactions with potential converts, but also an intervention in the political squabble over who should have access to the colony. Amerindian languages were deployed in the *Relations* as a privileged point of entry to the colony and thus to Amerindian souls. By portraying themselves as infants learning how to walk and as stammering schoolchildren, the Jesuit missionaries positioned themselves on the weaker end of the pedagogical relationships that they had already experienced as professors in Europe's Jesuit colleges. As mere schoolchildren in the early days of their work in New France, the priests could not be blamed for the initial slow pace of conversions, but also could claim likely future success, since diligent pupils, of course, eventually grow into knowledgeable adults. At the same time, rivals at home in France would be unable to replicate the Jesuits' linguistic progress, justifying their continued exclusion from the mission field.

Chapter three extends the examination of missionary linguistics undertaken in the previous chapter to Jesuit characterizations of Amerindian languages themselves, as objects of linguistic study. Once established in New France, the missionaries found the challenge of learning Amerindian languages to be the most obvious and immediate obstacle to their plan to preach in indigenous tongues, as well as a fertile site for reflection on some of the most pressing questions posed by the existence of the New World's distant and unfamiliar cultures. If Amerindians were indeed truly human, as papal decree had already determined, how could one account for the striking differences between them and Europeans? Even the Society's most gifted linguists in New France reported finding Amerindian languages vexingly difficult, a situation that not only posed a practical challenge but was also an implied affront to biblical accounts of the origin of humankind. In order for evangelization to be possible, Amerindian languages had to be shown to be sufficiently sophisticated to be up to the task. At the same time and without undermining their own argument, the missionaries had to characterize the languages in such a way that would excuse their own slow progress in mastering them, and in deploying them to communicate doctrine to potential converts. Chapter three shows that the Jesuit missionaries frequently met the challenge by characterizing Amerindian tongues as simultaneously "rich" and "poor," a dynamic that argued for the divine nature of Amerindian languages – and therefore their suitability for communicating Christianity – but also

suggested that they were deficient in some way that could only be remedied by missionary intervention, often cast as a process of enrichment.
The languages as they exist today – mostly in manuscript grammars and
dictionaries prepared by the Jesuits – are therefore the products of a
process of missionary invention as much as of careful linguistic study.
And passages in French in the *Relations* that purport to recount conversations between the priests and would-be converts may be considered
to be doubly translated between two languages that the priests believed
to be commensurate due to their supposed common divine authorship.
Points of doctrine first had to be translated into Amerindian languages in
order for conversation to take place, and then those conversations themselves were translated back into French when recounted in the *Relations*.
This process, as the missionaries themselves often admitted, inhibited
their ability to explain Amerindian cultures to their readers. The chapter
argues that these hidden processes open a dimension of meaning in the
Relations that regrettably cannot be accounted for without being able to
listen in on the actual conversations, but that nonetheless is revealing of
some of the fundamental assumptions of Jesuit missionary ethnography
and how those assumptions are reflected in the texts.

The initial rationale for learning Amerindian languages was, of course,
to facilitate the implantation of Christianity, a goal toward which the
Jesuit missionaries began working immediately upon their arrival. Chapter four examines this pedagogical process in relation to one of the most
sensational topics treated in the *Relations*: the stunning violence of various Amerindian groups toward their enemies. The chapter argues that
some of the most shocking scenes of cruelty in the *Relations*, which often
have been used to reconstruct the traditional practices of Amerindian
groups, are deployed not only to document bad behaviour, but also to
affirm the capacity of Amerindians to convert to Christianity. Although
often taken by modern scholars as an argument for the essential animality
of some Amerindians – particularly the Iroquois – such scenes on closer
inspection often turn out to mirror the pedagogical passion plays that
were a staple of Jesuit school stages in Europe, and are presented as proof
that Amerindians could be induced to convert in ways that would stand
up to the harshest test imaginable. Other instances of torture in the *Relations* – notably those carried out by the Iroquois – do in fact turn out to
suggest a degree of blood lust and instinctual violence that seems, at least

superficially, to contradict the Jesuits' efforts to describe the conversion of Amerindian groups as a feasible project. Closer examination of such passages, however, suggests that the distinction between edifying torture as a kind of passion play and the more reflexive cruelty elsewhere on display in the texts frequently was more a matter of distinguishing converts from non-converts than of parsing the humanity (or lack thereof) of the New World's various Amerindian groups.

Converting Amerindians was not, of course, purely an exercise in instruction. Priests also admitted that it often involved seeking lessons in pre-existing beliefs, and then discrediting them through reasoned argumentation. Chapter five examines Jesuit accounts of Montagnais beliefs about Creation. Drawing on the long Catholic tradition of catechistic questioning, the chapter shows how Jesuit accounts of Amerindian creation myths did as much to discredit such tales as unique knowledge, and reconcile them with Genesis, as they did to preserve and transmit non-Christian beliefs about the origin of humankind and its surroundings. By presenting the missionaries' encounter with the Montagnais myth as a teaching moment instead of as ethnographic description, the Jesuits' texts reverse the direction in which information at first appears to flow in the *Relations*, perhaps reassuring readers that the Jesuits – and, by extension, Catholic Europe – already knew all they needed to know about the origin of the Amerindians, and had more to teach on the subject than to learn. Jesuit descriptions of the creation myths of potential converts turn out to reflect a strategy to teach Christianity to the Amerindians and, at the same time, to reassure readers of the shared humanity of residents of the Old and New Worlds, and therefore of the enduring truth of biblical accounts of Creation. Because the two versions of the Montagnais myth contained in the *Relations* happen to straddle a pivotal moment in the history of the published series, the chapter also begins a reflection that is extended and developed in the following chapter on how the process of publishing the texts may have influenced subsequent instalments – that is, how the very process of communicating with Europe about the results of the mission may have shaped the form and contents of the texts.

Chapter six circles back to the point of view on the *Relations* that has been developed in this introductory chapter, by examining how a long-overlooked aspect of the ways in which the *Relations* were composed and then circulated may contribute to an understanding of Jesuit mission ethnography. The *Relations* often are presumed to have been the products of a circular movement beginning and ending in Europe, in which French priests travelled far from home to experience poorly known cultures and then shared the lessons learned with readers who had stayed home. There is a compelling case to be made, however, that the *Relations* also were sent back to New France after publication, where their authors could consult them and see the changes wrought by editors in Paris. Contrary to common assertion, the changes made by Parisian editors appear to have at least sometimes substantially altered the contents and meaning of the texts. There is evidence that the Jesuit authors in New France were attentive to these changes, as well as to feedback from Europe that arrived in other forms, such as the letters from readers and powerful benefactors that arrived with the ships each spring. This chapter argues for an alternate reading of the *Relations* as ethnographic texts and as travel accounts that conceives of them as the product of a colony-centric movement as much as a Eurocentric one. Manuscripts departed the colony each autumn, were altered during their brief stay in Europe, and then returned to the colony where they were collected in the library of the Jesuit college in Quebec, a perch from which they could influence the form and contents of the *Relations* for subsequent years. The chapter, then, applies to the publication and circulation of the texts the vision of Jesuit mission ethnography that has been developed throughout the present chapter. The *Relations* were not, or not only, the result of the more or less biased observations of Jesuits in New France, but also of an overlapping and bi-directional circulation of information between France and New France.

Although this book primarily is concerned with a relatively specific phenomenon – Jesuit mission ethnography in seventeenth-century New France – it also seeks to highlight some of the ways in which the legacy of the missionaries' textual project lives on, or is at least similar to patterns that can be discerned both in modern scholarship and in mainstream cultural phenomena. Accordingly, attention is paid throughout the book to how scholars have used and understood the passages examined here, in order to contrast Jesuit mission ethnography with its modern academic equivalent, but also, in some cases, to show how the particular nature of the missionaries' approach to describing Amerindian cultures continues to shape perceptions of those cultures. Also in the service of gesturing at questions that go beyond the specific focus of this book, chapters three, four, and five end with brief anecdotes about modern pop culture phenomena – both closely related to the New France mission and seemingly remote from it – that serve to summarize the argument of those chapters and to show how, almost four centuries after the fact, the ideas that informed Jesuit mission ethnography and that are traced in this book continue to operate in contemporary North America.

CHAPTER TWO

Amerindian Languages and the Beginning of the Jesuit Mission to New France

From the earliest days of European contact with the New World, explorers, traders, and missionaries sought ways to communicate with the Amerindian groups they encountered. Whether the goal was extraction of precious materials, exploration, or evangelization, "[t]he key to the continent was information – reliable, unambiguous, and digestible – and the quickest and best source of it was the Indians," writes historian James Axtell.[1] Knowledge of Amerindian languages was, in this context, jealously guarded in the early days of New France as various actors on the colonial stage sought to protect their advantage over rivals. Franciscan Recollet missionaries seeking language lessons, for example, sometimes encountered resistance from trading company interpreters who cited an oath to preserve the company's monopoly in all things as grounds for refusing to share their knowledge.[2] Familiarity with Amerindian languages was viewed as essential not only to commerce and diplomacy, but also, at least as far as Jesuit missionaries were concerned, to attempts to convert the non-Christians they encountered in what is today eastern Canada. As anthropologist Carole Blackburn remarked in her reading of the Jesuit *Relations*, "Language was the key to the interior consciousness – the 'minds and hearts' – of Aboriginal people, and when spoken properly, and in the manner associated with authority in indigenous cultures, it was an instrument of persuasion, command, and rebuttal."[3]

This chapter examines the ascent of the Jesuits, in the early 1630s, to the status of sole spiritual stewards of New France as it relates to how they wielded these linguistic "keys" to the continent and to Amerindian souls in the pages of the *Relations*. The first part of this chapter examines the political climate in which the Jesuits gained a monopoly on mission work in New France starting in 1632, after having been expelled along with their Recollet collaborators in 1629 when the English temporarily took over the colony. The Recollets' subsequent actions and arguments in their quest for re-entry to the colony created a climate of suspicion that may have threatened to delegitimize the Jesuits in the eyes of France's elite reading public – the very audience upon which any mission would rely for political and material support. The second part of the chapter shows how the Jesuit missionaries defended themselves against the perception – apparently actively but carefully encouraged by the Recollets – that they had no business having exclusive access to New France. Although the Jesuits did not address the controversy directly in the pages of the *Relations*, their characterizations of their efforts to gain mastery of Amerindian languages provided one way in which the missionaries could rhetorically grant themselves legitimacy as sole spiritual stewards of the colony, and also lock out meddlesome rival missionary groups. By casting themselves in their texts as temporarily weak in relation to their Amerindian interlocutors – mere pupils under the care of knowledgeable teachers – the Jesuits could defuse criticisms of the slow pace of conversions in the early years of their mission while simultaneously suggesting that future success was likely. By the same token, the inability of potential rivals who had been left behind in France to replicate the order's linguistic efforts would have implied that no one else – and perhaps especially not the spurned Recollets – could gain the kind of access to Amerindian souls that the Jesuits had procured for themselves.

In the early years of France's colonization of the New World, access – the ability to physically reach the colony and the right to conduct religious, commercial, or exploratory work there – was not necessarily easily procured. After nearly a century of occasional exploration and failed attempts to establish an enduring presence in the area that is today eastern Canada, France finally gained a permanent foothold in 1608, with the founding of Quebec by Samuel de Champlain. Champlain was a prominent and prolific writer on New France in his own right before his death in 1635, which left the physical and textual field open to the Jesuits. Although the establishment of Quebec lent a measure of stability to France's presence in North America after the previous century's half-hearted and disorganized efforts, the colony was slow to develop. According to historian Alain Beaulieu, "At the end of the 1620s, Quebec was still just a modest trading post occupied by several dozen Frenchmen, whose survival depended on goods imported annually from France."[4] The Crown, preoccupied with lingering civil strife and intra-European affairs, had little attention to spare for New France in the early decades of the seventeenth century, and instead sought to solidify French control there by tapping merchants to act as proxies. Consortiums of merchants were granted ten- or fifteen-year monopolies on New France trade in exchange for their agreement to administer the colony and oversee its growth. These trading companies had little apparent interest in promoting missionary work, despite the Crown's hope that New France would be settled and its inhabitants converted as a side effect of trade. The Franciscan Recollet missionaries who worked in the colony starting in 1615 were a thorn in the side of profit-oriented merchants, who viewed the missionaries' attempts to Christianize and Frenchify Amerindians as counter-productive, turning "good Indian hunters into poor French farmers at the expense of the fur trade."[5]

Like the rest of French activity in the New World, the Jesuit presence there proved difficult to establish and came only after extensive political wrangling, in which knowledge of Amerindian languages would come to play an important, if not usually recognized, role.[6] An initial attempt to found a mission at Port Royal in 1611 lasted just two years before British colonists from Virginia arrived to assert control over the area. When Jesuit priests arrived on the continent for the second time in 1625, they joined the Franciscan Recollet missionaries who already had been working the missionary field for ten years. Working in concert with Samuel de Champlain, who had been instrumental in bringing them to New France, the Recollets focused their efforts on convincing or forcing Amerindians to adopt the French language and lifestyle along with Catholicism.[7] Jesuit missionaries, on the other hand, attempted to bring religion to potential converts on their own terms, adapting Amerindian customs to Christianity and putting a premium on the use of local languages in spreading their message. Scholars differ as to whether these contrasting methodologies reflect philosophical or theological differences, or merely the different political and practical circumstances faced by each group.[8] Whatever the cause, it is clear that although allied by circumstance against the trading company, the Jesuits and the Recollets had different and potentially conflicting goals and methods in their respective work in New France. With trading companies, missionaries, and the Crown seemingly working at cross purposes, it is perhaps little wonder that the early years of the colony were not marked by resounding success in any domain.[9]

From the Jesuits' point of view, this arrangement surely was unsatisfactory, as it aligned poorly with the Society's vision for its missions. In New France and elsewhere, the Society of Jesus tended to conceive of its missions as closed, ideal religious communities, vice-free counterpoints to licentious European society. Inspired at least in part by the earlier communities of converts established by the Jesuits in Paraguay, Japan, and perhaps elsewhere, the New France mission was meant to become, the Jesuit authors suggested, a "Jerusalem blessed of God," a place that resembled France at its best, but without any of the moral shortcomings of the old country.[10] To cite just one example, mission superior Paul Le Jeune in 1635 expressed guarded optimism about New France's potential future as just such a place: "I fear very much that vice will slip into these new colonies. If, however, those who hold the reins of government in hand are zealous for the glory of our good God, following the desires and intentions of the Honorable Directors and Associates of the Company, there will arise here a Jerusalem blessed of God, composed of Citizens destined for Heaven. It is very easy in a new country, where families arrive who are all prepared to observe the laws that will be established there, to banish the wicked customs of certain places in old France, and to introduce better ones."[11] The colony's potential future as a uniquely pious community would depend, in Le Jeune's estimation, not only on the work of missionaries there, but also on the contributions of government and merchant authorities. Central to the effort to build a perfect religious society – in both New France and elsewhere – was the exclusion of European influences that interfered with the Jesuit vision for what that society should look like. As Michel Foucault argued in describing what he termed "heterotopias of compensation" – places that reflect and perfect or contest other sites such as colonies, museums, gardens, and even brothels – such places always feature a mechanism of opening and closing that simultaneously permits and prohibits access.[12] The early days of the Jesuit mission, in which the Society's representatives had to work alongside an order with different priorities and found themselves in conflict with merchants, fell far short of the Jesuits' preference for carefully regulated religious colonies to which access was tightly controlled.

It therefore may have been a blessing in disguise when French economic control of the colony, and missionary work along with it, was interrupted by the takeover of Quebec in 1629 by the Kirke brothers, British privateers who seized the colony and expelled the Jesuit and Recollet missionaries. Vexing though it surely was to have their missionary work interrupted, this coup also brought the Jesuits an opportunity to enhance their own role in the colony, possibly at the expense of their former collaborators. When England returned the colony to France following the 1631 treaty of St. Germain en Laye,[13] the Jesuits became exclusive missionaries to New France. From the seventeenth century to the present day, the blame for the Recollets' exclusion has been laid at the feet of Cardinal Richelieu and his confidant Père Joseph (a Franciscan Capuchin priest who apparently first tried to secure a monopoly for his own order before supporting the Jesuits), officials in the trading company, and sometimes even the Jesuits. Historian Caroline Galland recently has concluded that the Recollets were not excluded maliciously, but were instead "collateral damage" of the Jesuits' more skilful navigation of the political circumstances surrounding France's renewed possession of the colony.[14]

The Recollets, for their part, characterized their departure in terms that made it clear that they regarded it as only temporary, and that suggested that they had planned all along to return to New France. Gabriel Sagard, for example, claimed in his 1636 *Histoire du Canada* that his order had believed its claim to the mission to be so unassailable that they never bothered to completely move out when evicted by the English. Wrote Sagard, "It was necessary to be calm when prayers were useless and it was expected that the country would be returned to the French, for which our religious so hoped, and to return there at some point, that they contented themselves to bring only two trunks, and to hide the rest of their implements and furniture in various places under ground and in the woods, the greater part of our ornaments were enclosed tight in a leather box in a separate place."[15] In Sagard's retrospective telling of events, his order's departure from New France was meant to be only partial and temporary. The Recollets, who apparently saw no reason to doubt that they would soon have the opportunity take up their post once more in the New World, reportedly even left behind precious religious objects. In addition to signalling the Recollets' intention to return, the author's claim that the missionaries had intentionally left much behind when leaving New France would have reminded the reader of the order's long history there – long enough, in any case, to have accumulated possessions that were easier to store than to transport.

Indeed, when England transferred the colony back to French control in 1631, the Recollets apparently believed themselves to be first in line to resume missionary work there. Looking back on his order's exclusion from the end of the seventeenth century, Recollet missionary Chrestien Le Clercq claimed that the order had been surprised by this turn of events, given its long experience in New France: "We prepared for our return in the year 1631, and did not anticipate the least difficulty in the matter, as we had our establishments formed, patents from Rome and France in good form; a possession of fourteen or fifteen years, with untiring labors which we had undergone, rendered our right incontestable."[16] Le Clercq hung his order's claim to the mission on its many years of experience there, the infrastructure it had built, and the permission it had obtained from royal and papal authorities. Indeed, it seems that the order had good reason to believe that its return to New France was assured. A 1618 papal ruling, supported by King Louis XIII, had granted the Recollets exclusive stewardship of New France for as long as they cared to stay there, giving them what they believed to be an unshakable hold on the mission. The order apparently was so confident of its imminent return to the colony that it sought in 1631 to have a bishopric established there, making a case to the Congregation for the Propagation of the Faith in Rome.[17]

That the Jesuits were transported to New France in 1632 apparently came as a rude surprise to the Recollets, who seem to have had no prior knowledge that their former colleagues were preparing to return – alone – to the mission. Although they could not boast the same legal rights and long experience in New France as their former Recollet colleagues, the Jesuits had other strengths that apparently were enough to secure their place in the mission field, including their renowned political prowess. According to ethnohistorian Bruce Trigger, "Instead of seeking an alliance with Champlain, as the Recollets had done, the Jesuits undertook to control the highest echelons of the colonial administration in France itself, in order to ensure that no traders, officials, or other religious orders in France could oppose them."[18] As a "silent partner" in the formation of the Compagnie de 100 Associés, which held a monopoly on trade in the colony starting in 1627, the Jesuits had aligned themselves with the company's mission, set by the powerful Cardinal Richelieu, to "inscribe New France indelibly on the map of North America."[19] Indeed, instead of clashing with merchants, as had sometimes been the norm previously, the Jesuit missionaries appear to have actively encouraged the administration of the colony by the trading monopoly. The stage had thus been set in the late 1620s for an alliance between economic and religious interests in New France, but the English takeover of Quebec in 1629 halted the new arrangement before it had a chance to work. When England returned the colony to France in early 1632, the Jesuits were well positioned to claim a prominent role there thanks to their attention to mission politics in the previous decade, and seem to have viewed collaboration with governmental and commercial interests as essential to the success of their mission. As Le Jeune wrote in 1635, "The more imposing the power of our French people is made in these Countries, the more easily they can make their belief received by these Barbarians, who are influenced even more through the senses, than through reason."[20]

While the Jesuits supported the colonial and commercial ambitions of the new trading monopoly, the Compagnie de 100 Associés, in turn, aligned itself more closely with attempts to Christianize the colony than had previous traders. Unlike its predecessor, the Caen Group, which was made up of both Protestant and Catholic merchants who were perhaps naturally more concerned with extracting wealth than with presenting a single vision of Christianity to potential converts, the new company's duties explicitly included looking after the spiritual welfare of the colony. The royal edict establishing the company called for "a strong company for the establishment of a colony of naturalized Frenchmen, Catholics of both sexes, judging that it was the only way to advance in a short time the conversion of these people, and to enhance the name of France to the glory of God and the reputation of the crown."[21] The company's charter also forbade merchants to transport anyone other than French Catholics to the colony, and required them to provide material support for three missionaries at every settlement they established. Instead of working at seemingly conflicting goals, as they sometimes had previously, missionary and trade groups were poised to support each other's work when France regained control of the colony following the brief period of British control. In supporting the Crown's plan to govern the military, economic, and territorial affairs of the colony through the intermediary of a trading company, the Jesuits had aligned themselves with powerful French colonial interests, paving their way for a return to New France at the expense of the Recollets.

Political positioning aside, the Jesuits also had at least one unique strength that they were not shy about publicizing. From the very founding of the Society of Jesus, members emphasized the use of local languages in their missions. As Ignatius Loyola himself wrote in the *Constitutions*, "When a plan is being worked out in some college or university to prepare persons to go among the Moors or Turks, Arabic or Chaldaic would be expedient; and Indian would be proper for those about to go among the Indians; and the same holds true for similar reasons in regard to other languages which could have greater utility in other regions."[22] Accordingly, the priests undertook a major effort to analyze, document, and learn to speak well the languages of the peoples they hoped to convert in New France, a project that eventually would yield a sophisticated understanding of Amerindian languages and that will be examined in depth in the following chapter. Perhaps not surprisingly, the Jesuits' focus on and apparent relative success in acquiring language skills had been a point of emphasis in the missionaries' efforts to distinguish themselves from other groups from the earliest years of their presence in New France, before regular publication of the *Relations* began. Upon arriving in Acadia in 1611, the Jesuit Pierre Biard reported that Jessé Fléché, a secular priest — one focusing on ministering to believers but not a member of a religious order[23] — had baptized about a hundred Micmacs, despite the fact that they apparently possessed no knowledge of Christianity. Biard lashed out in a letter to his superior: "The trouble [mal] is, he has not been able to instruct them as he would have wished, because he did not know the language, and had nothing with which to support them; for he who would minister to their souls, must at the same time resolve to nourish their bodies."[24] In the Jesuit's estimation, Fléché's failure as a teacher of Christianity was linked to his concurrent failure as a student of Amerindian languages.

Although he admitted that the Jesuits who replaced Fléché were themselves still struggling to learn to teach their message in the language of the Micmacs, Biard followed his criticisms of Fléché with an account of conversations with some of the Amerindians that Fléché had baptized, as if to demonstrate that although imperfect, his knowledge was at least better than that of his predecessor. The word that Biard chose to register his disapproval of Fléché's actions also is significant. Instead of the more neutral "problème" or "défaut," Biard opted for the synonym "mal," a word that has moral connotations and highlights not only the practical problem posed by Fléché's poor grasp of the language, but also the absence of virtue in the "conversions" it produced.[25] Although the Jesuits would temper their direct criticism of other missionaries in their published comments in the following decades, Biard's letter reflects an argument that would become a point of emphasis in Jesuit portrayals of themselves as uniquely qualified for missionary work in New France well before regular publication of the Jesuit *Relations* began: one could not teach Christianity in New France without first having learned Amerindian languages, and the Jesuit missionaries had had more success in doing so than any of their rivals and collaborators.

The Recollets, although less liberal dispensers of baptisms than Fléché had been, apparently were only slightly more adept at acquiring Amerindian languages, a point that Jesuits were quick to bring to the attention of their readers. In a 1627 published letter to his brother Jérôme, later to become a prominent missionary author in his own right, Charles Lalemant recounted his efforts to enlist the help of trading company interpreter Nicolas Marsolet in his own attempt to learn the Montagnais language. Success was not likely, Lalemant wrote, because Marsolet had already refused to help others, and because negative impressions of the Society of Jesus were then prevalent in New France, at least partly due to the anti-Jesuit tract *L'Anticoton* that had been circulating among colonists. To Lalemant's apparent surprise, Marsolet proved himself a willing teacher. Wrote Lalemant, "Strange to say, he at once promised me that, during the winter, he would give me all the help that I could ask of him. Now in this a special providence of God must be admired ...

This Interpreter had never wanted to communicate his knowledge of the language to any one, not even to the Reverend Recollect Fathers, who had constantly importuned him for ten years; and yet he promised me what I have told you, the first time I urged him to do so, and he kept his promise faithfully during that Winter."[26] In a coup that Le Jeune would trumpet anew in 1633, the Jesuits claimed to have succeeded where the Recollets had failed by convincing Marsolet to share his knowledge of Montagnais. Having learned what he could from Marsolet, Lalemant reportedly turned to another, unnamed interpreter who similarly had kept the Recollets at arm's length, but who nonetheless immediately gave the Jesuits all of the lessons that they asked for.[27]

The successful extraction of information from both interpreters was presented in Lalemant's letter not only as a triumph of Jesuit persistence and diligence in their linguistic project, but also as a sign that God favoured their success. Indeed, in Lalemant's telling of events, his work with the interpreters threatened to be impossible, even if they cooperated willingly, due to the anticipated return to France of both of the language experts. Marsolet had been slated to return immediately to the Old Country, but was persuaded to stay in the colony. The other translator suddenly fell ill just prior to his own scheduled departure for France, and had to watch the boats leave without him. As the above passage indicates, Lalemant explicitly attributed the opportunity to work with Marsolet to divine providence, and the lucky illness of the second interpreter was no less an act of God, in the missionary's estimation. Wrote Lalemant, "It suffices to say that, before he recovered from this sickness, in which he expected to die, he assured us that he was entirely devoted to us; and that if it pleased God to restore his health, the Winter would never pass by without his giving us assistance, a promise which he kept in every respect, thank God. I have, perhaps, dwelt longer upon this than was necessary, but I am so pleased to relate the special acts of God's providence, as it seems to me every one must take pleasure in them; and in fact, if he had gone back to France that year, we would have made hardly any more progress than the Reverend Recollect Fathers did in 10 years. May God be praised for all!"[28] Gloating that the Jesuits, despite their recent arrival in the colony, were already better at Amerindian languages than their Recollet colleagues, Lalemant drew a sharp comparison between the two orders' linguistic prowess, all to the Jesuits' favour. And, Lalemant suggested, this relative success reflected the will of God, coming, as it did, despite circumstances that threatened the Jesuits' access to the interpreters' knowledge. Although the Recollets may have been able to boast experience in and apparent legal rights to the mission, the Jesuits had useful tools of their own in seeking a return to the colony: political savvy and a longstanding emphasis on the relative strength of their language skills.

When they arrived in New France in 1632 without their former Recollet associates, the Jesuits finally were fully ensconced in New France after many years of trying and two false starts, and were in a position to preach their message to the Iroquoian and Algonquian inhabitants of New France without the interference of Protestant traders or competing Catholic groups with whom they had already sometimes contrasted themselves in published texts. The Society's monopoly on missionary work in New France would last until 1657, when Sulpicians arrived in Montreal.[29] Not only would Jesuit voices be the only ones heard by potential converts, the organization had nearly monopolized the flow of information in the other direction as well, from New France to Europe. Samuel de Champlain's death in 1635 also brought an end to his frequent publications on the subject of life in the colony and the Amerindian groups that inhabited the area. Gabriel Sagard, a Recollet brother who had spent much of 1623 and 1624 in New France, including about a year among the Huron, parlayed his experiences into two books, the 1632 *Le Grand Voyage du Pays des Hurons*, and the 1636 *Histoire du Canada*. Published, as they were, many years after the fact, both tomes would have lacked the urgency and topicality of the Jesuit *Relations*, and could not hope to compete with the Jesuits' annual barrage of information. With no rival groups to publish competing yearly accounts of goings-on in the colony, the Jesuits, as modern scholarship's continuing reliance on them attests, were finally in a position to be the primary influence both on how Amerindian groups understood Europe and Christianity, and on how those groups would be understood by outsiders for centuries to come.

Although the Jesuits were in a position to conduct their mission to convince both Amerindians and Europeans to adopt their own ideas practically without competition, their rivals seem to have considered the matter far from settled. The Recollets mounted a vigorous campaign throughout the 1630s, '40s, and '50s to secure passage to the colony, writing, according to a later Jesuit observer, "memo upon memo to assert their rights, sparing no step."[30] They argued that they were the rightful owners of the New France infrastructure, and that royal and papal support, expressed in letters that were reproduced in texts destined for public consumption, should be enough to break down whatever barriers were preventing the order's return to New France.[31] Their efforts nonetheless were denied by officials of the trading company every year except 1633. In that year, trading company superintendent Jean de Lauson reportedly agreed to transport Recollet priests to the mission, but only when the ships that were to carry them were about to depart, leaving the would-be missionaries no time to make the necessary arrangements. The order took its case directly to the public as well, seeking and gaining the support of wealthy benefactors to counteract the perception, cited by some as a reason for the Recollets' exclusion, that the colony was too small, young, and fragile to support a mendicant order – one emphasizing poverty and frugality, and normally refusing to seek fixed revenues to support its communities.[32]

Despite the Recollets' apparent frustration at being shut out of the New France mission, the order seems to have maintained a generally cordial relationship with the Jesuits, both prior to and during the latter group's tenure as sole missionaries in New France, perhaps because the potential for inter-order squabbling sometimes was cited as a reason for the Recollets' continued exclusion. Both sides, at least publicly, dismissed those concerns.[33] Instead of resorting to overt hostility, each missionary group subtly undermined the other while promoting itself as the outfit best equipped to convert the New France Amerindians. Accounts by Recollet writers of the low-simmering dispute suggest that the order touted its own long experience and alleged successes in the colony, instead of directly criticizing the Jesuits, in its attempts to regain access to the mission field. One anonymous Recollet historian, for example, wrote the following in the unpublished 1689 *Histoire Chronologique de la Nouvelle France*: "The Recollet fathers served the land alone for ten years with much zeal and edification; they had cleared the first and very large difficulties of establishing the Catholic Religion in a new colony that was in the hands of an almost heretical company; they only needed to be supported a little and assisted to be able to continue their holy work; they addressed themselves for that to his eminence the Duke of Ventadour, to whom they showed that to work more fruitfully at the conversion of the *sauvages* they needed some some help to establish seminaries in the places where these barbarians resided."[34] Seeking only support for the continuation of their work, the author claimed, the Recollets appealed to Ventadour, the viceroy of New France, whose Jesuit confessor then convinced him to do nothing to help the Recollets directly, and to instead send the Jesuits to New France. This retrospective version of events suggests that the Recollets saw the Jesuits as unwelcome adjuncts to an already successful missionary operation, one that allegedly had, before the Jesuits' arrival, been successful in eliminating the most daunting obstacles to the Christianization of the colony.[35] By emphasizing their long experience in New France and the surprising and unwelcome arrival of the Jesuits, the anonymous author of the *Histoire Chronologique* and other Recollet writers maintained their claim to be the order best-equipped for the missionary task, and implied, without directly saying so, that the Jesuits were unqualified at best and usurpers at worst.[36]

Other Recollet writers claimed that their order itself had invited the Jesuits to join the New France mission in the first place, a claim that would make the Jesuits' elevation to exclusive spiritual stewards of the colony all the more unseemly. A 1636 memorandum produced by an unnamed Recollet that argues for the order's return to the colony, for example, claimed that the Jesuits only participated in the mission at the invitation of their predecessors: "They implore you to consider if it is just to have prevented them from returning to said country, having been there first and so long before having called the Jesuit Fathers there."[37] Although this claim occasionally has been repeated as fact since the seventeenth century, the most recent scholars to examine it have dismissed it as pure invention, and have reported finding no trace of any invitation from the Recollets that precipitated the Jesuits' arrival in the colony.[38] Whether true or not, the claim circulated by the Recollets that the Jesuits had begun their careers in New France as mere invited assistants to an already successful mission inevitably cast the newcomers and eventual replacements as less-qualified interlopers who had no business taking over the mission from the more experienced Recollets.

Recollet complaints about the Jesuits occasionally took the form of explicit accusations of underhanded dealings. In the 1636 memo mentioned above, the anonymous author accuses Jesuit priests of redirecting material support meant for the Recollets to themselves during their earlier stint together in New France: "Nevertheless, the Jesuits secretly had diverted the food of two Recollets to themselves, which monsieur de Ventadour, the viceroy, reversed upon learning of it."[39] Sagard repeated the accusation in his 1636 *Histoire du Canada*.[40] Although the charge does not seem to have been made explicitly at the time, the Recollets at least suggested, by citing a small example of Jesuit treachery, that their rivals were capable of the self-interested machinations that would have been required to unjustly exclude the Recollets once the colony returned to French hands after its brief stint under British control.

It was only decades later, after the Recollets had been granted a new role in New France in 1670,[41] that members of the order dared to directly accuse the Jesuits of purposely and maliciously shutting them out, and even then the accusation was apparently deemed too scandalous for publication. The anonymous author of the *Histoire Chronologique de la Nouvelle France*, looking back on decades of Recollet struggles to gain access to New France from his late-seventeenth-century perspective, was explicit in his accusation of Jesuit underhanded dealings, reflecting the long years of frustration his order had endured in attempting to loosen the Jesuit stranglehold on the New France mission: "my goal is only to make known the injustices that some Jesuit politicians create by means of the secular power that they wield in the manner the most adroit and the least fair in the world. I do so without passion and only to make known their passion that rages in Canada against a small number of Recollets. I know that it is inconceivable in France that the Jesuits, that seminarians, that religious communities even, are crossing the sea to apply all of their zeal to ruin a small community of friars of Saint Francis. That is nonetheless what is happening under the greatest guise of friendship in the world."[42] Not only did the Jesuits steal the rightful place of the Recollets, the author claimed, they purposely set out to destroy their predecessors by skilfully manipulating secular authorities, without any concern for justice. Although it may never be known for certain why the *Histoire Chronologique de la Nouvelle France* was not published until 1888, the author of the preface to the first edition, the journalist and lawyer Eugène Réveillaud, suggested that it was due to a continuing desire among Recollet authorities to maintain at least the appearance of civil relations with the Jesuits.[43] Whatever the reason, the text makes it clear that the

Recollets had a motive to undermine the Jesuits whenever the opportunity arose, and the spurned missionaries' most potent argument seems to have been that the Jesuits were unqualified at best, and quite possibly had purposely and maliciously excluded the Recollets who had previously worked alongside them.

The authors of the *Relations*, for their part, did not address the controversy directly.[44] And according to some sources, the Jesuits actively supported the Recollets' efforts to regain access to the colony. In his nineteenth-century account of Jesuit activity in New France, Camille de Rochemonteix, himself a member of the Society of Jesus, claimed that the Jesuits did nothing to block their former coworkers from returning to the colony, and indeed repeatedly wrote to them to express the hope that they might again collaborate.[45] But even such statements in support of the Recollet campaign to return to New France indicate that a climate of suspicion surrounded the Jesuit presence in the colony, to the extent that Jesuit outreach was needed to defend the Society from the suspicion that they had intentionally excluded the Recollets. The Recollet Chrestien Le Clercq, for example, professed to believe that the Jesuits had done nothing to shut out his order, but nonetheless characterized the Jesuit outreach as a defensive move intended to counter perceptions that the Jesuits had conspired to steal the mission from the Recollets: "the reverend Jesuit Fathers saw themselves suspected of preventing the return of the Recollects. They chose to exculpate themselves by a certificate, by protestations, by authentic letters which I have read, one from the Reverend Father Le Jeune, Superior of the mission ... another from the Reverend Father Charles Lallemant ... and a third from the same Father Lallemant to Brother Gervase Mohier, in which he complains greatly that the Fathers of the Society were suspected in France and in Canada of being opposed to our return."[46] The first two letters mentioned by Le Clercq are listed as "lost" in Jesuit scholar Lucien Campeau's massive collection of documents related to the mission, and it is in vain that one searches for traces of the third.[47] These absences regrettably make it impossible to evaluate the Jesuits' efforts to defend themselves, or Le Clercq's interpretation of those efforts, but the letters' contents are, in any case, irrelevant for the current discussion. Le Clercq either accurately represents a level of suspicion that necessitated Jesuit outreach, or invents it, casting aspersions even as he pretends to applaud the good will between the two orders. Both possibilities suggest that the Jesuits were, in at least some quarters, suspected of culpability in the exclusion of their predecessors from New France.

Whether the Jesuit missionaries fully supported Recollet aspirations regarding New France or secretly worked to have them excluded may remain unknown, but it is clear that the circumstances leading to the Society's monopoly on the mission and the climate of suspicion that it produced posed challenges to the Jesuits' legitimacy in New France. Even if the Jesuits did nothing to obstruct the Recollets, their presence in the colony and the resistance encountered by their rivals left them vulnerable to the perception – apparently actively but carefully encouraged by the Recollets – that they had usurped the rightful place of the more experienced order that claimed to have invited their participation in the first place. Asserting its authority and demonstrating its capacity to effect change in the New France mission were therefore necessary moves if the Society were to be accepted as a legitimate force for converting Amerindian groups, and if the information about indigenous cultures in its *Relations* were to be taken seriously by readers and potential financial backers in France. With access to the New France mission in dispute, and with skill in languages already established as a strong point of Jesuit strategy, it is perhaps natural that descriptions of Amerindian languages and Jesuit attempts to learn them would serve, as the rest of this chapter will show, as assertions of the order's ability and legitimacy as sole spiritual steward of the colony, and as an indirect critique of its would-be collaborators.

And yet, this longstanding point of emphasis was not necessarily an unalloyed strength in the case of the Jesuit mission in New France, because it had yet, in the early 1630s, to yield the desired result: large-scale conversion of Iroquoian and Algonquian inhabitants of the area. Perhaps not surprisingly, progress in converting Amerindians to Christianity was extremely slow in the earliest years of the Jesuits' tenure in New France. During the forty-year period in which the *Relations* were published, the Jesuits claimed to have baptized more than 16,000 Amerindians, mostly Huron. But only 55 conversions were reported in the first five years after the Jesuits' arrival in 1632, 49 of which were deathbed baptisms.[48] Indeed, poor use of Amerindian languages in the early years of the mission apparently drew ridicule from potential converts, and allowed the missionaries' religious message to be easily brushed aside.[49] And resistant interlocutors also reportedly sometimes feigned incomprehension to avoid co-operating with Jesuit requests. For example, Le Jeune reported in 1636 the result of a colleague's attempt to convince the Montagnais to allow a dead relative to be buried in the Christian manner: "a Savage answered him, 'Go away, we do not understand thee.' This is an answer that the Savages occasionally make to us, when we urge them to do something that does not suit them. It is true that, as yet, we speak only stammeringly; but, still, when we say something which conforms to their wishes they never use these reproaches."[50] The linguistic resistance that the priests reported sometimes encountering suggests that they were not alone in understanding Amerindian languages as an entry point that might lead to cultural change.[51] Feigning incomprehension and co-operating only when there was a clear advantage to doing so could be interpreted as an effort by Amerindians to slow the Jesuits' linguistic progress, and thereby to keep them at arm's length and limit the changes they could introduce to Amerindian cultures. Not only were languages a potential key to the continent for merchants and missionaries, they were also, potentially, a mechanism by which Amerindians could close the door on meddlesome outsiders, or at least slow their advance.

These daunting obstacles notwithstanding, comments in the *Relations* suggest that readers and financial backers in France were impatient for results in New France, and the missionary authors pointed to continuing struggles to express themselves in local languages as the culprit. To cite just one example, Le Jeune's 1636 *Relation* counselled patience to readers:

> If nothing else were needed than to propose a few truths stammer-
> ingly, in order to fully convince the Savages, this would soon be
> done. But one must question and answer, satisfy inquiries, dis-
> pose of objections, and prepare one's hearers. In short, our truths,
> which are newer to these Barbarians than the operations of Algebra
> would be to a person who could only count to ten, must almost
> make them forget their own language, when we use it to explain
> these to them. In the same way, are we far from being sufficiently
> familiar with it, in so short a time, for the explanation of myster-
> ies so deep. And then they ask why it is that we have advanced so
> little in the conversion of these Barbarians. Great affairs are usually
> concluded only in a long time.[52]

For the Jesuit mission superior, facility with Amerindian languages was of primary importance in convincing potential converts to embrace Christianity. The above passage goes on to recount the vexingly long process of the construction of a "miracle of human ingenuity," the Temple of Saint Sophia in Constantinople. Like that achievement, Le Jeune implies, learning Amerindian languages well would require time and patience, but would be worth the wait. At the same time as he counselled patience and insisted on the enormity of the task, Le Jeune also compared the project to teaching algebra. It might be difficult initially, but like algebra, he suggested, Christianity was a clear and unambiguous truth that could not fail to persuade, once the student had the necessary background knowledge and once the new material was effectively communicated.

Simultaneously insisting on language as a privileged entry point to the colony and the mission and admitting temporary weakness was a delicate balancing act for the Jesuit missionaries in their early efforts to describe their attempts to convert Amerindians to Christianity. While language barriers, whether naturally existing or purposely placed in the Jesuits' way by reluctant prospective converts, might have been an acceptable excuse for disappointing results, Jesuit missionaries still were under pressure to justify their presence in New France in response to Recollet claims that they were the rightful stewards of the mission, due to both experience and legal rights. In writing about Amerindian languages, then, the priests had to justify their slow progress by pointing to their lack of full fluency in the unfamiliar tongues, while simultaneously justifying their position as sole New France missionaries by suggesting that the needed skills would soon be acquired, and that they knew more than anyone else. As the rest of this chapter argues, the ways the priests described their efforts to attain fluency asserted rhetorical control over the languages, reminding readers that the Jesuits – and only the Jesuits – were in a position to obtain what they regarded as the most important tool for bringing Christianity to the Amerindians. The authors openly acknowledged the flawed state of their linguistic knowledge, and the resultant slow pace of conversions, but also cast success as inevitable. Jesuits had their foot in the door, so to speak, and suggested that before long they would have unfettered access to Amerindian souls. And although the missionaries were not in a position of direct control over who could travel to the colony, their near monopoly on the flow of information across the Atlantic during their tenure as exclusive missionaries to New France's Amerindian populations gave them an opportunity to rhetorically close the door on any would-be competitors or colleagues, at least temporarily. As the public's almost sole source of news from the colony and the mission, the authors of the *Relations* were well-positioned to set the terms for missionary access to New France, and to define for French and religious authorities, as well as potential financial backers of any missionary effort, what it would take to successfully bring Christianity to the Amerindians.

And yet, it would be years before missionaries would be able to meet the lofty goal of oratorical skill they had set for themselves. When Le Jeune disembarked in 1632, he had only a small handwritten and error-filled Montagnais dictionary on which to rely, the fruit of one of the Society's earlier, brief stints in Canada.[53] Even the Jesuit Jean de Brébeuf, who was reputed to be a gifted linguist and who had demonstrated such aptitude for learning Montagnais during his first tour of duty in New France starting in 1625 that he was soon sent to learn the Huron language, was not yet ready to speak eloquently in the earliest years after his second arrival in the colony in 1633, even if he was able to communicate. As the priest's 1635 *Relation* put it, "As for me, who give lessons therein to our French, if God does not assist me extraordinarily, I shall yet have to go a long time to the school of the Savages, so prolific is their language."[54] Brébeuf's simultaneous casting of himself as both pupil and teacher summarizes the paradoxical quality of the entire Jesuit ethnographic enterprise, explained in detail in the previous chapter. As the order's best linguist, Brébeuf was responsible for helping his colleagues learn Amerindian languages, much the same way Le Jeune and the other priests who would eventually be charged with composing the *Relations* were responsible for communicating accrued knowledge, shaped to support the Jesuits' particular point of view, to readers in France. But this position of power was balanced by a corresponding weakness: reducing himself to a mere écolier, Brébeuf suggested that he still had much to learn, and was therefore in no position to bring about large-scale conversion, or even to learn much about the beliefs and practices of potential Amerindian converts.

The two roles that Brébeuf found himself occupying simultaneously, those of master and student, were roles with which each missionary was already intimately acquainted. The role of master – transmitting new lessons to the uninitiated – would have been familiar to Brébeuf and his colleagues before their arrival in New France. Each Jesuit spent at least two years as a teacher in Europe's Jesuit colleges as part of his training. Also familiar, therefore, would have been the role of student, and the rules and standards governing the Jesuit colleges in which future missionaries were formed shed light on Brébeuf's characterization of himself in such terms. In Jesuit colleges – and in contrast to the modern connotations of the word – a "student" was not merely a person engaged in a course of study. Instead, students in such colleges were purposely and thoroughly alienated from all that was familiar for the purpose of instilling in them the supposedly superior culture of the ancient Romans. Use of French was prohibited in favour of Latin and Roman culture and history were emphasized, whereas French equivalents were ignored, and students' contact with the world outside the school was sharply curtailed. In short, Jesuit colleges sought not only to instruct their students, but also to do so in a way that cut them off from all that was familiar, thereby constantly reminding them of how little they knew and of their status as lowly students.[55] By characterizing himself as a pupil going to the Amerindians' school, then, Brébeuf was not only emphasizing his own lack of knowledge of the languages of potential converts, but was also suggesting a degree of powerlessness and alienation that is not usually understood, anymore, to be part of being a student. The experience of having been immersed in an unfamiliar culture and language in the Jesuit colleges of Europe was one that all of the missionaries shared, and was therefore an easy point of reference for describing contact with the Amerindians' "prolific" and wholly unknown languages.

Brébeuf was not the only New France Jesuit who, having already graduated from pupil to master in Europe, cast himself in the less powerful of the two positions in the pages of the *Relations*. To Brébeuf's lament mentioned above could be added Le Jeune's similar remark in 1633 casting himself as a pupil under the guidance of Pierre Pastedechouan, a Montagnais man who had been baptized and taught French during a stay in France under the care of the Recollets.[56] Wrote Le Jeune, recounting the extreme difficulty of learning Montagnais: "I begin to work incessantly. I make conjugations, declensions and some little syntax, and a dictionary, with incredible trouble, for I was compelled sometimes to ask twenty questions to understand one word, [so much did my master, unaccustomed to teaching, vary]. Oh, how grateful I am to those who

sent me some Tobacco last year. The Savages love it to madness. Whenever we came to a difficulty, I gave my master a piece of tobacco, to make
him more attentive."[57] Casting the relationship between missionary and
potential convert as one of master and pupil – as opposed to enlightened
European and uncivilized native, or participant-observer and anthropological subject – suggests a relative weakness on the part of the missionaries that was certainly accurate,[58] but also implies that their place in the
less powerful role was only temporary. Pupils, after all, do not remain
forever under the control of their master. As the Jesuits would themselves have known well from their own formation and early careers, it is
through long study that one becomes a master, and one can hardly blame
a pupil for not equalling his teacher's status immediately upon beginning
to study, or even quickly, if his master is not a gifted teacher. Le Jeune's
master, in particular, was not portrayed as an adult authority figure, but
rather a child-like possessor of knowledge who had to be bribed to pay
attention. If Le Jeune found himself under the instruction of such a
master, it surely meant that progress could hardly be swift, even if it did
not imply permanent powerlessness.

Similarly, the Jesuit authors sometimes cast themselves as children in
matters of language, left to observe and learn from adults – Amerindians who spoke the way the priests hoped they themselves would, one
day. Of the missionaries' understandably shaky language skills in 1633,
Le Jeune wrote, "Certainly, one must speak in order to be understood;
and this is what we cannot do yet, except as children."[59] Four years later,
the priest again characterized himself this way after reporting that a new
convert had recounted the Christian creation and flood stories to other
Amerindians in better terms than the priest could have done it himself:
"Oh, what a difference between a man who talks and a child who only
stutters! I do not doubt that, if we knew the language perfectly, we might
obtain much from these people."[60] In his repeated depiction of himself
as a stammering child, Le Jeune admitted his linguistic incompetence,
but again suggested that the condition was not permanent. Just as a student through long study becomes a master, a child grows into an adult
over time.

François-Joseph Le Mercier's 1637 description of the short speeches on
Catholic doctrine given to inhabitants of a Huron village similarly infant-
ilized the Jesuits, depicting their linguistic efforts as similar to learning to

walk. Wrote Le Mercier: "We derived considerable advantage from this little exercise, by improving ourselves in the language. Besides teaching the children, we took occasion to explain some of our mysteries to the fathers and mothers, for which we usually made some preparation; these talks, however, were not very long; one must learn to put one foot before the other, before he can walk. We were greatly consoled to see that we were understood, and that a Savage occasionally took up the conversation and repeated what we had said."[61] Describing the study of languages this way suggests inevitable, natural progress: in the same way that a child taking his or her first steps will, in time and with additional practice, walk more steadily, the Jesuits, through a "first step" of their own – giving very short religious lessons in Huron – would gradually gain proficiency in the language and therefore the power to effect widespread conversion. In addition to suggesting inevitable progress, these characterizations of the Jesuits' efforts to learn Amerindian languages shift responsibility for the slow pace of conversions and their still imperfect knowledge away from the missionaries. At the mercy of "masters" who were not particularly gifted at teaching, the Jesuits could hardly be blamed if their language-learning was not swift, and their communication skills were not yet advanced enough to bring about mass conversions. Though they could not yet boast of conversions of large numbers of Amerindians, reducing themselves to mere crawling infants and schoolchildren may have excused the poor results of their missionary efforts, but also suggested that the future was bright.

The self-infantilization that often marks the Jesuits' early descriptions of their attempts to acquire language skills sometimes has been interpreted as a sign of the missionaries' frustration with their difficult situation. Historian Edward G. Gray, for example, has suggested that the Jesuits were shamed by their position as mere schoolchildren in relation to their Amerindian teachers. Wrote Gray, "For Jesuits, many of whom had served as teachers of Latin in their native France, to find themselves abandoned to the whims of Indian teachers must have been to experience the deepest humiliation and confusion. The notion that one must learn fundamentals from students before even an elementary lesson could be taught meant that far from the sort of generally accepted superiority enjoyed by a Jesuit schoolmaster, Jesuit missionaries were at once the pupils and the spiritual fathers of their Christian charges. This instructional relationship represented a total reversal of usual channels of authority in Jesuit education."[62] In the context of the political climate surrounding the beginning of Jesuit missionary work in New France, however, it seems that the simultaneous positions of submission and authority that characterized the linguistic enterprise – the positions of student and teacher – would have served to define a relationship between the missionaries and the unfamiliar cultures that, although perhaps humiliating, was also politically useful. By casting themselves as students, the Jesuits could suggest ever-increasing mastery and control over Amerindian languages, which they had already suggested was indispensable to the conversion of Amerindian groups. In other words, portraits of humiliation and confusion may be thought of as having served a useful purpose in the missionaries' efforts to explain their work to European readers, as long as they were accompanied and balanced by suggestions that the situation was only temporary. At the same time, highlighting the challenge would make even rudimentary knowledge all the more impressive to readers – a marvelous feat that would enhance the reputation of the Jesuits as capable and qualified missionaries in the face of the doubts that were expressed both privately and publicly at home in France.

Perhaps belatedly recognizing the political stakes of the Jesuits' emphasis on learning the languages of potential converts and the need to compete in that domain, the Recollet missionary Gabriel Sagard published a Huron dictionary in 1632 as an appendix to his *Grand Voyage au Pays des Hurons*, about eight years after his own departure from New France. The decision to publish what he knew of the Huron language, particularly in the same year his order found itself unexpectedly shut out of the mission, could be seen as an effort to bolster his order's credentials in an area that Jesuits had long been claiming as their own strength.[63] Wrote Sagard in a brief introduction to the dictionary, "And even though I am little versed in the Huron language, and very incapable of doing anything of value, I will nonetheless share with the public … the little that I know of it."[64] By his own account of his motives, Sagard's intention in publishing the dictionary was to share this knowledge with the public, not merely to preserve it for the education of future missionaries and colonists. Although it suggests that the Recollets may have come to understand the political stakes of proficiency in Amerindian languages, Sagard's single effort to establish the Recollets as competent language-learners in their own right was not likely to be more convincing than the case that the Jesuits made year after year in their *Relations*.

Perhaps not surprisingly given his order's position on the outside of the mission looking in, the relationship that Sagard described with potential informants was different from the Jesuits' frequent suggestions of current weakness and future strength. In his 1636 *Histoire du Canada*, Sagard recounted his efforts to convince Huron convert Pierre Pastedechouan, who had spent time in France, and Nicolas Marsolet to help him learn the Huron language:

> Sorry that I wasted my effort and my care, with all the study
> I had done with no other master than the little Pastedechouan,
> I addressed myself to the interpreter Marsolet, to have some
> instuction, but he told me frankly in our boat at Tadoussac that
> he could in no way do it and that I should ask another ... I asked
> him again to teach me some words of this language, for there was
> no one else more capable than he, and that I would help him on
> another occasion, but he continued in his refusal, not wanting, he
> said, to violate his oath and to do anything contrary to his prom-
> ises. Nevertheless, in the end he threw me these two Montagnais
> words, *Nomakinistitototiu*, which means, in French, "No, I do not
> understand you," for in Huron one says *Danstantearonca*. That is
> all that I could draw from him with all of my effort ...[65]

Sagard refers to Pastedechouan as a "master," but simultaneously dimin-ishes his power by labelling him "little." And the Recollet author's ac-count of his attempts to persuade Marsolet to give him lessons paints a similarly muddled portrait of the power dynamic between them. Mar-solet holds all the cards, but Sagard nonetheless manages to badger him into sharing a few precious words, and thereby violating his oath to the trading company, which, as noted earlier, required its interpreters to help preserve the company's monopoly in all things, including linguistic knowledge. Sagard goes on to report seeking the "help" and "assistance" of French interpreter Etienne Brûlé, a formula that casts his informant as a servant or a helper, rather than an authoritative master. Finally, Sagard concludes that the Recollets' attempts to learn Amerindian languages would not depend on submission to any master other than themselves.

Wrote Sagard, "Our principal masters in this art had to be our efforts and frequent communication with the savages."[66] Whereas Jesuit authors had portrayed themselves as temporarily occupying a position of weakness in relation to Amerindian masters, Sagard admitted his inability but placed responsibility on his own shoulders. He was his own master, in dialogue with Amerindians and interpreters instead of under their tutelage. Coming after his order had been excluded from the mission, and in the context of its ongoing efforts to regain access, this characterization no doubt reflects the political context surrounding the New France mission. Unlike the Jesuits, who had a disappointing record of conversions to defend in the 1630s, Sagard placed himself in a position of relative responsibility in his account of his efforts at language-learning, perhaps in order to minimize any signs of weakness that might have been used as an excuse to keep his order out of New France.

The ways in which the Jesuit missionary writers characterized their own linguistic efforts at the start of their tenure in New France offer a compelling way of understanding the Society's approach to the mission work that would produce the famed *Relations* from New France. In particular, Jesuit characterizations of themselves as initially and temporarily weak in relation to potential converts shed light on the bi-directional and overlapping flow of information that, as this book seeks to illustrate, characterized their missions in New France. Indeed, Jesuit accounts of their interactions with Amerindians in their attempts to learn the local languages not only paint a useful portrait of the encounter between French Jesuits and Amerindians, but also shed light on the European institution that was responsible for the missionaries' presence in the New World in the first place. The description of the Society of Jesus as a militaristic organization is as old as the order itself, and is likely at least partly born of the personal history and writing habits of its founder. As James Axtell has put it, "Ignatius Loyola, the founder of the order, had been an audacious officer in the Spanish forces of Navarre before his conversion to the religious life while recovering from wounds suffered in a French attack. A noble son of Spanish chivalry, he fell naturally into the language of war when he penned the Institutes for his new Society of Jesus."[67] And Pope

Julius III reinforced Loyola's militaristic vision of the fledgling order by referring to its members as "soldiers of God" in his papal bull authorizing its creation.[68] Modern scholars have often embraced the metaphor as a way of insisting on the highly organized, hierarchical, and zealous nature of the Society of Jesus itself. Axtell, for example, began a chapter on Jesuit missionary work in New France this way: "From the first coastal assault on Acadia, the Jesuit invasion of pagan America was suitably cast in a military mold."[69] And it is true that Jesuits themselves – both in New France and throughout the world – sometimes characterized their enterprise in these terms. As Carole Blackburn has remarked, the authors of the *Relations* made much use of the rhetoric of conquest, and "[a] key feature of this rhetoric was the Jesuits' representation of themselves as soldiers of Christ, engaged in the liberation of a country ruled and oppressed by Satan ... Their portrayal of their missionary work in New France as a military endeavour was consistent with aspects of their training; the same approach had been used to characterize their work in Europe, Asia, and South America."[70]

Linguist Victor Hanzeli has applied the military metaphor directly to the order's linguistic pursuits in New France, calling knowledge of Amerindian languages a "*machine de guerre*" for the missionaries.[71] And historian Alain Beaulieu discussed the Jesuits' linguistic efforts under the heading "Of the Weapons Necessary for War," and wrote that mastery of Amerindian languages permitted the missionaries to "attack" their religious systems.[72] Le Jeune himself in 1638 referred to languages as a weapon in describing missionary strategy: "First, we make expeditions to go and attack the enemy upon their own ground, with their own weapons – that is to say, by a knowledge of the Montagnais, Algonquin, and Huron tongues."[73] It is interesting to note that Le Jeune's characterization of the missionaries as troops brandishing arms and advancing on the enemy, as opposed to helpless schoolchildren, came only as the Jesuits' linguistic efforts were beginning to bear fruit in the final years of the 1630s,[74] an achievement that, as this chapter has suggested, would have been understood in the Jesuit conception of and strategy for religious conversion to come with considerably increased ability to Christianize New France's Amerindian groups.

Although it is true that militaristic rhetoric can be found in the *Relations*, embracing the metaphor as a defining characteristic of the Society's work in New France carries the risk of reducing Jesuit missionaries to mere robots who only had the power to influence life there, and perception of Amerindian cultures in Europe, by virtue of being instruments of Rome and the Catholic Church's authority. And yet, the *Relations* do not – on language or any other subject – reflect only the exercise of Rome's or Paris' power in the New World. As this chapter has argued, the missionaries were powerful in their own right, and used their texts to further their own interests in struggles with representatives of other branches of the Church over access to and control over the mission. Although derived from the writings and life of Loyola himself, the common portrait of the Society of Jesus as a troop of religious soldiers taking and carrying out orders from the pope is, as others have argued in different contexts, ripe for revision.[75] At least on the subject of language, it is clear that the New France Jesuits characterized themselves in the early years less as a dominant force than as children and students who eventually would grow into positions of authority from which they could effect religious conversions among their Amerindian masters. Simultaneously suggesting current weakness and future strength in this way would have bolstered Jesuit claims to the mission while excusing disappointing early results. Functioning in the *Relations* as an assertion of increasing control over Amerindian languages and therefore the missionary field, this was power exercised at the local level by Jesuits – not handed down to them by Rome – that also had implications for political affairs on the other side of the Atlantic.

The relationships of power between Amerindian groups, Jesuit missionaries, and their detractors in France that are on display in the Jesuit *Relations*, and particularly on the subject of the language acquisition project, add nuance to common perceptions of the texts that Jesuit missionaries produced. As this book will argue in relation to various other aspects of the texts, passages of the *Relations* that depict Jesuit engagement with Amerindian cultures are not only a record of encounters between a European force and the populations it acted upon, but also a record of the political, intellectual, and religious pressures acting on the Jesuits' budding proto-anthropology. Upon their arrival in New France, Jesuit missionaries were less like soldiers of Rome pursuing a mission handed down to them by authorities in the Society of Jesus than like agents in their own right, negotiating the fraught political waters of early-seventeenth-century French colonialism. They described their efforts to accumulate information in New France in terms that suggested current weakness, but also future strength. They wielded Amerindian languages as a political and religious key to New France, and they used it in the pages of their *Relations* to lock out meddlesome would-be competitors and erstwhile collaborators who, left behind in France, could not hope to procure that key for themselves.

The political dispute over access to the New France mission that surrounded the Jesuits' arrival alone in the mission field in 1632 would not be the end of the missionaries' engagement with Amerindian languages. Missionaries, after all, are teachers at least as much as they are students, and the Jesuit authors sometimes suggested as much even as they emphasized their own weakness relative to Amerindian masters. Jérôme Lalemant, for example, commented in 1639 that the Hurons who came to visit him in his cabin were there to both teach and learn. Wrote Lalemant, "For, whatever the number of barbarians that come to see you, they are so many Masters and pupils visiting you, and saving you the trouble of going to them, Masters, I say, in the use of the language; Pupils, as regards their salvation and Christianity."[76] Although the lack of a record of encounter from an indigenous perspective limits opportunities to assess Amerindian attitudes and practices with regard to the Jesuits' efforts to learn their languages, the Jesuits' record of linguistic work in the *Relations* allows for an understanding of the language encounter in which both Jesuit and Amerindian were, at times, powerful masters and submissive students. Political conditions and the need to excuse slow mission progress may have given the Jesuits a reason to emphasize their role as students and metaphorical children in the earliest years of the mission, but their long-term success and credibility also would depend on the cultivation of an ability to teach Amerindians about Christianity in their own languages. In order to become teachers of doctrine as much as they were students of Amerindian tongues, the Jesuits would need to procure for themselves a rigorous and complete knowledge of those languages. That effort is the subject of the following chapter.

CHAPTER THREE

Very Rich and Very Poor: Jesuit Missionary Linguistics in New France

Once established in New France, Jesuit missionaries undertook a concerted and rigorous effort to gain mastery of the languages that they found there. Amerindian languages were not only useful in Jesuit efforts to establish their legitimacy in the colony and rhetorically close the door on rivals, but were also critical to their efforts to teach Christianity to their would-be converts in the New World, and to convince French readers that Amerindians, despite their sometimes alarmingly different customs and behaviour, were children of God and could one day be made to believe it. In the winter of 1633–34, mission superior Paul Le Jeune embarked on a daring voyage, his detailed account of which can serve to illustrate the lengths to which the Jesuits were willing to go in order to gain mastery of the unfamiliar tongues of potential converts and can reveal their understanding of what was at stake in that project. Over the course of nearly six months, Le Jeune would travel with a band of Montagnais in their hibernal wanderings in search of food, all for the opportunity to learn their language. Although he knew that this decision might lead to his premature death, he nonetheless characterized a season in isolation among the Montagnais as indispensable to the success of the Jesuit mission in New France. Explained the priest in his 1633 *Relation*, "One of our Frenchmen, who lived with them last winter, told us that during two days he ate nothing but a small piece of candle, that he had accidentally carried in his pocket. This is the treatment that I shall perhaps have next winter; because, if I wish to learn the language, I must necessarily follow the Savages. I fear, however, that our growing family may keep me here this year; but sooner or later I must go. I would like to be there already, I am so sick at heart to see these poor straying souls, without any help because of our inability to understand them. We can die but once; the soonest is not always the worst."[1] The winter-long sojourn among the Montagnais that Le Jeune was contemplating would not be undertaken out of curiosity, but rather, the text suggests, out of necessity. Le Jeune portrayed himself as perfectly willing – and indeed impatient – to risk his life and endure much hardship in order to obtain the ability to communicate with the Montagnais, whose souls he understood to be at stake.

Although the experience did not kill him, Le Jeune found much to complain about, and his isolation from his countrymen and forced intimacy with the Montagnais apparently did not provide a particularly easy path to fluency. One of the priest's chief interlocutors during this difficult winter was Pierre Pastedechouan, mentioned in chapter two, a Montagnais man who had spent the years 1620 to 1625 in France, where he had been baptized and learned French. Le Jeune complained in his *Relation* that Pastedechouan sometimes purposely gave him the wrong word when the priest asked for a translation, leading Le Jeune to label him "the apostate" for his treachery and apparent abandonment of his former Christian beliefs. The food that the Montagnais sporadically procured was practically inedible in the priest's estimation, and made him sick. Sleeping in makeshift tents in which he could not stand fully erect, Le Jeune's clothes and limbs closest to the fire were prone to burning, while his extremities closest to the tent walls froze. And the smoke from the fire was so thick that the priest's eyes watered constantly, forcing him to put his mouth to the ground in order to breathe. Driven outdoors for an occasional respite from the smoke, heat, and general discomfort of sharing an enclosed space with the Montagnais and their dogs, Le Jeune was exposed to the brutal cold of the Canadian winter. Perhaps not surprisingly, in the face of resistant interlocutors and a constant struggle for survival, Le Jeune was forced to admit that he had not advanced much in his study of Montagnais by the end of the winter.[2] And yet, rather than abandon the project, the Jesuits, at least to judge from their comments in the *Relations*, continued to prioritize the study of local languages in the years following Le Jeune's hard winter among the Montagnais.

This chapter examines representations in the Jesuit *Relations* of Amerindian languages, and of the stakes and results of the missionaries' efforts to learn them. It seeks in particular to interpret the Jesuit language-learning project in light of the overlapping and simultaneous missions that serve as the lens through which this book reads the Jesuits' texts: the conversion of Amerindians and the representation of the missionaries' contact with those groups in a way that would convince readers of the project's value and likelihood of success. At stake was not only the missionaries' need to distinguish themselves from rivals at home in France in squabbles over access to the colony, but also the credibility of their claims to effect spiritual change in New France. In describing Amerindian languages and their own efforts to master them, the Jesuits sought to persuade readers that the striking differences between New and Old World cultures – of which languages were an obvious example from the missionaries' earliest attempts to learn them – were not the impediments to conversion that they may have appeared to be. Drawing on a scripture-based understanding of the nature and origin of linguistic difference, the missionaries argued that Amerindian languages were beautiful and complex – or as the Jesuits put it, "rich" – due to their divine origin, and therefore were not evidence of the radical difference of Amerindian cultures but rather of a link between Worlds Old and New. And yet, the Jesuit *Relations* also often characterized the languages of potential converts as "poor," due to their apparent lack of terminology related to Christianity. By insisting on the simultaneous "richness" and "poverty" of the unfamiliar tongues, the missionaries could suggest to readers that they were suitable for preaching Christianity, but also deficient in a way that necessitated missionary intervention. The lack of exact equivalence that the Jesuits reported finding between Amerindian and Old World languages also could be useful in asserting the missionaries' credibility as ethnographic observers, since, they suggested, their use of French signifiers to describe Amerindian concepts forced them to give readers only an imperfect and incomplete version of their own knowledge. Far from merely learning to communicate in the Algonquian and Iroquoian languages, the missionaries used them in their published *Relations* in ways that would attract support for their efforts, and lend credibility to their words.

At the same time, this chapter investigates the particular nature of Jesuit mission linguistics in New France, and seeks to bring nuance to the missionaries' modern reputation as precocious and gifted scholars of language. That reputation rests, in large measure, on the startlingly rich linguistic data, in the form of handwritten grammars and dictionaries, that were the fruits of the Jesuits' enthusiasm for learning Amerindian languages. Those texts, many of which are housed at the Musée de la Civilisation in Quebec, have been much appreciated by modern scholars.[3] Ethnolinguist John Steckley, for example, wrote that "[y]ou could say with no fear of contradiction that, in terms of grammar and dictionary development, these works are superior to any comparable material in and about the English language (though not the French language) during the same period."[4] And as Victor Hanzeli has pointed out, the manuscript dictionaries are quite precise in their transcription of Amerindian words and in morphology. Hanzeli went so far as to claim that the missionaries' linguistic methods resembled current procedures, despite the lack of a modern theory of linguistics to inform their efforts.[5] Indeed, the Jesuits themselves sometimes characterized their linguistic work in ways that call to mind twentieth-century ethnographic methods. In one oft-cited passage, for example, François-Joseph Le Mercier wrote that he and his colleagues were actively collecting Huron words like "so many precious stones," a formula that evokes the collection of discrete facts that early anthropologists viewed as their task, and calls to mind Bronislaw Malinowksi's well-known admonition that the fieldworker should "be an active huntsman" in the search for "concrete data."[6] Due in no small part to the relative rigour that they brought to the study of Amerindian languages, the Jesuit missionaries' unpublished linguistic work has since formed the basis of several modern studies of Iroquoian and Algonquian languages.[7] Rather than focus individually on Jesuit attempts to learn each of the languages they encountered, their linguistic efforts here are treated more holistically. Although the Iroquoian and Algonquian language families are distinct, there are signs in the *Relations* that the priests viewed the challenges posed by the various languages as similar. In 1633, to cite just one example, Le Jeune remarked that Algonquin differed from Montagnais only in pronunciation, and that Huron was "of the same construction."[8]

Devant. coram me, aent. echieont coram te no te viets pas
Reg. moy. ennonchien eskeontak. aller devant ahenton is, t. se se.
+ aller au devant de gl. Kgatrandihou.
Devenir. voy. les verb. en. et Aton in gram. i. Rad.

Deuil. pleurer etre enduil. Astaron. etre veuf. Atonnensk ga.

Deviner. arendio. yanne. deviner. chi atoen. jay deviné
chi gaetoen user des superstition p. deviner. Kg atoxgi.

+ developper q. c. agennondiaskagan in cp.

Devoir. per mod potentialem exprimunt. is mutant per voces
bien ou mal fait.

Diable. oki ondechionronnon voy. Aki.

Diacre. ond. harihgagasendik hatsihenstatsi S'ahachenk.

Diarrée. voy. flux de venere.

Diette, la f. Ensontiehi. jeusner.

Dieu. Die. hagendio.

Diffamer. atehene, & atehenchae. arihondati. arihontiensenni.

Different. ga arihgennon. 2. ch. differentes. ga Kirihgennon.

Differer. andiseyan s. f. differer. andiseyatandi. R.

Difficile. andoron vonk von vonde s. Atendovonkxgandi. trouver
difficile q. c. satendovonkxyandik is as tu de la peine a cela?

Digerer. Atekxichiai. voy. consumer.

Digue. chaussée. ocha

Diminuer. aeniesti. aeniestandi. R. arihgas Kgati. voy. petit.

Diner. voyez. Repas. Atsataion

Dire. En. g. o u in vru nisi in pr at. Aton in vru tu in vroes. et imps.
ihon. in fut. et Aor. dire degsq. ent ond. iit ichit. i itak ichitak. isa
iont, je parle de soy. aeren ivrirse Kond. ihoeven, sa dit cela
andoton & Atindoton. iprie racontes dire arse glq. hivre sa voix
agendaienton. entendre dire Aronen

Scholars drawing on the Jesuits' rich linguistic materials have not been wrong to see the Society's tenure in New France as a turning point in the study of Algonquian and Iroquoian languages. Earlier French visitors to the area tended to emphasize basic communication with their Amerindian interlocutors, and did not attempt the kind of careful study of the local languages that the Jesuits undertook. French explorer Jacques Cartier, for example, described the frantic and sometimes fruitless gestures he used with the Iroquoian group he encountered during his first voyage to New France in 1534.[9] The inadequacy of that method of communication revealed itself in an incident in which Cartier and crew ended up using a cannon to make a point that hand gestures had failed to convey: "And because we only had, as I already said, one of our boats, we did not want to trust their signs, and made signs to them to withdraw, which they did not want to do, and rowed with such force that they surrounded our boat forthwith, in their seven boats. And since, despite the signs that we made, they did not want to withdraw, we shot two cannon balls over their heads."[10] Perhaps recognizing that gestures alone – whether by hand or cannon – would not suffice, Cartier also compiled word lists, aiming not at complete knowledge of the subtleties of Amerindian tongues, but at acquiring a few basic expressions only to facilitate navigation, trade, and the procurement of sustenance.[11] Similarly, the Recollet missionary Gabriel Sagard's Huron dictionary, published as an appendix to his 1632 *Grand Voyage du Pays des Hurons*, is in the form of a phrasebook, and the author acknowledged that he did not possess a comprehensive understanding of the language. Indeed, he claimed that the dictionary was intended not to fully document the language's vocabulary, but rather "for the convenience and use of those who have to travel in the country and do not have knowledge of said language."[12] For Sagard, the emphasis was squarely on communication.

In addition to gestures and rudimentary word lists, pidgins also had their place in the early days of encounter, when conversations between Amerindians and French merchants and traders largely concerned practical matters such as bartering and procuring directions. The blending of various languages in the New World was so advanced in some cases that an early-seventeenth-century visitor to Acadia reported that the language of the Amerindian groups of that region was "half-basque" due to decades of contact with Europeans.[13] And the Jesuits themselves did not fail to notice that contact between various languages had produced crude linguae francae that were used for the purpose of rudimentary communication. As mission superior Paul Le Jeune wrote in his 1633 *Relation*: "I have noticed in the study of their language that there is a certain jargon between the French and the Savages, which is neither French nor Savage; and yet when the French use it, they think they are speaking the Savage Tongue, and the Savages, in using it, think they are speaking good French."[14] The dismissive term that the priest used to describe the crude linguistic blend that he encountered – "jargon" ("barragoin") – attests that even at this early stage in the Society's long tenure in New France, its members recognized the limitations of the methods of communication upon which other visitors had relied prior to the arrival of the Jesuits. Although they did not entirely abandon the use of gestures, images, and other communicative strategies, the Jesuits put a premium on learning to speak – and speak well – the languages of potential converts.[15] Accordingly, and unlike their predecessors, the priests made a concerted effort to master Amerindian languages upon their arrival in New France. In 1635, superior Paul Le Jeune reported that a part of the Jesuit contingent among the Montagnais had been devoted to "an arduous and thorough study of the language." Jean de Brébeuf reported in the same year a similarly rigorous group effort to learn Huron.[16]

Although it certainly is true that the Jesuits brought unmatched sophistication and dedication to the task of learning Amerindian languages, their project has much to tell us aside from the grammatical and lexical characteristics of those languages.[17] For one thing, the glaring differences between the Jesuits' manuscript dictionaries and the published *Relations* on the subject of Amerindian languages provide a clue about the relationship between Jesuit knowledge of Amerindian cultures more generally and the representations thereof that they prepared for readers. Perhaps not surprisingly in light of the importance that the missionaries attributed to the project, language is practically a leitmotif in the Jesuits' published texts. Entire chapters and lengthy passages are devoted to the subject, and the missionaries peppered their texts with offhand comments about, and samples of, Amerindian tongues. Despite the considerable time and ink they devoted to the project, Le Jeune and his colleagues tended to emphasize their efforts rather than display their results in detail, and usually described Amerindian languages in general terms instead of providing specific linguistic data. Indeed, the distance between Jesuit knowledge of Amerindian languages as demonstrated in their private, internal documents and in texts crafted for public consumption is vast, perhaps explaining why the missionaries' manuscript dictionaries – and not the more accessible and voluminous *Relations* themselves – generally serve as the basis for studies of Amerindian languages as they existed at the time of contact.[18] This suggests, at a minimum, that the information on display in the missionaries' published texts must be regarded as only a partial record of their knowledge of Amerindian cultures. Information could be shared or withheld, it seems, depending on how doing so aligned with the Society's interests, a point that will be developed further in later chapters of this book.

The paucity of linguistic data in the published *Relations* has been attributed to several causes since the seventeenth century. One modern linguist blamed the priests' failure to recognize the intellectual value of their work for their failure to publish dictionaries and detailed grammatical descriptions of Amerindian languages.[19] The missionary linguist Jean de Brébeuf himself attributed it in his 1636 *Relation* to the rapidly changing state of Jesuit knowledge on the subject. Wrote the priest in an account of Jesuit activities over the course of the summer, "Finally we busied ourselves in revising, or rather in arranging, a Grammar. I fear we shall often have to make similar revisions; for every day we discover new secrets in this science, which for the present hinders us from sending anything to be printed. We know now, thank God, sufficient to understand and to be understood, but not yet to publish."[20] Another possibility is that the political factors involving the role of Amerindian languages in missionary arguments over access to New France that were examined in the previous chapter might very well have encouraged the Jesuits to keep their hard-won linguistic data close to the vest. Indeed, it is perhaps telling that the Jesuits never published any of the dictionaries or grammars that they produced in New France, even after decades of work had produced a sophisticated understanding of the languages. One scholar has suggested that the lack of a printing press in New France – despite a Jesuit request for one – may have prevented the more widespread dissemination of linguistic knowledge. And yet, it seems that if the missionaries and their superiors had deemed truly important and

desirable the widespread diffusion of their accumulated linguistic knowledge, they could have simply sent copies to France for publication, as
Brébeuf himself suggested in the passage cited above and as was already
common practice for the annual *Relations*.[21] Whatever the reason, the
Relations tend to contain far more in the way of general commentary on
Amerindian languages than detailed data, making them a useful tool for
understanding how the Jesuits understood their linguistic project and
described it to readers in order to support their mission. Scholars reading
the missionaries' unpublished linguistic materials have usually concluded
that the Jesuits were exceptionally rigorous and knowledgeable proto-
linguists, but the explicit commentary on Amerindian languages that is to
be found in the missionaries' published texts and that is absent from the
manuscript dictionaries offers different lessons about the Jesuits' project.

Perhaps the clearest lesson that the *Relations* can teach us about the
Jesuits' language-learning project is that the missionaries were not motivated by academic curiosity alone. Indeed, the missionaries consistently
portrayed the ability to speak well in the languages of potential converts
as key to convincing them to embrace Catholicism.[22] As Le Jeune put it
in his 1633 *Relation*, "*Fides ex auditu*, faith enters by the ear. How can a
mute preach the Gospel?"[23] Accordingly, Jesuits described their work as
an effort not only to communicate, but also to master the conventions
of Amerindian oratory and to adapt them to their own purposes, focusing on the discursive strategies associated with authority.[24] Wrote Le
Jeune in his 1635 *Relation*, "When you speak to them of our truths, they
listen to you patiently; but instead of asking you about the matter, they
at once turn their thoughts to ways of finding something upon which
to live, showing their stomachs always empty and always famished. Yet
if we could make speeches as they do, and if we were present in their
assemblies, I believe we [would be very powerful] there."[25] The Jesuits
frequently characterized their efforts to learn Amerindian languages not
merely as an exercise in academic research, but rather as an activity that
was indispensable to their mission to Christianize the inhabitants of the
New World. Rudimentary knowledge of the kind on display in Cartier's
word list or Sagard's dictionary would not, they suggested, be enough
to earn the respect that apparently came, in Amerindian societies, with
speaking eloquently.[26] As Le Jeune would put it in the *Relation* for 1636,

cited in the previous chapter, the ability to engage Amerindian interlocutors on complex questions, to satisfy their doubts, and to argue against their objections was expected to yield real power to effect religious change.

The prize for learning to speak Amerindian languages well, the missionaries suggested, would be direct access to the souls of thousands of potential converts. As Le Jeune remarked in his 1633 *Relation*, "Secondly, he who knew their language well would be all-powerful among them, however little eloquence he might have. There is no place in the world where Rhetoric is more powerful than in Canada, and, nevertheless, it has no other garb than what nature has given it; it is entirely simple and without disguise; and yet it controls all these tribes, as the Captain is elected for his eloquence alone, and is obeyed in proportion to his use of it, for they have no other law than his word."[27] The priest's repetition of the word "powerful" (*puissant*) reinforces the message that skill in local languages was no mere tool for tourists, but a means of obtaining the power to effect change. Indeed, the Jesuit missionary Barthélemy Vimont literalized the transformative power of God's word in his 1640 *Relation*: "There is no heart so hard that the word of God does not soften it in time. A rude and haughty fellow said to me some time ago, 'I have a hundred times made sport of the speeches of Father de Quen; I have opposed Father Buteux, trying to prevent him from instructing us; as for thee, I could not endure thee, —I took pleasure in quarreling with thee, and, when I had done so, I went through the cabins and spoke of it as a great feat. But now your words seem good to me; they are going down little by little into my heart; I believe my ears will get accustomed to hear them.'"[28] It is the words themselves, in Vimont's account, that convince the Algonquian interlocutor of the validity of the Jesuit message, entering by the ear and wending their way to the heart. By emphasizing the words themselves as the cause of progress toward conversion – as opposed to the message – Vimont foregrounded the importance of language in conveying religious truth. Speaking well to a potential convert in his own language, this passage suggests, was the key to securing a change of heart.

Central to the belief that the Jesuits expressed in their *Relations* in the power of Amerindian tongues to communicate Christianity were two key tenets of the Christian tradition concerning language. The first is an explicit link between religion and language. The term "author" and its French and Latin equivalents signified, in the seventeenth century, both "originator," in a general sense, and producer of a written text.[29] God is sometimes referred to as an "author" both in the Jesuit *Relations* and in the Bible, an appellation that refers to the deity's role as the creator of mankind and its surroundings, but also to textual authorship. The biblical Gospel according to John begins thus: "In the beginning was the Word, and the Word was with God, and the Word was God ... And the Word became flesh and lived among us, and we have seen his glory, the glory of a father's only son, full of grace and truth."[30] Belief in God and his son, then, is fundamentally also receptivity and attention to a message, a divine communication. And it is also through this "Word" – Christ – that man is understood to communicate with God.[31] Christ is, in the Christian tradition, not only a God to be worshipped, but a medium, a language through which God's will is transmitted to man and through which man responds to God. Christianity is therefore simultaneously belief in and worship of the Christian God and participation in a conversation that is carried out in the divine language of Christ – receptivity to the "Word made flesh" and response to God through prayer to Christ. The New France Jesuits themselves frequently drew a link between belief in God and language, pointing to a transcendent "word of the heart" or "word of God" that they claimed moved Amerindians to convert.[32] As father/author of a son/Word, God was understood to be the creator of language. And language, by virtue of its divine origin, was portrayed by the Jesuits as an authoritative medium between the worlds of grace and nature, one that could put man in communication with God.[33]

The link between belief in a Christian God and the understanding of language as a divine medium also, according to the biblical tradition, manifests itself in the world's various tongues. Amerindian languages could theoretically be as powerful a tool for religious change as any other language, owing to the biblical account of the origin of linguistic difference. The story of the tower of Babel, contained in Genesis, claims that early man shared a single tongue, but that God found it necessary to "confuse their language ... so that they will not understand one another's speech" because a project by humans to build a tower to reach heaven convinced God that as long as humans had a common language, "nothing that they propose will be impossible for them."[34] Since God had deliberately scrambled the world's languages, differences between them could be understood as beautiful, and evidence of God's work, instead of as distortions caused by wandering and poor record-keeping, as in the case of the Amerindian creation myths discussed in a later chapter of this book. As divinely created languages, Amerindian tongues were thought to be as suitable to effecting spiritual change as any other language. And the Babel incident also provided a central motivation for missionaries in the New World: reunification of the groups that had diverged culturally and religiously in the wake of God's linguistic intervention.[35]

In the context of the reasons that the Jesuits gave readers for their attempts to master Amerindian languages – their utility in effecting conversions – and their scripture-based understanding of linguistic difference, it is perhaps not surprising that the missionary authors seem to have been less interested in displaying their knowledge than in interpreting it in order to provide a compelling answer to a particularly vexing question, one that had to be addressed if readers were to take seriously and support the Jesuits' mission: how to account for the startling differences between Amerindian and European cultures? Although Europe had long been aware of the existence of culturally different non-Christians in Africa and Asia, the newly discovered Amerindian was so radically different as to uniquely constitute "a challenge to a whole body of traditional assumptions, beliefs and attitudes," as historian J.H. Elliott put it.[36] Issues raised by Europe's contact with the Amerindian Other have long been acknowledged to have been vexing for European travellers and thinkers, and have attracted a fair amount of scholarly attention in recent decades.[37] Were Amerindians human? If so, were they created in Eden with Europeans' ancestors? How could one explain their presence in America, with little apparent knowledge of their origin as documented in the Bible? And if they were human and of the same stock as European Christians, how could one explain the fact that their beliefs and behaviour were so different from those of their French Christian interlocutors?[38] In a sign that the question was regarded as an urgent one by Europeans anxious to determine how New World related to Old, a papal pronouncement just one year after Columbus' 1492 voyage, and another in 1535, affirmed that Amerindians were indeed human, and therefore theoretically able to understand the Catholic religion.[39] Nonetheless, the debate over Amerindians' intelligence and capacity for conversion continued across Europe, no doubt fuelled by the alternately pessimistic and optimistic assessments of Amerindian nature in travellers' accounts. As Dominique Deslandres has remarked, making the existence of North American peoples fit within Christian traditional knowledge about the origins of mankind and the Earth was a challenge Europe could not fail to meet. Wrote Deslandres, "by his very existence, this Other is disturbing, incongruous, out of place to the highest degree because he corresponds to nothing, to no known model. If one accepts him as is, all of the authority of Scripture collapses, it is truly the end of the world."[40]

Amerindian languages were an obvious example of this puzzling diversity, and one that the Jesuits – who, as noted, above, were more focused on learning languages than any other early visitors to New France – remarked on in their earliest *Relations*. Wrote Le Jeune in 1633 of the Montagnais language, for example, "I do not think that I have ever heard any language spoken which is formed in the same manner as this. Father Brébeuf assures me that the language of the Hurons is of the same construction. People may call them Barbarians as much as they please, but their language is very regular. I am not yet a perfect master of it; I shall speak of it some day with more assurance. If I were not afraid of being tedious, I should note here a striking and radically strange difference between the languages of Europe and those of this country."[41] It is telling that Le Jeune's comments on the uniqueness of Amerindian languages and their radical differences from European tongues is not particularly negative. Indeed, Le Jeune called the languages "very regular," as if to say that the languages, despite being dissimilar to more familiar models, had a recognizable structure and could therefore be mastered, given sufficient time.

Other passages in the *Relations* are even more explicit in characterizing Amerindian languages as admirable, reflecting the missionaries' understanding of the divine origin of linguistic difference, discussed above. Jérôme Lalemant went so far in singing the praises of Algonquian and Iroquoian tongues as to cite them in 1646 as proof of God's existence: "Their compounds are admirable; and I may say that, though there should be no other argument to show that there is a God than the economy of the Savage languages, that would suffice to convince us. For there is no human wisdom nor skill which can unite so many men, so as to make them observe the order which they maintain in their languages, wholly different from those of Europe; it is God alone who holds the guidance thereof."[42] Similarly, Brébeuf's 1636 description of the Huron language calls a particularly complicated grammatical structure a "marvel." And in the eyes of the enthusiastic priest, verb forms and proverbs were "remarkable," and gendered verb conjugations were "most extraordinary."[43] The differences that the Jesuits noted between Amerindian and European languages were presented in the *Relations* not merely as intellectual curiosities or impediments to rapid language-learning, but also as a sign of the divine origin of the unfamiliar tongues and, by extension, the people who used them.

The ways in which Le Jeune and his colleagues tended to characterize those differences simultaneously underscored for readers the potential of Amerindian languages to convey Old World truths and the factors that limited their immediate use in that project. After working with Pierre Pastedechouan prior to his winter among the Montagnais, for example, Le Jeune offered a broad summary of what he termed the richness and poverty of the language, a formula that would be repeated by the priest's colleagues in later *Relations*. Wrote Le Jeune: "I shall say, in passing, that this language is very poor and very rich. It is poor, because, having no knowledge of thousands and thousands of things which are in Europe, they have no names to indicate them. It is rich, because in the things of which they have a knowledge, it is fertile and plentiful."[44] Two years after Le Jeune's winter journey with the Montagnais, Brébeuf concluded his remarks on the grammatical complexity of Huron and prefaced his comments on its lack of definite articles in similar terms: "that is [rich]. Here is one which is not so."[45] It is worth examining in turn what was implied in describing the languages as "rich" and "poor."

In his account of his winter spent following a band of Montagnais, Le Jeune began his comments on that group's language by complaining about its perceived deficiencies, but then provided examples of the "riches" that he found in their language, and compared those features to aspects of the more familiar languages of Europe:

> Let us now turn the tables and show that this language is fairly
> gorged with richness. First, I find an infinite number of proper
> nouns among them, which I cannot explain in our French,
> except by circumlocutions. Second, they have some Verbs which
> I call absolute, to which neither the Greeks, nor Latins, nor we
> ourselves, nor any language of Europe with which I am familiar,

have anything similar. For example, the verb *Nimitison* means absolutely, "I eat," without saying what; for, if you determine the thing you eat, you have to use another Verb. Third, they have different Verbs to signify an action toward an animate or toward an inanimate object; and yet they join with animate things a number of things that have no souls, as tobacco, apples, etc. Let us give some examples: "I see a man," *Niouapamaniriniou*; "I see a stone," *niouabatè*; but in Greek, in Latin, and in French the same Verb is used to express, "I see a man, a stone, or anything else."[46]

In describing each of these "riches," and the four more that followed, Le Jeune compared the Montagnais language to the more familiar tongues of Europe.[47] The abundance of proper names could not be explained in French, and unique verb structures were unlike anything to be found in Greek, Latin, or French. Brébeuf's 1636 chapter on the Huron language similarly drew comparisons to the more familiar languages of Europe. Wrote Brébeuf, to cite just one example, "As for the verbs, what is most remarkable in their language is: 1. That they have some to signify animate things, and others to signify things without life. 2. That they vary their tenses in as many ways as did the Greeks."[48]

The fact that the Jesuit authors portrayed unique aspects of Amerindian languages – their "richness" – as sure signs of divine authorship and, by extension, suitability for the missionary task, suggests that in spite of the priests' modern reputation as precociously rigorous linguists, their work was less a matter of investigating the particularities of the languages than of figuring out how they had been scrambled by God in the Babel incident.[49] And indeed, this would be precisely the message that missionaries would want to convey to their readers: Amerindian languages were not difficult due to their inherent deficiency, but rather because of their marvelous richness, which was proof of their capacity to communicate Catholic doctrine even if the process was not easy. Remarked Le Jeune in 1634, "the difficulty of this language, which is not slight, as may be guessed from what I have said, has been no small obstacle to prevent a poor memory like mine from advancing far."[50] Though Le Jeune acknowledged that the challenge was daunting, his comments would have reassured readers that Amerindian languages were a problem with a solution, a complex set of information that would require an impressive feat

of memory to master, or an enigma that, once unlocked, would give the
missionaries the capacity to preach their message in the languages of the
people they sought to convert, and thereby to introduce Christianity into
those cultures.

Despite the doctrinal foundation for their appreciation of Amerindian languages, Le Jeune and his colleagues seem to have been unique
among Frenchmen in New France in framing as admirable those languages' complexities. The Recollet Gabriel Sagard, for example, offered a
far less appreciative assessment of the Huron tongue, highlighting what
he viewed as its flawed and unstable nature in the prefatory comments to
the dictionary appended to his 1632 *Grand Voyage du Pays des Hurons*. He
described it as "a wild language, almost without rules, and so imperfect
that one more able than myself would be hard put to do better."[51] Sagard's complaints about the difficulty he encountered – that the language
was wild, imperfect, and devoid of rules – suggest that unlike his Jesuit
rivals he did not view the language as a divine creation that was adequate
to expressing doctrine. As Sagard apparently saw it, the problem was with
the language itself, not the inadequacy of his own skills. Perhaps naturally, in light of his order's preference for preaching in French, discussed in
the previous chapter, Sagard described the language in terms that cast it
as an inferior New World system to be replaced as soon as possible with
a superior language from Christian Europe.

Although they clearly did not share Sagard's unfavourable opinion of
Amerindian languages, it is true, as mentioned earlier, that the Jesuit
authors sometimes cast the languages they encountered in New France
as "poor." Like the vexing "richness" or complexity of Amerindian languages, their lack of the vocabulary needed to explain Christian concepts
and ignorance of European referents, coupled with the limitations inherent in the Jesuits' perspective and training when it came to adapting their
message to the languages, posed challenges to the Jesuits' efforts.[52] In the
year after Le Jeune's *Relation* commented on the simultaneous richness
and poverty of Montagnais, he elaborated on the linguistic deficiencies
that he had encountered during his winter among that group:

All words for piety, devotion, virtue; all terms which are used to
express the things of the other life; the language of Theologians,
Philosophers, Mathematicians, and Physicians, in a word, of all

learned men; all words which refer to the regulation and government of a city, Province, or Empire; all that concerns justice,
reward and punishment; the names of an infinite number of arts
which are in our Europe; of an infinite number of flowers, trees,
and fruits; of an infinite number of animals, of thousands and
thousands of contrivances, of a thousand beauties and riches, all
these things are never found either in the thoughts or upon the
lips of the Savages. As they have no true religion nor knowledge
of the virtues, neither public authority nor government, neither
Kingdom nor Republic, nor sciences, nor any of those things of
which I have just spoken, consequently all the expressions, terms,
words, and names which refer to that world of wealth and grandeur must necessarily be absent from their vocabulary; hence the
great scarcity.[53]

Due to an apparent complete absence of referents in Montagnais culture
related to abstract Christian theological concepts, signifiers for those concepts also reportedly were lacking, an observation that would illustrate
for readers the difficulty of delivering religious lessons in the languages of
potential converts, even if their simultaneous "richness" meant that it was
certainly possible to do so.

Le Jeune was not alone in his claim that Amerindian languages were
"poor." As the Jesuit Jérôme Lalemant would later lament, even the sim-
plest Bible stories proved difficult for the Jesuits to express in Huron:
"Not only do words fail them to express the sanctity of our mysteries,
but even the parables and the more familiar discourses of Jesus Christ
are inexplicable to them. They know not what is salt, leaven, stronghold,
pearl, prison, mustard seed, casks of wine, lamp, candlestick, torch; they
have no idea of Kingdoms, Kings, and their majesty; not even of shep-
herds, flocks, and a sheepfold, – in a word, their ignorance of the things
of the earth seems to close for them the way to heaven."[54] Without such
basic vocabulary, how could one explain the fate of Lot's wife, the parables of the mustard seed and the yeast, or any other of Christianity's classic stories? Such assertions that Amerindian languages lacked the words
needed to convey biblical knowledge are common in the *Relations*.[55]

The Jesuits sometimes also claimed that the grammars of Amerindian
languages were inadequate to the task of expressing doctrine. Perhaps

the most famous example is Jean de Brébeuf's oft-cited 1636 request for approval of a translation of the Trinity, a concept that he reported struggling to express in Huron. Wrote Brébeuf,

> A relative noun with them includes always the meaning of one of the three persons of the possessive pronoun, so that they can not say simply, Father, Son, Master, Valet, but are obliged to say one of the three, my father, thy father, his father. However, I have translated above in a Prayer one of their nouns by the word Father, for greater clearness. On this account, we find ourselves hindered from getting them to say properly in their Language, *In the name of the Father, and of the Son, and of the holy Ghost.* Would you judge it fitting, while waiting a better expression, to substitute instead, *In the name of our Father, and of his Son, and of their holy Ghost?* Certainly it seems that the three Persons of the most holy Trinity would be sufficiently expressed in this way ... Would we venture to employ it thus until the Huron language shall be enriched, or the mind of the Hurons opened to other languages? We will do nothing without advice.[56]

Catholic faith holds that the three entities of the Trinity – the Father, the Son, and the Holy Spirit – are "one Being, three Persons."[57] Changing the formula to "Our Father, His Son, and Their Holy Spirit" might adequately express the three persons of the Trinity, as Brébeuf asserted, but it does little to capture their unity in a single being.[58] Brébeuf himself acknowledged the inadequacy of the translation with the phrase "while waiting a better expression," but blamed not his own awkward rendering, but rather the characteristics of the language itself. Until the Hurons' language could be "enriched" with new signifiers and their culture supplemented with corresponding concepts to facilitate a more faithful translation, this imperfect solution would have to do.[59] It is telling of the Jesuit missionaries' motivations in collecting information on Amerindian languages and cultures that Brébeuf cast the peculiar grammatical characteristics of the Huron language that he encountered when attempting to translate the Trinity as obstacles to preaching Christianity that had to be overcome, rather than as a sign of the language's profoundly relational nature that might have revealed how the Huron viewed and situated themselves in the world. Whether discussing Amerindian vocabularies or grammar, the missionaries portrayed themselves as struggling to find ways to express the Old World ideas that they were attempting to teach to potential converts, and the "poverty" of Amerindian languages was the culprit.

Although this insistence on the deficiencies of Amerindian vocabularies and grammars would at least superficially seem to undermine the argument that the Jesuits made, based on the "richness" of the unfamiliar tongues, that Amerindian languages were suitable for communicating Christianity, casting the languages as poor had the advantage of suggesting that missionary intervention was necessary, helping justify to readers the Jesuit project. Indeed, the Jesuits suggested that they were, to at least some degree, inventors of the languages as much as they were students. This suggestion would later be made explicit by Joseph-François Lafitau, himself a former Jesuit missionary among the Iroquois, in his 1724 *Moeurs des Sauvages Américains*. Wrote Lafitau, "they have had to make a more individual and much more painful study to draw from the very depths of these languages, as it were, a new language, which serves to make known to the Indians, matters pertaining to God and abstract truths."[60] In Lafitau's account of the project, the New France Jesuits did not have to invent new languages out of whole cloth, but rather needed to extract them from the "very depths" of the languages as they existed. This formulation preserves the notion that Amerindian languages, as divine media, were adequate to the task of preaching Christianity, but also suggests that the Jesuits stretched them beyond common usage.

In the year before his famous voyage with the Montagnais, Le Jeune himself claimed that linguistic innovation was required in his efforts to teach Christian concepts to that group, and characterized that process in a way that reversed the dynamic of power that one would expect to find between an Amerindian and an outsider seeking language lessons. Wrote Le Jeune: "I explain to them, very crudely, the mysteries of the Holy Trinity and of the Incarnation, and at every few words I ask them if I speak well, if they can understand [well]; they all answer me: *eoco, eoco, ninisitoutenan*, 'yes, yes, we understand.' Afterwards I ask them whether there are several Gods, and which of the three persons became man. I coin words approximating to their language, which I make them understand. We begin the Catechism by this prayer, after having made the sign of the

Cross: *Noukhimami Jesus, ïagoua Khistinohimaonitou Khikhitouinacaié Khiteritamouïn. Ca cataouachichien Maria ouccaonia Jesu, cacataouachichien Joseph aïamihitouinan.* 'My Lord, or Captain, Jesus, teach me your words and your will! Oh, good Mary, Mother of God! Oh, good Joseph, pray for us!'"[61] Although Le Jeune suggested that the words he used were inventions, and did not exist in the Montagnais language, they were at least good approximations of the Montagnais language, and were, to judge from the self-reported comprehension of Le Jeune's interlocutors, easily enough incorporated into the language, he claimed. Remarkably, Le Jeune's account of this process of invention that he claimed was necessitated by the poverty of the Amerindian language turns on its head the language encounter. In using invented words for Christian concepts, Le Jeune appears not, in this passage, as a student of an unfamiliar tongue, but rather a master teaching the Montagnais' own language to them. In this way, the potentially troubling "poverty" that the missionaries saw in Amerindian languages actually furnished an opportunity for the Jesuits to assert greater mastery over them.

The Jesuits' characterizations of Amerindian languages as simultaneously "rich" and "poor," and of their own interventions as a process of invention or enrichment, have consequences for our understanding of how the missionaries went about collecting information about the Amerindian cultures of New France and then rhetorically fashioning it to suit the tastes and needs of readers at home in France. The case of Amerindian languages in the Jesuit *Relations* suggests that providing a complete portrait of unfamiliar cultures was, in at least some instances, less important to the Jesuit ethnographic project than the way in which it was represented. Instead of offering up their data to readers – or, as Sagard did, labelling Amerindian languages fundamentally defective – the Jesuits described linguistic difference in terms that would validate the Society's preference for conducting missionary work in local languages, suggest that Amerindians were as much children of God as were Europeans, and demonstrate the necessity of the missionaries' own work. The Jesuits framed Amerindian languages in the *Relations* in such a way as to suggest that Iroquoian and Algonquian cultures were like the more familiar examples of home and that their conversion was possible, but also that they were deficient in some way that would require extensive missionary intervention. As later chapters in this book will confirm, emphasizing the simultaneously admirable and flawed nature of Amerindian cultures was a common way in which the Jesuits argued to readers that their project was both much needed and likely to succeed.

The characterization of Amerindian languages as both beautiful and flawed also would have served to bolster the Jesuits' authority as uniquely knowledgeable commentators on Amerindian cultures. Because the priests conducted their missionary work in Amerindian languages, they were in an unrivalled position to understand and change the cultures of the groups they encountered in New France. But by the same token, they were unable, they suggested, to perfectly explain all that they knew to European readers without pressing French terms into the service of an ill-fitting message in the same way they used Amerindian languages in novel ways. Indeed, the priests sometimes attached disclaimers to their translations of Amerindian expressions indicating that the languages' differences from French prevented them from telling readers precisely what an Amerindian word or speech meant. Just as Christian parables were hard to explain in Amerindian languages, local customs, it seems, did not always translate well into French, since the language was as lacking in Amerindian concepts and their corresponding signifiers as Huron and Montagnais were in French ideas and terms. In his 1637 *Relation*, for example, Le Jeune added the following caveat to his use of the word "sorcier" to describe Montagnais religious figures: "Not that the Devil communicates with them as obviously as he does with the Sorcerers and Magicians of Europe; but we have no other name to give them, since they even do some of the acts of genuine sorcerers, – as, to kill one another by charms, or wishes, and imprecations, by the abetment of the Manitou, by poisons which they concoct."[62] Le Jeune opted for the word "sorcerers" when describing Montagnais healers to his francophone audience, but also paused to critique his own translation. Readers, he suggests, would have to be content with an approximation, since their lack of knowledge of the language prevented them from grasping the true meaning of the Montagnais word. Nor was "sorcerer" the only example of this kind. As noted earlier, the priest reported in his 1634 chapter on the Montagnais language that there were many such terms: "I find an infinite number of proper nouns among them, which I cannot explain in our French, except by circumlocutions."[63]

Even Amerindian speeches that were directly quoted in the *Relations* were often presented as imperfect, if faithful, renditions of actual utterances. Le Jeune, for example, closes his long quotation of a speech by a

Montagnais "captain" in his 1633 *Relation* with a disclaimer of the accuracy of his account: "This is [more or less] the answer of this Savage." In 1638, the Jesuit missionary François-Joseph Le Mercier similarly suggested that something had been lost in his account of a speech by a Huron elder, prefacing his translation with a disclaimer: "One of them spoke [nearly] in these terms." The following year, Le Jeune cited a speech made by an Algonquin convert, and suggested again that his translation failed to capture the beauty of the speech he heard: "He made this speech to us in better terms in his own language than I can report in ours." And in 1642, Vimont similarly pointed to the inadequacy of his translation of an Amerindian speech, and the eloquent reply of another Amerindian who was in attendance: "To this harangue – which was more eloquent in the Algonquin tongue than I can render it in French – Paul Atondo replied still more eloquently, in his own language."[64] Not only were readers reliant on Jesuit translations, but those translations, it was often suggested, were only approximate. Readers could get the general idea, but truly intimate knowledge of Amerindian cultures, it seems, was reserved for the Jesuits, who spoke the local languages. In this way, the challenges posed by the simultaneous "richness" and "poverty" of Amerindian languages allowed the missionaries to remind readers of their status as privileged observers of culture who would always know more than anyone else.

Indeed, frequent insistence on the consequences of the incommensurability of French and Amerindian tongues was not the only way in which the missionaries claimed control in the pages of the *Relations* over the languages of their would-be converts. Ironically, in light of the Jesuits' stated aim of learning to speak with authority, the missionaries often presented their efforts to master Amerindian languages as a matter of writing more than speaking. In the year before his trying winter spent following a small band of Montagnais, Le Jeune suggested that learning to communicate was not, for the Jesuits, a mere question of conversational practice, but also of careful composition, of writing as much as of speaking.[65] In describing his efforts to learn Montagnais under the tutelage of the ever-unreliable interpreters Nicolas Marsolet and Pierre Pastedechouan, Le Jeune reported that his effort to learn local languages unavoidably would entail the creation of books. Wrote Le Jeune, "Before knowing a language, it was necessary for me to make the books from which to learn it; and, although I do not hold them to be so correct, yet now, at the time when I am writing, I make myself understood very well by the savages. It all lies in composing often, in learning a great many words, in acquiring their accent, and my occupations do not permit it. I was thinking of going with them next winter into the woods, but I foresee that it will be impossible, tied as I am. If my teacher had not left me, I should have made considerable progress in a few months."[66] The text-based approach to learning Amerindian languages evoked by Le Jeune had its roots in longstanding Jesuit pedagogical practice. The *Ratio Studiorum*, the 1599 Jesuit treatise on pedagogy, called for Latin to be the exclusive language of the Jesuit colleges where missionary priests received their training and served as professors before being sent to New France, and the Society's *Constitutions* called for students to attain "a good foundation" in Latin above all other subjects.[67] Unlike modern language textbooks that tend to be activity-based, inductive, and centred on teaching communication skills, the Latin texts that were used in Jesuit schools and that, as linguistic Victor Hanzeli put it, "constituted the hard core of the Jesuits' approach to language" emphasized the clear statement of grammatical rules and a demonstration of the rational ordering of Latin.[68]

Book-learning was not only the ideal, as far as Le Jeune and his colleagues were concerned, but also the method actually used in the mission field. The Jesuits' rich linguistic manuscripts were as much pedagogical tools as they were reference books, since copying and revision of the dictionaries apparently was part of the training of new arrivals among the Society's New France contingent.[69] Indeed, the Jesuit authors often portrayed language-learning as a process of writing as much as a matter of speaking. Le Jeune depicted himself attempting to write down the Montagnais language as a means of learning it during his winter among that group, a method that apparently left him vulnerable to an Amerindian interlocutor's cruel sense of humour. Cataloguing his complaints about Carigonan, a Montagnais man reputed to have supernatural powers and whom Le Jeune called "le sorcier," Le Jeune wrote, "In the fourth place, wishing to have sport at my expense, he sometimes made me write vulgar things in his language, assuring me there was nothing bad in them, then made me pronounce these shameful words, which I did not understand, in the presence of the Savages."[70] Jean de Brébeuf provided a similar glimpse into the missionaries' text-based methodology when he wrote in 1635 that "[i]n the first place, we have been employed in the study of the language, which, on account of the diversity of its compound words, is almost infinite. One can, nevertheless, do nothing without this study. All the French who are here have eagerly applied themselves to it, reviving the ancient usage of writing on birch-bark, for want of paper."[71] To cite just one more example, shortly after his arrival in New France and as his own efforts to learn the Montagnais language were just beginning in earnest, Le Jeune characterized the language-learning process as a matter of writing things down, apparently including, in the earliest years, things written down in error. Wrote Le Jeune: "I wrote a few words of it last year that I characterized as Savage words, believing them to be so. For example, the word, *Ania*, which I have mentioned above, is an alien word, the Savages making use of it on every occasion in speaking to the French, and the French in speaking to the Savages, and all use it to say 'my brother;' but in the real Savage Tongue of the Montagnaits, *Nichtais* means 'my eldest brother,' *Nichim* 'my youngest'; the word *Sagamo* is used by only a few here to say 'Captain.' The correct word is *Oukhimau*; I believe this word, *Sagamo*, comes from Acadia; there are many others like it. When a person first visits a country, he writes a great many things upon the word of others, believing them to be true; time reveals the truth."[72] It is clear that writing was, for the Jesuit missionaries, key to their efforts to gain mastery of Amerindian languages.

The missionaries' emphasis on the role of writing in their attempts to learn how to speak reflects an assumption that will be examined further in later chapters of this book: real knowledge was understood to be textual, not oral. Indeed, it is telling that both Le Jeune and Brébeuf, instead of describing the absence of specific sounds in Amerindian speech, claimed that their alphabets lacked several letters, as if the essential form of the language were written even if the Amerindians only knew its oral form.[73] As Walter Mignolo has remarked of a different set of language encounters in the colonial Americas, this bias toward textual knowledge, and the accompanying act of writing comprehensive grammars and vocabularies, converts a dynamic language from a communicative process into an object that can be possessed, and that becomes a point of reference against which actual use of a language is subsequently judged.[74] By characterizing their language-learning project as a process of writing down unfamiliar tongues, then, the Jesuits were also suggesting that they were taming the marvelously complex oral languages of the New World into a form that would be recognizable to Europe as knowledge, and over which the Jesuits, as authors of dictionaries and grammars, would have control. Although the rich unpublished materials left to posterity by the New France Jesuits may have cemented in place their status as the premier source of information on Amerindian languages, it is clear that their characterizations of the unfamiliar tongues of potential converts also have much to tell us about how the missionary authors perceived and represented for readers the inhabitants of the New World. Interpreting new information in relation to old models, the Jesuits sought not so much to describe the unfamiliar as to reconcile it with received knowledge and thereby reassure readers of its utility in effecting conversions. That rhetorical move, as other chapters of this book will confirm, played a prominent role in Jesuit mission ethnography.

Driving into Wendaké, the Huron-Wendat *réserve* near Quebec City, I encountered in the summer of 2007 a sure sign that contact between European and indigenous languages had left an enduring mark on the town. In this case, the sign was of the literal variety – a bilingual stop sign on the Rue du Loup at its intersection with the Rue Chef Stanislas-Koska that interrupted my progress toward a tourist site where visitors can stroll through a reproduction of a traditional Iroquoian village, complete with longhouse and protective palisades. The sign – reading "arrêt" in French and "seten" in Huron-Wendat – was a stark reminder of the linguistic encounter between French colonizers and Amerindian groups centuries earlier, and its very existence illustrates the points this chapter has made regarding the linguistic work of the Jesuits. Le Jeune and his colleagues suggested that as divine media, French and Amerindian languages must have been directly related to each other, in the same way the stop sign I found myself contemplating suggested an exact equivalence between the two words painted on it. The richness and beauty of Amerindian languages were presented as further proof that the existence of Amerindian groups could be explained in terms of the Christian tradition, and that their languages eventually could be comprehended in terms of Latin, Greek, French, or any other language, albeit with great difficulty and only after long, hard work. By characterizing the languages this way,

3.2 · A bilingual stop sign in the Huron-Wendat reserve: Wendaké, Quebec.

the Jesuits suggested to readers that observing Amerindian cultures was from the beginning a matter of cataloguing their particularities, but also of illustrating their relationship to known models in order to reassure readers that conversion would be possible. But at the same time, drawing Amerindian languages into a direct relationship with the more familiar languages of Europe required invention. Without the intervention of the Jesuits, and to a lesser extent other early observers like Sagard, it would have been impossible for "seten" to be painted on a sign – or written at all, for that matter, a fact that can serve to remind us that the Jesuit observers did not only observe the cultures they wrote about, but no doubt also changed them in some ways as well, and then fixed their interpretations in texts that influenced how those cultures were perceived in Europe, and how they continue today to be perceived by scholars.

Proceeding on from the stop sign, I joined a tour at the cultural site, conducted by a French-speaking tour guide who proudly informed us that a linguistic renaissance was under way among the residents of Wendaké, that despite the fact that the language is no longer spoken,[75] children were learning its written form in school. Although it is certainly laudable that modern descendants of the Jesuits' missionary targets today have stop signs and school texts in their traditional language, it is important to remember that the language as it exists today is the one perceived, altered, and preserved for posterity by outsiders. Not only did the priests introduce new words into the languages they studied, they fixed their versions of the languages in writing, rendering permanent their understanding of the languages and their relationship to more familiar European tongues and ensuring that their influence would be durable. Indeed, it could be said that the one-time Jesuit students of the Huron-Wendat language have belatedly become masters, with their linguistic work now shaping ongoing efforts to revive and preserve the language. According to an account of Huron-Wendat efforts to resuscitate their language in the Montreal *Gazette*, the project relies heavily on the Jesuits' linguistic work. Wrote reporter Mark Abley, "of all of North America's native languages, Huron may offer the finest models. Though a few early 20th-century recordings of Huron exist, most of the credit goes to the 17th- and 18th-century Jesuits who sailed here from France."[76] Is the language that the descendents of the Huron now study in school and write on road signs the tongue of their ancestors, or a version thereof filtered through a Western culture and passed through the sieve of orthographic encoding? The answer is surely both. This chapter has argued that the Jesuits were not wholly disinterested students of Amerindian languages and cultures and that their treatment thereof in the *Relations* bears the marks of the intellectual challenges that the Old World had to confront when considering cultures that were startlingly different from previously known models. And yet, the language clearly was not altered so much as to lose its distinction from other tongues, since writing "stop" in French and Wendat still requires two separate words.

Amerindian languages, then, paradoxically function in the *Relations* to illustrate to readers the difference between inhabitants of Old World and New, but also to frame the challenging nature of the unfamiliar tongues as an initially puzzling symptom of cultural diversity that could, over time, be made to fit within Christian Europe's worldview. The missionary authors' descriptions of the challenges posed by Amerindian languages add nuance to their modern image as rigorous linguists and ethnographers. By casting themselves in their accounts of interactions with Amerindian interlocutors simultaneously as diligent students and as inventors adding to and modifying the local languages to make them suitable for expressing European ideas (and vice versa), the authors of the *Relations* demonstrated the extent to which the two aspects of their mission work – teaching Christianity and learning about an exotic culture – were intertwined. Learning Amerindian languages was also a matter of teaching new uses for the languages to would-be converts. And the Jesuits' portrayal of Algonquian and Iroquoian languages as simultaneously rich and poor also was useful in emphasizing to readers the necessity of the Jesuits' work, as well as its likelihood for success.

CHAPTER FOUR

Religious Conversion and Amerindian Cruelty in the Jesuit *Relations*

Few aspects of the Jesuit *Relations* are as sensational – or as often studied in modern ethnohistorical scholarship – as the missionaries' descriptions of the brutal torture, often followed by cannibalism, that various groups meted out to their enemies. From Le Jeune's 1632 *Brième Relation* on, scenes of vicious attack, physical torment of captives that could last for days, and consumption of human flesh were staples of the Jesuits' annual reports. In the context of uncertainty in early modern Europe about the relationship between the inhabitants of Europe and the New World discussed in the previous chapter, Amerindian violence was a charged topic indeed, and one that the Jesuits would need to confront both in their mission to Christianize those groups and in their efforts to transmit to readers messages about the unfamiliar cultures on the far side of the ocean. In the context of prevailing ideas about the inhabitants of the New World, the stunningly violent treatment of enemies – whether ritual torture or spontaneous attack – would seem to constitute a challenge to the Jesuits' belief that Amerindians could be convinced through reason to convert. As Cornelius Jaenen has noted, "The ultimate proof for many of the devilish nature of the land and its people was their general resistance to conversion, their practice of scalping enemies and subjecting captives to barbaric platform torture, and their supposed cannibalism."[1]

This chapter argues that the extreme violence depicted in the *Relations* frequently, and perhaps counter-intuitively, constitutes a part of the Jesuits' affirmation of the rationality of Amerindians, and their capacity for thoughtful conversion. Torture was often not, in the *Relations*, included as a sign of the absence of civilization or humanity among Amerindians, but rather as proof that it was possible to induce them to embrace Christianity in an informed and enduring way. Attempts to separate the violent details of such incidents from the Jesuits' religious message have led to the missionaries' comments on the stoicism displayed by captives facing physical torment being interpreted incorrectly as depictions of romantic Amerindian courage, rather than the sign of newfound Christian faith that the missionary writers suggested it was. And what appears, in modern ethnohistorical accounts, as proof of a precocious predilection for detailed and careful observation of Amerindian cultures actually serves instead to illustrate the degree to which the Jesuits' evangelical ends influenced their proto-ethnography. Even a subject as seemingly far removed from religious conversion as the violent torture of enemies often proves, on closer examination, to be intimately connected to the Jesuits' efforts at religious instruction of the Amerindians, and also to serve the message that the missionary authors attempted to communicate to readers about the effectiveness and potential of their religious mission. This chapter is not intended to be a comprehensive catalogue of torture and the way it was decribed by the Jesuits, but rather to focus on some of the most often studied descriptions of violence in the *Relations*. The passages of the texts that tend, in modern ethnohistorical scholarship, to serve as key illustrations of typical Amerindian behaviour toward captured enemies also, as the following pages will show, record the missionaries' attempts to teach specific lessons both to the Amerindians and to readers at home in France.

The single best-known account of Amerindian torture in the Jesuit *Relations* surely is François-Joseph Le Mercier's 1637 description of the torture and execution of an Iroquois prisoner at the hands of his Huron captors.[2] The victim, one of seven men taken prisoner following a Huron raid on a group of Iroquois fishermen, was given to an influential Huron leader as a replacement for a nephew who had been captured by the Iroquois, as custom apparently dictated. Wrote Le Mercier, "for it is customary, when some notable personage has lost one of his relatives in war, to give him a present of some captive taken from the enemy, to dry his tears and partly assuage his grief."³ At least according to modern scholars, the fate of such captured enemies depended on how the loss that they were meant to remedy could best be offset. Women and children almost always were adopted, living out their days as replacements for deceased members of their new community. Although male captives could also replace a deceased enemy, they were much more frequently tortured and killed.⁴ At the time of his arrival in the Huron village where Le Mercier first encountered him, it was clear that the prisoner was fated for a violent end, given that he already showed the signs of abuse inflicted during his captivity. One hand, which had been crushed by a rock, was missing a finger. The other hand was missing the thumb and a finger, and the joints of the captive's arms were burned and deeply cut. The Jesuit witnesses reportedly wasted no time reaching out to the captive to begin trying to convert him, promising him eternal happiness in heaven. The captive, according to Le Mercier, listened with pleasure and understood so well that he was able to recite back to the priests what he had learned about heaven, hell, and the immortality of the soul.

Over the course of several days, the Iroquois man was treated with kindness by his captors, behaviour that Le Mercier cynically viewed as intended to make the torture to come more unbearable. "All those who surrounded him, with their affected kindness and their fine words, were so many [torturers] who showed him a smiling face only to treat him afterwards with more cruelty."⁵ Meanwhile, the Jesuits continued to instruct him in the Catholic faith, baptizing him and naming him Joseph on his first night in the village when they found themselves sharing a cabin with him. As Le Mercier hastened to point out, the successful conversion of Joseph made him the very first convert among the Onondaga nation of the Iroquois League, a doubly significant event heralding not only the gain of a single soul to Christianity, but also the potential opening of an entire nation to conversion. The following day brought more opportunities to instruct the new convert, and more chances for him to reaffirm his faith, since the Jesuits once again found themselves sharing sleeping space with Joseph, this time in a nearby village where the prisoner had been taken for reasons that are not explicitly given in the text. On the third day, when the prisoner's torture was set to begin, Joseph again was approached by the Jesuits and instructed in the Catholic faith, and affirmed once more his desire to die a Christian and to go to heaven. With his execution imminent, the priests told him once more about the happiness that awaited him after death, counselled him to perform an act of contrition for his sins, and then watched as his captors took him away.

The torments that ultimately cost Joseph his life began at sundown on the third day. Le Mercier painted a frightening image of the torture scene prepared for Joseph. Eleven fires ringed the interior of the cabin belonging to Atsan, the village war captain. The cabin was so full of eager would-be tormentors that they were practically stacked one on top of the other, gleefully shouting and preparing embers with which to burn Joseph. The captive was made to run around the fires in the cabin, while spectators burned him with fiery pokers on his way by. He often was stopped at the end of the cabin, where bones in his hands were broken and his ears were pierced with sticks, among other torments. After each trip around the cabin's fires, he was allowed to catch his breath while standing in a bed of hot coals. Finally, on his seventh trip around the cabin, the captive's strength failed him. The fires were extinguished and he was given water to revive him. But the respite was short. Joseph's remaining fingers were broken, and the burning of his skin with hot pokers was resumed, with each tormentor reportedly striving to outdo his comrades in cruelty. The torture continued through the night. At daybreak, the villagers began preparations for Joseph's death by building fires outside the village. Once again, Jesuit onlookers managed to speak alone to the captive, giving him absolution after a hasty lesson on sin and divine forgiveness. He was led outside, where he was burned even more cruelly than before. Whereas previous instances of burning focused mostly on his legs, Joseph's tormentors this time left no part of his body unburned, targeting even his eyes. Finally, when the long-suffering captive no longer appeared able to move, his hand and foot were cut off, immediately followed by his head, which was saved for presentation to a war captain. His torso was, Le Mercier implies, destined to be eaten by the Huron the same day.

It is surely due to the unsurpassed detail of the plight of Joseph the Iroquois prisoner that the incident described above has become a standard account of Iroquoian torture practices for students of Amerindian cultures at the time of contact with Europeans. Indeed, the tale could be thought of as a kind of poster child for an imagined and precocious ethnographic rigour, thanks to its frequent and generally uncritical use in scholarly accounts of Iroquoian torture rituals. Nathanial Knowles, in his classic study of the torture rituals of various eastern Amerindian groups, claimed that the incident was "reasonably typical of the tortures inflicted by Iroquoian speaking peoples of upper New York State and Canada" and also a good indication of the customs of some Algonquian groups, since the Montagnais, Knowles claimed, imitated Iroquoian torture and cannibalism practices. Relying heavily on his lengthy quotation of Le Mercier's account, Knowles listed the distinguishing characteristics of what he termed Iroquoian "platform torture," so named for the outdoor area where victims typically were displayed for the amusement of onlookers.[6] In such torture, the captive was free to move at all times, and the abuse was carried out overnight in the cabin of a war chief and then outside at dawn. The torments lasted many hours, and were preceded by continuous, more minor abuse inflicted by men in the chief's cabin and by the entire village population outside at dawn. The captive was generally not tortured to death, but was killed with a knife or a blow to the head outside, on a platform before onlookers. Scalping was part of the torture process, and cannibalism reportedly was customary.[7] As one of the most detailed incidents in the written record that fits this pattern, the story of Joseph's plight has been influential in studies of Iroquoian torture. To mention only a few prominent examples, Bruce Trigger used Le Mercier's account as the basis for a general description of Huron torture rites in his authoritative ethnohistory *The Children of Aataentsic*. Elisabeth Tooker offered a detailed summary of the incident as an example of typical Huron torture customs in her *Ethnography of the Huron Indians*, as did Peggy Reeves Sanday in a wider discussion of Iroquoian torture and cannibalism in her book *Divine Hunger*.[8]

Although the story, like other similar accounts in the *Relations*, now is prized primarily for its value in illuminating the violent behaviour of Amerindian inhabitants of the New World toward their enemies – for the lessons that the Jesuit authors learned in New France and then transmitted to Europe and to posterity – understanding its significance in light of the Jesuits' efforts to teach Christianity requires placing it in the context of Europe's ideas about Amerindian cruelty at the time. The *Relations* were published at a time when Europe was, as mentioned in the previous chapter, preoccupied with much more fundamental questions: how were Amerindians related to the inhabitants of Europe? And, by extension, could they be convinced to convert through reasoned argumentation, or would it be necessary to impose a Christian lifestyle by force? According to Cornelius Jaenen, "Great debates in Spain and Rome had determined, at least for the intelligentsia who paid heed to such arguments, that the native peoples of the Americas were fully human according to two criteria: first, they were reasoning creatures, therefore qualified according to Aristotle to be called human; secondly, they seemed capable of understanding the Christian gospel and receiving divine grace, therefore were part of the Adamic family in need of redemption and salvation. Finally, there was the observation that unions with Europeans did produce fertile offspring."[9] Early papal interventions and successful breeding may have established the humanity of Amerindians for Europe's religious authorities, but the earliest explorers and colonizers in the New World did not reach a similar consensus. Travellers and colonizers of the period offered a range of assessments of Amerindian nature, from child of Eden to diabolical wildman, and many degrees of wildness or sophistication between. While travellers offered complex and nuanced assessments of Amerindian nature, the academic debate at home in Europe over how to colonize and convert newly encountered peoples quickly organized itself loosely along two general conceptions of Amerindian nature, one pessimistic about the prospects for voluntary conversion, and the other optimistic that Amerindians could be convinced through education and evangelization to embrace European customs and religion. Although assessments of Amerindian nature varied widely, European observers were unanimous on at least one point, that Amerindians were deficient in matters of religion and civilization.[10] Europe's colonial engagement with the inhabitants of the New World, then, was a question as much methodological as religious and philosophical. As Robert Berkhofer summarized the question in reference to the Spanish context, "Was the nature of the Indian so bestial as to demand force and ultimately enslavement to accomplish his conversion to Christ and Spanish ways, or was the Indian sufficiently rational and human to achieve these goals through peace and example alone?"[11]

Perhaps not surprisingly, alleged brutality toward enemies was a fixture of negative conceptions of Amerindian nature – and therefore also a justification for a more aggressive stance toward potential converts – from the earliest days of contact. Christopher Columbus described the people he encountered as kind and intelligent, inaugurating a line of positive conceptions of Amerindians, but he also described fierce, man-eating pillagers, a first negative image from which would follow a tradition of describing Amerindians as wild and violent by nature.[12] And in a well-known 1550 debate at Valladolid against Bartolomé de las Casas, Juan Ginès de Sepúlveda cited the cruelty of Amerindians toward their enemies and their much-discussed cannibalistic practices in refuting his opponent's more positive portrait of the inhabitants of the New World: "And don't think that before the arrival of the Christians they were living in quiet and the Saturnian peace of the poets. On the contrary they were making war continuously and ferociously against each other with such rage that they considered their victory worthless if they did not satisfy their monstrous hunger for the flesh of their enemies."[13] Both Columbus and Sepúlveda portrayed Amerindians engaged in violence as reflexively ferocious, killing and eating their enemies impulsively, to satisfy a hunger for human flesh. In such assessments, violence was not a rational act of justice, or defence of self or others, but an animalistic one driven by base instinct. Thus, many of the earliest European portraits of the inhabitants of the New World established their violence toward enemies as an argument for pessimistic assessments of Amerindian nature, and in support of the theory that efforts to "civilize" them would have to be more coercive than convincing.

French debates about the nature of the New World's inhabitants followed the example of their Spanish predecessors in organizing themselves along positive and negative lines. As Berkhofer notes, Spanish thought likely directly influenced French perceptions of the Amerindian Other, but even if it did not, "French and English explorers saw Native Americans in light of the Christianity and civilization they knew and valued and therefore made the same comparisons as had the Spanish adventurers and settlers earlier."[14] And in sixteenth-century France, opportunities to contemplate the nature of the Amerindian Other were abundant. Translations of Spanish works about the inhabitants of the New World were published in Paris, including the well-known works of Oviedo and Gomara, which appeared in French in 1555 and 1558, respectively, and presented Amerindians as sub-human, godless, and lawless.[15] Later in the same century, the essayist Michel de Montaigne would famously offer a more positive assessment of the inhabitants of the New World, one in which even the supposedly horrifying torture practised by Amerindians was not proof of their intellectual and spiritual inferiority to Europeans, especially given the Old World's own inclination for torture and other violent punishment.[16] The French also would have been influenced by the opportunity to contemplate Amerindians brought home by travellers and put on public display in the decades before French activity in New France began in earnest. The first such Amerindian to appear in France was a Brazilian man named Essomericq, who arrived in 1503 and reportedly lived in France until 1538. In 1509, several Amerindians from Brazil were put on display in Rouen, and the early seventeenth century also saw Tupinamba transported to France for display in various cities. Exhibition of individuals eventually progressed to more elaborate public festivals such as those held in Rouen, Troyes, and Bordeaux in 1550, 1554, and 1565, respectively, and that sometimes included reconstructions of Amerindian villages and mock battles. Such spectacular festivals kept Amerindians, and especially, in the sixteenth century, Brazilians, in the public eye in the century before the colonization of New France.[17]

By the time the authors of the *Relations* began intervening in the discussion, French economic activity and missionary efforts far to the north of the Spanish and Portuguese colonies had begun in earnest, and the debate over whether the inhabitants of the New World were rational, spiritual creatures of God fully capable of embracing Christianity or reflexively violent, instinctual humanoids who would not listen to reason often broke down along political and religious lines. The Jesuits, perhaps not surprisingly in light of their religious mission, claimed that Amerindians were indeed capable of thoughtfully embracing Christianity. As mission superior Paul Le Jeune observed, to cite just one example, "As to the mind of the Savage, it is of good quality. I believe that souls are all made from the same stock, and that they do not materially differ; hence these barbarians having well formed bodies, and organs well regulated and well arranged, their minds ought to work with ease."[18] That the Amerindian groups described in the *Relations*, and especially the Huron, later came to loom large in the "noble savage" myth of Enlightenment France often has been attributed to the Jesuit authors' favourable assessments of their capacity for reason and reflection.[19]

The Jesuits' detractors, spurned would-be Recollet missionaries to New France in particular, offered a much less flattering portrait of the

Amerindians' rational and spiritual faculties.[20] The Recollet missionary Louis Hennepin, for example, described Amerindians in his 1697 *Nouvelle Découverte d'un très grand pays situé dans l'Amérique* as "barbarous nations who have not any regard of any Religion true or false, who live without Rule, without Order, without Law, without God, without Worship, where Reason is buried in Matter, and incapable of reasoning the most common things of Religion and Faith. Such are the people of Canada."[21] In keeping with his own order's practice of imposing French language and customs on the Amerindians – for revolutionizing their entire lives rather than attempting to convince them to embrace an idea – Hennepin rejected reasoning with potential converts as a viable strategy in New France. The Baron de Lahontan, an aristocratic French military commander in the seventeenth century and author of several texts about the colony and its Amerindian inhabitants, similarly attributed to the Recollets a sharply pessimistic view of Amerindian capacity for conversion, and contrasted it with the Jesuits' more optimistic assessment. The difference, he claimed in his 1703 *Nouveaux Voyages de M le Baron de Lahontan dans L'Amérique Septentionale*, was due to the fact that "these two Orders [do not get along very well] in Canada."[22] Accordingly, claims that conversions performed by the Jesuits amounted to training Amerindians to parrot the Jesuits' religious deportment, with no real understanding of its significance, were staples of complaints by spurned rivals of the Jesuits in the seventeenth century. Chrestien Le Clercq mockingly called Jesuit claims to progress "the pretendedly great success which is boasted of without even the appearance of truth."[23] And the anonymous Recollet author of the 1689 unpublished *Histoire Chronologique de la Nouvelle France* similarly derided Jesuit publications as "[b]ooks stuffed with stories that they make up to fool the public."[24] Under the pen of spurned Recollet missionaries, familiar negative images of men too simple and backward to be converted to Christianity by evangelization alone would serve the political project, discussed in chapter two, of casting doubt on the successes claimed by a rival missionary group.

Despite the Jesuits' consistent defence of Amerindians' capacity to thoughtfully embrace Christianity, it cannot be said that the priests portrayed their would-be converts as exemplars of humanity at its best. Indeed, startlingly unflattering portraits of Amerindian behaviour exist in the texts alongside more positive assessments. George Healy provided a concise summary of the *Relations'* negative comments on Amerindians in his influential 1958 article. Wrote Healy, "The documents do contain some remarkably laudatory comments on the Indian; but they are much more copiously filled, and especially in the early accounts, with tediously detailed descriptions of the cruelty, lust, gluttony, thievery, polygamy, sodomy, cannibalism, filth, superstition, lying, blasphemy, and general barbarity of the Jesuits' reluctant neophytes."[25] For Healy, brutal torture was one item in a long list of unsavoury topics that added up to a negative portrait of Amerindian nature in the early *Relations*, to be replaced gradually in later years by a more positive assessment. Other scholars also have pointed out that descriptions of violence toward enemies were a key ingredient in negative Jesuit comments about potential converts. Carole Blackburn, for example, claimed that torture and cannibalism in the *Relations* were taken as signs of "savagery" by the Jesuit writers, Yvon Le Bras affirmed that even the normally relativistic Paul Le Jeune condemned torture practices as contrary to civilization, and Réal Ouellet and Mylène Tremblay placed the torture scenes in the *Relations* in a tradition of depictions of Amerindians as "diabolical savages."[26]

The prevalence of such passages in the Jesuit *Relations* begs a question that has implications for the Jesuits' religious mission, their proto-ethnographic attempts to represent Amerindian cultures in their texts, and the reciprocal influence of those two simultaneous projects: how could the Jesuits insist on the capacity of Amerindians to convert while simultaneously describing actions that often have been interpreted as symptomatic of the wildness or inherent wickedness of the inhabitants of the New World? A closer look at some of the most prominent such descriptions of Amerindian cruelty in the *Relations* suggests that they often participate fully in the Jesuit project of asserting the capacity of New World inhabitants to embrace Christianity and defending their own claims of progress against skeptics in France. Although Jesuit accounts of torture often have been understood to depict the routine brutality of Amerindian groups toward their enemies, restoring them to their original context often reveals that the cruelty in question is inextricably and perhaps counter-intuitively linked to a favourable assessment of the capacity of Amerindians to change and to the Jesuits' own abilities to bring about that change. In other words, Jesuit accounts of torture served not only to document bad behaviour, but also to reconcile that behaviour with Jesuit claims about and hopes for their religious mission.

The case of Joseph the Iroquois captive recounted earlier is a particularly compelling example of how the missionary writers put torture to
work in the service of their religious mission, both on the ground in New
France and in the pages of their published texts, due to its rich detail
and the use to which it has been put in reconstructing Iroquoian torture
rituals. As should be clear from the summary of the story at the beginning of this chapter, Joseph was portrayed as an attentive and enthusiastic
student of Catholicism in addition to being a victim of torture. After an
initial lesson on heaven, hell, and the immortality of the soul, the prisoner demonstrated his receptivity, Le Mercier claimed: "Your reverence
would have felt consolation in seeing with what attention he listened
to this discourse. He took so much pleasure in it and understood it so
well that he repeated it in a few words, and showed a great desire to
go to Heaven."[27] By prefacing his comments on Joseph's reaction to the
message with speculation about the favourable impression he expected
it to make on the Society's provincial in Paris, Le Mercier indicated that
he was aware that more was at stake in Joseph's conversion than a single
soul in New France. The story also, he suggested, was important for the
lessons it would communicate to readers in France who were hungry for
news of progress, and perhaps were even skeptical that such conversions
were possible. Later, after a lesson on God's universal love, to which, the
reader is told, the captive listened attentively, the priests found him so
well disposed to conversion that they opted to baptize him immediately,
naming him Joseph. Le Mercier's repeated insistence on the attentiveness
with which the Iroquois prisoner listened to the Jesuits' message, and
the pleasure and comprehension he displayed, suggests that the conversion described in the passage was not merely mimicry of the Jesuits, but
a profound spiritual change. Reinforcement of that message comes as
the new convert affirms his faith at least three more times, including
after suffering brutal torments at the hands of his captors. Readers addi-
tionally would have been reminded that the captive had converted each
time he was referred to by his new Christian name or as "nostre nouveau
Chrétien."[28]

In addition to these explicit reminders of the captive's conversion, Le
Mercier draws on a favoured technique of Jesuit education, that of pedagogical theatre, to transform the violent scene of torture into an edifying
spectacle of steadfast faith in the face of adversity. Theatrical performance of inspiring and instructional scenes had a place in Jesuit pedagogy

from its earliest days. The 1599 *Ratio Studiorum* required that students of rhetoric write and deliver "Latin or Greek orations or verses on some subject which will be of spiritual benefit and inspiration to students of the college and to externs."[29] Tragedies and comedies with pious themes were also to be periodically staged in the Jesuit colleges, and such presentations were common both in European schools and in Jesuit missions around the world in the sixteenth and seventeenth centuries. Subjects including the fall of man in the Garden of Eden, the Passion of Christ, and the martyrdom of saints were presented on Jesuit school stages, usually penned by a professor and acted by students. The New France mission was not immune to the practice. One such presentation to the Algonquin, described in the 1640 *Relation*, depicted an unconverted man being chased by two Algonquin-speaking demons, who eventually cast him into hell. That spectacle, apparently intended to frighten its audience into converting so as to avoid eternal damnation, reportedly made such an impression that those who had witnessed it continued to talk about it for days afterward. Concludes the episode in the *Relation*, "In brief, these poor peoples are giving themselves up to Jesus Christ from day to day."[30]

Indeed, a closer examination of Joseph's ordeal reveals that it is framed in the *Relations* not as the straightforward account of Amerindian cruelty for which it has so often been taken, but as an edifying spectacle of the sort with which Le Mercier, like all of his Jesuit colleagues both in New France and Europe who had been students and teachers in Jesuit colleges, would have been intimately familiar. Le Mercier's account frames Joseph's plight as a reenactment of a foundational Christian scene of suffering, a staging of the Passion of Christ that served to demonstrate the capacity of Amerindians to sincerely convert, and that suggested that brutal torture was not, or not only, an act of barbaric wildness, but an effective tool for inducing onlookers to learn about Catholic doctrine and eventually convert. Much the same way Jesus was turned over to the governor Pontius Pilate who then delivered him into the hands of his executioners, Joseph reportedly was given to "one of the chief men of the country," who decided his fate and then turned him over to his Huron compatriots to be tortured. And just as Jesus was dressed by his captors and adorned with a crown of thorns, Joseph was dressed in a beaver robe and made to wear a crown of *Pourcellaine* – decorative shells.[31] After recounting a brutal round of torture, Le Mercier makes the comparison explicit:

"Yet a soul closely united to God would have here a suitable occasion to meditate upon the adorable mysteries of the Passion of our Lord, some image of which we had before our eyes."[32] Suggesting that the suffering endured by the Iroquois captive was more a passion play than a typical scene of Amerindian cruelty was perhaps the highest praise Le Mercier could bestow on the dying convert – and the most persuasive argument he could muster that Joseph's conversion was genuine – since the imitation of Christ was a particularly esteemed sign of faith for the Jesuits.[33] In Le Mercier's account, the captive was clearly no mere captured wild man superficially imitating the actions of friendly Jesuits while stoically enduring torture as custom dictated, but a devoted Christian following in the footsteps of Christ.

Although Le Mercier's account of Joseph's demise is certainly the most well-known torture scene in the Jesuit *Relations*, it is far from the only such description. Some scholars have prudently drawn on more than one account of torture to reconstruct the practices of the groups that the Jesuits wrote about.[34] But even such composite summaries cannot entirely evade the fact that torture scenes often double as accounts of religious conversion in the Jesuits' texts. Many of the victims of torture whose torments were chronicled in the *Relations* are depicted, like Joseph, as devout Christians bravely facing their impending demise, secure in the knowledge that their suffering would be compensated after death. Le Jeune reported in his 1636 *Relation*, for example, that the Jesuit Antoine Daniel instructed and baptized an Iroquois man who was being held captive by the Huron. One night while the priest was ministering to the new convert, his captors reportedly commenced their torture, binding and burning the victim, who endured the pain "[w]ith a firmness worthy of admiration."[35] Coming on the heels of comments about the victim's conversion, his stoicism, like that displayed by Joseph, reads more like an act of faith than traditional Amerindian bravery in the face of torture. Three years later, missionary Jérôme Lalemant's *Relation* contained a detailed account of the torture of an Iroquois captive named Pierre, who endured the torments of his Huron captors with courage before dying with his eyes cast heavenward. Wrote Lalemant: "Several Savages have reported with wonder, and a sort of conviction of the truths that we preach to them, that, shortly before he received the last blow which caused his death, he raised his eyes to Heaven and cried out joyfully, 'Let us go, then, let us go,' as if he were answering a voice that invited him. Surely it would seem that he had in mind no other journey except that to heaven, to which, without distinction, the captive, if he so will, has as much right to admission as he who is free."[36] In closing his tale this way, Lalemant, like Le Mercier before him, explicitly related a captive's bravery in the face of severe torture to his newfound faith and the expectation that he would go to heaven after death. And, since Lalemant reportedly received this news from admiring members of the audience, it seems that the spectacle had its desired effect on potential converts. Although Lalemant's account of the cruelty he witnessed is, like Le Mercier's, frequently cited in studies of Amerindian torture customs, its clear religious significance has not been considered as an element of the Jesuits' proto-ethnographic theory and method.

Also not usually considered in ethnohistorical accounts of Amerindian torture is the possibility that the stoicism of Amerindian Christians in the face of torture may itself have caused alteration of the normal torture ritual that the Jesuits apparently thought they were describing. When torturing a captured enemy, the Huron apparently believed that the failure of the victim to cry out and plead for mercy would bode ill for future success in conflict with enemies.[37] It seems plausible, then, that the Huron would have redoubled their normal cruelty when confronted with stoic, converted captives, in an effort to break them and thereby avoid bringing bad luck to their own future battles. The very presence of the Jesuits, and their conversion of torture victims, may then have altered the Amerindian custom that such scenes in the *Relation* appear to record, by making them more violent than normal. Because all existing accounts of Amerindian torture in this period were penned by outsiders, this point must remain speculative, but there are other signs in the Jesuits' texts that the Amerindians themselves may have understood that the presence of the Jesuits interfered with their normal torture practices. As Jérôme Lalemant wrote in his 1639 *Relation*, tortured converts "displayed so much fortitude in their torments that our Barbarians resolved no longer to allow us to baptize these poor unfortunates, reckoning it a misfortune to their country when those whom they torment shriek not at all, or very little."[38]

Although the examples above of torture serving to prove a new Christian's faith pertain only to torture conducted by the Jesuits' Huron allies, the dynamic also holds true when the Iroquois – allies of the Dutch and enemies of the Huron and, by extension, the French – are doing the tormenting. Jérôme Lalemant opened his 1647 *Relation* with a chapter entitled "Of the Treachery of the Iroquois," in which he tells the story of a Huron convert named Jean, who is burned all night long by Iroquois captors, from the bottom of his feet to his waist. The following day, he is again tormented until he finally loses strength in the evening. Then, his entire body is thrown on the fire. The account resembles in its mechanics the actions that Le Mercier had attributed to the Huron. As in the case of Joseph the Iroquois convert that Le Mercier described in 1637, Lalemant's account gave spiritual significance to the scene, and insisted on the victim's newfound faith. Wrote Lalemant, "never, according to the report of a person who saw him in his sufferings, did he utter any cry, or give any sign of a dejected heart. He raised his eyes to Heaven in the midst of his flames, looking fixedly at the place whither his soul was aspiring."[39] In dying stoically, with his eyes on the celestial prize, the victim was understood by the Jesuit authors to have reaffirmed his newfound faith, and to have died a Christian.

It is fair to say, then, that Christian victims of platform torture are frequently depicted in the *Relations* as steadfast and unwavering in their new faith, regardless of who their tormentors are, bolstering arguments about the capacity of Amerindians to embrace Christianity and contributing to a positive assessment of Amerindian nature. Indeed, many, if perhaps not all, of the victims of prolonged torture described in the *Relations* turn out upon careful reading to be converts to Christianity.[40] Equally significant is that there do not seem to be any passages in the *Relations* that chronicle a convert's days-long test of faith by torture and that end in renunciation of faith. Although it is certainly possible that some converts renounced Catholicism and cried out in pain when tortured, such cases (not surprisingly) do not receive attention in Jesuit accounts that served to raise funds for the mission and report on its progress. Torture of converts often serves in the texts – and especially in some of the most frequently studied instances of torture – to prove to readers the capacity of Amerindians to sincerely and permanently convert, and not merely to showcase cruelty and the missionaries' abilities to document it in minute detail.

So effective were captivity and torture in securing converts that the Jesuit Paul Ragueneau claimed to be torn between wishing for new converts to be tortured in order to solidify their faith, or for them to live peacefully and contribute to a supposedly growing community of Christian converts. In his 1648 *Relation*, Ragueneau commented on the spiritual bounty that Amerindian torture of captured enemies brought to the mission:

> We desire neither sufferings nor misfortune for our Christians; but still I cannot refrain from praising God for those that happen to them, because experience has shown me that their Faith is never livelier, nor do their hearts belong more fully to God, than when, considering matters with too human vision, we have most fear and compassion for them. All those whom I have seen who have fallen into the hands of the enemy, and have afterward escaped, have admitted that, at the height of their misfortunes, they felt more Christian courage and sweeter consolation, and had more complete recourse to God, than at any time in the whole of their past lives, or even after their deliverance. Thus we know not what to wish for our Christians and for ourselves; and, however great may be the losses that this church may suffer, we shall praise God therefore, because we see clearly that he derives his glory from these to greater advantage than we could have hoped for by any other means.[41]

The value of Amerindian torture in spreading the faith was clear to Ragueneau, for whom the practice, though certainly disturbing, was not merely an unsavoury Amerindian practice described for the sake of providing to readers an accurate portrait of Amerindian culture. Instead, it was nothing short of the most effective means of ensuring the salvation of new converts.

Indeed, so fruitful would Amerindian torture rituals prove for the Jesuits' missionary enterprise that they eventually came to explicitly characterize such ordeals as an indispensable test of faith for the Iroquois, among whom the Jesuits struggled to establish a mission. Wrote Jérôme Lalemant in his 1660 *Relation*: "Who would believe that the torture by fire – which often overwhelms the victim with despair, and sometimes shakes the constancy of the best Christians – opens to some of the Iroquois the road to heaven, and that these fires are the surest means, *quibus certissimè liberantur quicumque liberantur?* – So sure are they, that we have scarcely ever seen an Iroquois burned without regarding him as on the way to Paradise; nor have we considered a single one as certainly on that road whom we have not seen pass through this torture."[42] With endurance of torture coming to serve in the *Relations* as the ultimate proof of the new faith of Iroquois converts – a test that assured salvation and without which salvation could not be assured – descriptions of the prolonged torture of captives in the texts must not be read solely as accounts of traditional cruelty of Amerindian groups toward captured enemies.

Contrasting Jesuit accounts of Amerindian stoicism and torture with one that was recorded by a non-missionary observer, one that is perhaps less known and certainly less cited than Le Mercier's account, underscores the specific nature of Jesuit ethnographic writing that this book attempts to illuminate. Samuel de Champlain recounted the treatment of an Iroquois prisoner at the hands of his Montagnais captors in his 1632 *Voyages de la Nouvelle France*. His account resembles later Jesuit descriptions in its details, including the burning of the captive with hot pokers and the ripping out of his fingernails, and Champlain notes, but does not explain, the captive's bravery in the face of these torments: "This poor wretch uttered strange cries, and I pitied him when I saw him treated this way; and yet he showed such endurance that one would have said that, at times, he did not feel any pain."[43] Absent from Champlain's account are the explicit comparisons to the Christian tradition and the insistence on the religious instruction and conversion of the victim that mark Jesuit treatments of Amerindian torture. Whereas Champlain described Amerindian torture practices and judged them to be cruel, Jesuits went further, giving religious significance to behaviour that Champlain had merely described as part of the astonishingly cruel event he witnessed. Although Champlain and the Jesuits recorded similar details about Amerindian torture, the different explanations that they provided for Amerindian stoicism reflect the Jesuits' particular brand of ethnographic writing, one influenced by not only a proto-scientific mission, but also a religious one. The vexing challenge to the notion that Amerindians were human and therefore capable of conversion that was posed by their apparently barbaric and cruel torture of members of enemy groups was resolved by establishing a relationship between Amerindian customs and Europe's Catholic traditions. Shocking and prolonged violence reportedly motivated by revenge could be reframed as a literally hellish test of faith, with the victim's suffering cast as an edifying performance of the Passion of Christ. This rhetorical move simultaneously responded to claims that the inhabitants of the New World were incapable of conversion and recast their seemingly animalistic cruelty as a harsh but ultimately useful step in the process of converting Amerindians to Christianity.

In addition to serving to convince readers of the sincere conversion of torture victims, scenes like that endured by Joseph also reportedly had a profound effect on audience members – Amerindians assembled to witness and participate in torture. While preparing the captive for baptism, the priests also instructed others in Catholic faith, since those attending to and guarding Joseph inevitably heard what the Jesuits said, Le Mercier claimed. Wrote Le Mercier, describing a colleague's exploitation of the large audience while preparing Joseph for baptism:

> A goodly band of Savages who were present, not only did not interrupt him, but even listened to him with close attention. Upon this, he took occasion to talk to them about the goodness of God, who loves all men the world over, – the Iroquois as well as the Hurons, the captives as well as the free, the poor and the miserable equally with the rich, – provided they believe in him and keep his Holy Commandments. What a great advantage it is to have mastered their language, to be loved by these peoples, and to have influence among them! You might have said that all this crowd had flocked together, not to while away the time around the prisoner, but to hear the word of God. I do not think that Christian truths have ever been preached in this country on an occasion so favourable, for there were present some from nearly all the nations who speak the Huron tongue.[44]

Not only did torture serve to prove and solidify the faith of Joseph and other victims like him, but Amerindians who happened to hear their preaching and witness the spectacle of Joseph's Christ-like suffering also showed interest in Catholicism. In Le Mercier's version of events, then, the torture of a hapless captive was a particularly advantageous context in which to teach Christianity. Indeed, Joseph's ordeal reportedly furnished several more such opportunities.[45] In addition to a stomach-churning scene of the slow destruction of a human life, Le Mercier's account depicted an especially effective missionary tactic – one that had antecedents in longstanding Jesuit pedagogical practice – and also sent to readers an optimistic lesson about Amerindian nature, the order's progress in the very new Huron mission, and the potential for future successes. What could be seen as very bad news about potential converts becomes, under Le Mercier's quill, a reason to believe that the Jesuits were indeed able to induce the inhabitants of the New World to convert in a thoughtful and enduring way.

If Joseph's behaviour was presented to readers and, apparently, to Amerindian onlookers as an edifying spectacle of faith in the face of adversity, the demeanour and actions of his tormentors also can be interpreted in this light. Le Mercier himself described in religiously loaded terms the scene that awaited Joseph in the cabin where his torture was to take place: "One must be there to see a living picture of hell."[46] The tormentors, shrouded in smoke, packed so tightly into the space that they were practically stacked one on top of the other, and brandishing hot pokers, were said to resemble demons, and the cabin itself seemed to be consumed by fire, calling to mind biblical descriptions of hell as a fiery place.[47] Joseph himself "shrieked like a lost soul" when his tormentors burned him as he ran past them.[48] As Carole Blackburn has rightly pointed out, such descriptions of torture in the *Relations* often appear "as a visible manifestation in this world of the consequences of the absence of belief and the abandonment of and by God," and indeed, the Jesuits reported using comparisons between torture and hell to frighten the Huron into converting.[49] In Jérôme Lalemant's 1646 *Relation* from the Huron mission, for example, a convert addresses the crowd assembled to torture a captive. Wrote Lalemant, "Never had there been heard, in the midst of these cruelties, the like harangue; the tormentors desist at the threats, so astonishing, of this new preacher. 'No, no, my brothers,' he adds, 'do not think that I wish to seize that captive from your hands, or to procure his liberty; the time of all his happiness is past, and, now that he burns in the flames, death alone can put an end to his miseries. My compassion is for yourselves; for I fear for you, infidels, woes a thousand times more terrible, and flames more devouring – for which your death will furnish a beginning, and which will never have an end.'"[50] Although comparisons between visibly excruciating torture and hell may well have been a useful

threat for winning converts, this insight does not explain why the missionary authors would use this tool in a text destined for French Catholic
readers. The inclusion of hell imagery in a text designed to win material
support for the Jesuits' missionary efforts is perhaps better explained by
a desire to convince readers of the sincerity of Joseph's conversion. In the
context of the prisoner's instruction, conversion, and repeated protestations of faith, Le Mercier's observation that the torments endured by the
new Christian resembled those that occur in hell serves to amplify the
severity of the test of Joseph's faith. The more hellish his ordeal, the more
convincing and impressive his reported conversion would have been to
French readers.

In addition to the religious implications of the cruelty displayed by
Joseph's torturers, it also likely would have fostered a sense of connection
to events in New France in readers, as if distant events and customs were
not so different from goings-on in the home country. As Mary Baine
Campbell observed in her analysis of torture scenes in Lafitau's *Moeurs
des Sauvages Américains*, the exhaustive and graphic nature of Lafitau's
descriptions of torture – traits that, it could be argued, are shared by Le
Mercier's account – impose on the reader an invitation to engagement,
whether in the pain of the victim or in the sadistic gratification of the tormentor.[51] Readers were, as shown above, invited to recognize and empa-
thize with Joseph as a Christ figure, but as Campbell points out, rejection
of that invitation would entail identifying with his tormentors, whose
zeal for public punishment of an enemy may have been recognizable to
seventeenth-century readers. Public torture as a form of punishment was
not uncommon in Europe at the time of Le Mercier's writing, and ceded
nothing in cruelty to the Amerindian practices described by the Jesuits.
As Cornelius Jaenen has pointed out, the seemingly chaotic violence of
a large group against a single person would not have been so unfamiliar
to French readers. Wrote Jaenen, "judicial torture and capital punishment were just as vicious and cruel in contemporary European societies.
Heretics, for example, like people accused of sorcery, could be gnawed
by starving rats or torn by raging swine; they could be made to endure
the most refined tortures of rack and wheel and other devilish devices,
and later beaten with rods in public, hanged, have their entrails burned
before their yet living eyes, and their corpses dragged away to the dung

heap. That was the measure of mercy and justice of French society against which evaluations of comments about Amerindian barbarism and cruelty should be measured."[52] Whether drawn to Joseph as a Christian acting out the Passion or to the sadistic cruelty of his tormentors, then, readers could have seen something of their own beliefs and customs in Le Mercier's account. Far from marking the horrifying difference of Amerindian cultures, torture scenes such as that involving Joseph the Iroquois captive can be understood to bridge the gap between the Old World and the New, and to render the exotic familiar.

Although European torture practices may have offered an easy point of reference to readers seeking to understand violent Amerindian customs, Le Mercier himself explicitly rejected the comparison. Wrote the priest, in quoting his own reply to a Huron's question about French customs, "'Yes, indeed; we kill them, but not with this cruelty ... fire is only for enormous crimes, and there is only one person to whom this kind of execution belongs by right; and besides, they are not made to linger so long, – often they are first strangled, and generally they are thrown at once into the fire, where they are immediately smothered and consumed.'"[53] For Le Mercier, the preferred French analogue to Amerindian torture was not the public torment and execution of criminals, but instead old and childish customs that were proof more of youthful hooliganism than an absence of humanity. Wrote Le Mercier, "Superstitions and [customs that are outdated] and authorized by the lapse of so many centuries, are not so easy to abolish. It often happens in the best cities of France that when a troop of children get to fighting with their slings, a whole town with its Magistrates has considerable difficulty in quelling this disorder; and what could two or three strangers, who would like to interfere, accomplish, unless it were to get killed?"[54] By comparing it to what he regarded as bad and childish behaviour in France, Le Mercier cast the Hurons' treatment of their prisoner in terms that humanized it, and minimized its seriousness as a challenge to the Society's evangelical mission by suggesting that it was not so different from the indiscretions of France's youth. For the missionary author, ritualized torture and execution was not evidence of a system of justice analogous to that of the French, and nor was it a sign of irredeemable animalistic wildness. Instead it was merely errant and immature conduct to be outgrown and corrected, and therefore no fateful indication of the character of full-grown adults. And in the meantime, it was at least proving useful for the purpose of putting new converts to the test.

The dynamic traced above holds true for many passages in the *Relations* depicting the ritual torture of captured converts, but it must be recognized that there is much violence in the *Relations* that is not so clearly presented as a childish custom that could be redirected to serve as a passion play until it could be displaced. Indeed, one group stands out as particularly cruel in the missionaries' accounts, even outside of the context of the ritual torture of captured enemies. The Iroquois lurk constantly in the background of the Jesuit *Relations*, apparently waiting for opportunities to pounce on unsuspecting Algonquians, Hurons, and even the Jesuits themselves in seemingly random acts of cruelty that bear little resemblance to the ritualistic, revenge-based platform torture exemplified by the tale of Joseph the Iroquois convert.[55] The opening chapter of Jérôme Lalemant's 1647 *Relation* begins with the murder of the Jesuit missionary Isaac Jogues at the hands of the Iroquois, and then goes on to describe those groups as cold-blooded killers motivated primarily by bloodlust: "Immediately after these murders, of which we had no knowledge until Spring, they spread themselves about in various places in order to capture, kill and massacre as many French, Algonquins, and Hurons as they could. Let us follow them in their raids, and mark the times of their attack and of their [hunt for] men."[56] Labelling the Iroquois hunters of men, Lalemant details a series of seemingly random acts of violence. The carnage catalogued in the chapter starts with the murder of the Jesuit missionary Isaac Jogues and Jean Lalande, a young Frenchman who was accompanying him on his mission to the Iroquois. The rest of the chapter details one violent, unprovoked attack after another. No one is immune: Algonquins, Hurons, and Frenchmen fall victim to the marauding Iroquois. In contrast to the ritualistic, if stunningly violent torture examined above, Iroquois violence, in Lalemant's estimation, was often not a focused act of revenge that sought to offset one specific death with another, but a machine that aimed to consume everything in its path.

Perhaps not surprisingly, Lalemant's rhetorical reduction of the Iroquois to hunters of men who were motivated by nothing but their hunger for flesh often is accompanied in the *Relations* by accusations of actual cannibalism. The practice of eating human flesh sometimes appears in the *Relations* as the finale of the ritualistic spectacle analyzed earlier in this chapter, but Iroquois cannibalism often is depicted in the Jesuit *Relations* as random violence, indiscriminate and reflexive, rather than the prescribed end of customary torture. Barthélemy Vimont's 1644 *Relation* from New France describes the events leading to the murder and consumption of a travelling companion of the Jesuit priest Joseph Bressani: "The enemies landed, with their prisoners; broke open all the packages containing the articles needed by our Fathers, who have received nothing for three years; tore up the letters that we sent them; and equally divided the spoils. They then threw themselves on the body of the man whom they had killed; they tore his heart out of his breast, and scalped him; they cut off his lips, and the most fleshy parts of his thighs and legs, which they boiled and ate in the presence of the captives."[57] Eating human flesh is, in this scene, the last step in a frenzy of destructive Iroquois behaviour. After ripping open packages, shredding letters, and dividing up the loot, the attackers threw themselves on the fleshiest morsels of the victim's corpse. Conspicuously absent from Lalemant's account is any indication that the Iroquois' actions were linked to a customary wartime ritual of vengeance. Instead, greed for loot and hunger for human flesh seem to motivate the attack.

Indeed, the Iroquois sometimes are depicted as actually enjoying eating the flesh of their enemies. In his 1647 *Relation*, Lalemant recounted the story of a prisoner who overheard her Iroquois captors talking about their appreciation for enemy flesh: "She had also heard, at her departure, some young men, who, not supposing that she understood their language, were asking one another which part of the body they would find the most dainty. One of them, looking at her, answered that the feet roasted under the ashes were very good."[58] Instead of an obligatory part of the torture ritual, the anticipated consumption of human flesh is in this account a rare treat, and the captive herself is clearly marked by her captor's gaze as an intended victim. The fact that the source of this account was a captured enemy of the Iroquois who may or may not have understood perfectly their language goes unexamined by the missionary author, who uses it to paint the Iroquois as relishing the taste of flesh.

In contrast to the enthusiastic and ravenous cannibalism of the Iroquois, French allies reportedly participated in cannibalism for the same reason they tortured captive enemies: out of respect for tradition. At least some of the Huron who consumed enemy flesh were, according to Brébeuf's 1636 *Relation*, barely able to choke down pieces of a captive's heart: "some taste of this [dish], or of all the rest of the body, only with great horror. There are some that eat it with pleasure."[59] The Huron in Brébeuf's account are expected to participate in the ritual regardless of the pleasure or disgust they feel upon doing so, which the priest characterized as a matter of personal preference rather than an inborn hunger or taste. In fact, it is fair to say that instances of cannibalism by allies of the French are usually depicted as having a cause that is, in some way, understandable and probably correctible. The very first mention of cannibalism in the published Jesuit *Relations* came in 1632, in the inaugural instalment in the series, as part of a description of the torture of an Iroquois prisoner at the hands of the Montagnais: "At last, as a final [catastrophe], they eat and devour them almost raw ... So enraged are they against every one who does them an injury, that they eat the lice and other vermin that they find upon themselves, – not because they like them, but only, they say, to avenge themselves and to eat those that eat them."[60] By classifying the Montagnais' cannibalism as an act of vengeance akin to eating a parasitic insect, Le Jeune placed the act squarely in the realm of justice and custom, in contrast to acts of cannibalism carried out by the Iroquois that were portrayed as being motivated mostly by that group's predatory nature, depravity, and craving for human flesh.

As attentive readers of the *Relations* have frequently pointed out, the Jesuit authors often applied a variety of labels to the Iroquois that seem to denote their lack of humanity, especially in the context of the violent and reportedly unprovoked attacks described in the missionaries' texts. Most notably, the Jesuits often called the Iroquois "wolves," but sometimes also opted for "ferocious beasts," "tigers," and other varieties of predatory big cats, echoing the language of other early French visitors to the New World.[61] Blackburn cites the comparison of the Iroquois to animals as evidence of Jesuit "fear and anxiety" over the Iroquois threat, and Le Bras has commented that such characterizations attribute the traits of wild animals to the Iroquois and suggest that they had more in common with wild beasts than with men.[62] Indeed, the word "loup" appears to have denoted a kind of cruelty and ferocity particularly worthy of fear in seventeenth-century France. Antoine Furetière's *Dictionnaire Universel* defines the term thus: "Ferocious animal that lives in the woods, and is very damaging to livestock, because it is the most gluttonous, the most carnivorous, and the sharpest of the animals."[63] It is the essential ferocity of the wolf toward domesticated animals that Furetière highlighted in describing the animal, and the string of superlatives that he employed in his definition emphasizes that the animal represented an extreme form of violence.

The Jesuits' frequent application of a term connoting such extreme violence to the Iroquois has led some to conclude that the missionaries regarded that group as animalistic by nature. As Yvon Le Bras, for example, has remarked, "Closer to animals than to men, the Iroquois become under Le Jeune's quill the most barbaric of the savages."[64] Referring to the Iroquois as beasts like wolves and tigers may seem, at first glance, to reduce them to particularly dangerous and cruel animals, but the word "loup" also had metaphorical meaning in seventeenth-century France, a fact that has not escaped scholars.[65] Wrote Furetière, "Wolf, said figuratively … of a heretic, hypocrite, or enemy of the church." The word "tiger" similarly had metaphorical value at this time, serving to designate not only wild animals, but also men who shared their least desirable traits. Furetière defined "tigre" as "Ferocious and cruel animal … said figuratively of a mean, furious and cruel man."[66] Although comparing the Iroquois to dangerous animals may superficially appear to reduce them to beasts, the metaphorical value of both terms in French suggest that the Jesuits were calling the Iroquois flawed human beings and enemies of the Church as much as they were highlighting their violent, animalistic nature.

The full significance of the metaphor only comes into focus when it is extended beyond the Iroquois to account for their relationship to other actors on the New France stage. Furetière's "wolf" was not, after all, cruel only in isolation, but rather preyed on domesticated animals. The missionaries' Amerindian allies are often cast in the *Relations* as the livestock to the Iroquoian wolves, a rhetorical move that not only suggests the mortal peril in which the Huron, the Jesuits, and Algonquian groups sometimes found themselves, but that also has clear religious resonance.

New converts to Christianity are often referred to in the *Relations* as "lambs," a name that links them to both Christ and his flock. Christ himself is referred to as the "Lamb of God" both in the Bible and in the *Relations*, and the New France mission sometimes is characterized in the missionaries' texts as a mechanism for drawing people closer to this lamb. Of the likelihood that Jesuits would be martyred in New France, for example, Jérôme Lalemant wrote in his 1646 Relation that "the principal design of this denomination is that this Mission may be assisted with the influence and favor of those blessed and consecrated victims who have the honor to approach nearest to the Lamb, and to follow him everywhere."[67] Applying the name to new converts suggests the same kind of alignment with Christ that Joseph the Iroquois prisoner displayed while being tortured. In the Jesuits' deployment of the wolf-lamb metaphor, new converts were Christ-like, but vulnerable to lupine enemies of the faith. With descriptions of the Iroquois as ferocious animals serving as a metaphor for their religious status at least as much as for their supposed animalistic nature, it is perhaps not surprising that the Jesuits sometimes suggested that transformation from wolf to lamb was possible. Despite the lurking threat that the Iroquois represented for the Jesuits, the missionaries eventually expanded their mission to the Iroquois, but it was not until 1667 that all five Iroquois groups were finally at peace with the French.[68] Earlier attempts famously ended in tragedy. Father Isaac Jogues, for example, attempted to minister to the Mohawk after being ambushed and taken captive in 1642, and was rewarded for his efforts with brutal torture. In 1646, the same priest tried again, only to be blamed for an epidemic that broke out, tortured again, and killed.[69]

Despite their difficulties in establishing a mission among the Iroquois and frequent application of animalistic metaphors that seem to suggest an essential lack of humanity in that group, the Jesuits consistently suggested that the poor conduct of the Iroquois was no proof that they could not ultimately be converted. As Jean de Quen wrote in his 1657 *Relation*, the Jesuits hoped to "change those Wolves and Tigers into Lambs, and bring them into the fold of Jesus Christ."[70] One year earlier, the priest had framed the project in the same terms, and explicitly compared it to the work carried about by the apostles of Jesus: "These nations are composed only of rogues, and yet we must trust ourselves to their fickleness, and surrender ourselves to their cruelty. Father Isaac Jogues was killed by those traitors while they were showing him the most love. But since Jesus Christ sent his Apostles as Lambs among wolves, to convert them into Lambs, we should not fear to lay down our lives in like circumstances, for the sake of establishing Peace and the Faith where war and infidelity have always held sway."[71] De Quen's recourse to the Bible places the wolf-lamb metaphor squarely in the realm of religious conversion. Framed this way, Iroquois cruelty appears not as a permanent, natural trait, but rather as a flaw that might be corrected through the establishment of religion. The already sheep-like allies of the French Jesuits were, according to the logic of the wolf-sheep metaphor, predisposed both to follow Christ and to be victimized by vicious enemies of the faith, at least until those enemies could be turned into sheep themselves.

Bruce Beresford's 1991 film *Black Robe*, an adaptation of Brian Moore's 1985 novel of the same name, illustrates the degree to which descriptions of Amerindian cruelty in the Jesuit *Relations* have been taken at face value, and divorced from the other Jesuit mission that this book traces, their efforts to communicate Christianity to the inhabitants of the New World. The film is based on the novel, which in turn took its inspiration both from the Jesuit *Relations* and from Francis Parkman's famous nineteenth-century study of the Society of Jesus' mission in New France.[72] The story follows a fictional Jesuit priest named Father La Forgue on a seventeenth-century journey to Huron country, accompanied by a band of Algonquins and under constant threat from the Iroquois who lurk in the woods. As in the *Relations*, groups other than the Iroquois are shown to have cruel streaks. For example, the priest's travelling companion, a young Frenchman named Daniel, narrowly escapes death at the hands of the Amerindians with whom the pair is travelling. A specific reason for the threat to his life is clear, as is the reason he is ultimately spared: a member of the band, led by a man named Chomina, nearly kills Daniel, who has struck up a love affair with Chomina's daughter. After the Amerindians abandon the two Frenchmen to pursue their own interests, Daniel persists in following Chomina's daughter. A jealous member of the group nocks an arrow on his bow with the intention of ending Daniel's life. Daniel is spared at the last moment by Chomina himself,

whose conscience ultimately will not allow him to abandon the Frenchmen after promising to accompany them to Huron country. Chomina's
decision reflects his concern for honouring his commitments. Violence is
not, for Chomina, an uncontrollable urge, but a potential solution to a
problem that is ultimately rejected as dishonourable.

Huron violence in the film follows a similar pattern. Upon his arrival
in the Huron village where he is to take up residence and help two priests
already there, the fictional Father La Forgue finds one of his fellow missionaries dead in the chapel, brutally murdered with a hatchet. Again,
a specific reason for the violence is provided to viewers. La Forgue ar-
rives just as epidemic disease has swept the village, taking a heavy toll on
its Huron inhabitants. The surviving missionary explains the murder to
La Forgue: "Some months ago the fever struck this village. The Indians
thought that we brought it to punish those who would not accept our
faith. Many died. One man who lost his child killed Fr. Duval."[73] Although still a tragedy and grounds for disapproval, the fictional murder
is at least explained, and can be partially sympathized with as the action
of a desperate but misguided person attempting to protect his family
and village.

The Iroquois in the film, in contrast, are portrayed as violent by nature.
As the Frenchman Daniel remarks at one point, "The Iroquois are not
men. They are animals." When Chomina's band returns to the spot where
they left La Forgue after their aborted abandonment, an Iroquois band,
invisibly hidden in the underbrush, strikes without warning, killing several of them and taking others prisoner along with the priest and his
French companion. No motivation is apparent for the brutal assault on
Chomina's group other than the Algonquin band's misfortune to cross
paths with a group of Iroquois. Later, when La Forgue and what remains
of Chomina's band arrive at the home village of their captors, they are
exposed to one act of cruelty after another. The men are forced to run
through a gantlet of villagers who beat them mercilessly with clubs, La
Forgue's finger is cut off with an oyster shell by a village leader who visibly
enjoys watching his enemies suffer, and Chomina's young son's throat is
slit while his father watches helplessly. In each violent act, the Iroquois
tormentors evidently are enjoying themselves. Violence appears in these
scenes as a sport for the Iroquois, a reflexive part of their nature carried
out for no rational purpose. Thus, more than 250 years after the Jesuits

first characterized the relative violence of Amerindian groups in terms sympathetic to their allies and disparaging of their enemies, the dynamic can still be found today in pop culture depictions of those cultures, testifying to the enduring influence of the *Relations* in their own right and through the intermediary of the scholarship and pop culture artifacts that draw on them.

And yet, strikingly absent from the film is any suggestion of the relationship that the Jesuits established between violence and religious status, testifying to the degree to which cruelty in the Jesuit *Relations* has so often been taken as a straightforward recounting of Amerindian custom. As Georges Sioui – himself a Huron-Wendat – has pointed out, much was at stake in the Jesuit descriptions of torture: "We know that evoking the Amerindians' bloody cruelty was a powerful means used by the colonial (mainly religious) authorities to attract the favour, sympathy, and financial support of their country's upper classes. Aside from this self-seeking attitude, some sources, particularly oral accounts, indicate that torture and its corollary, cannibalism, never had the importance attributed to them."[74] Sioui argues that colonial writers exaggerated torture and cannibalism in their haste to titillate readers and spur them to action in support of the colonial and missionary enterprise, and that modern scholars basing their assessments on accounts such as those found in the Jesuit *Relations* have been duped into giving Amerindian violence more cultural importance than it actually had at the time of contact. Others are surely more qualified than this author to judge the importance of torture and cannibalism in early contact Amerindian cultures,[75] but the analysis offered in this chapter supports Sioui's assertion that Jesuit chroniclers of Amerindian cruelty were motivated by more than a concern for careful documentation of the cultures they encountered. Contrary to interpretations of violence in the *Relations* as evidence of a pessimistic Jesuit attitude toward Amerindian nature, such passages tend to convey optimistic messages about the capacity of Amerindians to embrace Catholicism and to remain true to their new religion. Events that might reasonably be considered steps backward for the fledgling mission – the torture and death of some of the precious few converts and of some of the missionaries themselves, and vicious surprise attacks on French allies by enemies of the faith – are rhetorically transformed into evangelical opportunities by the authors of the *Relations*, and cause for optimism among readers at home in France. Converts such as Joseph who are tortured to death are depicted as having survived hell on earth without losing faith, reinforcing the Jesuits' message that Amerindians were capable of embracing Christianity and that Jesuit methods were effective in leading them to do so, and pushing back against the competing European viewpoint that Amerindians were too brutish and unreasonable to convert. And while depictions of the stunning brutality of the Iroquois suggest the relative deficiency of that group compared to the Jesuits' Huron allies, the animal metaphors that the Jesuits deployed suggested not permanent and radical beastliness, but rather a state of religious backwardness that could be remedied: wolves could, in the Jesuits' estimation, become lambs.

CHAPTER FIVE

Messou the Great Restorer: Questioning Montagnais Religious Knowledge

In Europe's attempts to make sense of the inhabitants of the New World in the wake of first contact, the Beginning was considered an excellent place to start. As Giuliano Gliozzi remarked in his exhaustive study of early modern European theories of Amerindian origins, "No self-respecting travel book fails to dedicate one of its first chapters to discussion of the problem of the 'origins of the Americans.'"[1] Even European writers who did not make the trans-Atlantic voyage themselves almost always attempted to resolve the question in some way when commenting on the New World. At stake was a fundamental theological question: what did the existence of geographically remote non-Christians, for which scripture provided no obvious explanation, imply about the Amerindians' relationship to the rest of humanity? The answer to that question had political consequences as well, especially when France began to take an interest in exploring and colonizing the New World. The 1494 Treaty of Tordesillas had divided the New World between Spain and Portugal, and a papal bull that preceded it by one year forbade the French to colonize the Americas or to engage in trade or missionary work there. One exception to that prohibition was that lands held by a Christian king prior to Columbus' voyages were not to be redistributed.[2] France therefore could justify its lack of adherence to this ban by arguing for a Gallic connection between the inhabitants of New France and the Old Country. Whether motivated by religion or politics, attempts to answer the question of Amerindian origins were of primary importance in European texts describing the New World's unfamiliar peoples during the age of exploration and colonization.

Jesuits in New France were no less interested in Amerindian origins than others who visited and/or wrote about the New World, but as missionaries who were hoping to convert to Christianity the area's inhabitants, their interest was not restricted to Old World political and theological debates. This chapter examines the subject of Amerindian origins in the Jesuit *Relations* from the standpoint of the priests' two simultaneous missions – preaching Christianity in the New World and transmitting to European readers the lessons they had learned as result of their contact with its inhabitants. The Jesuits frequently attempted to teach the biblical creation story to their potential converts in the New World, and the Amerindian myths that the Jesuits learned from their Native interlocutors also frequently appear in the texts. The term "myth" is used in this chapter not in its popular sense of fable or fiction, but instead as defined by Mircea Eliade, to designate a sacred belief about the origins of the world, humankind, and its surroundings.[3] Although such passages have sometimes been cited as indicative of Amerindians' unique, traditional knowledge about the creation of the world and its inhabitants, this chapter argues that the Jesuits approached Amerindian creation myths not as proto-ethnographers gathering and shaping information about a unique belief system, but as catechists or pedagogues who already knew the correct answer about the origin of Amerindian people, and were seeking signs of that knowledge, as well as its absence, in the belief systems of their potential converts. Casting their engagement with Amerindian myths as a teaching opportunity instead of an exchange of ideas also would have sent a specific lesson to the Jesuits' readers at home in France, serving to explain the relationship between Amerindians and Europeans in a way that would not threaten to invalidate biblical knowledge on the topic.

The examination of the problem of Amerindian origins in the Jesuit *Relations* that is contained in this chapter focuses on two passages that describe what the missionaries apparently believed to be a Montagnais creation myth. The two versions of the story appeared in the *Relations* in two consecutive years, 1633 and 1634, and straddle the moment in the history of the published series in which the missionary authors seem to have become aware that their texts – initially conceived as internal reports – were being published in France. This happy coincidence provides an opportunity to assess how the knowledge that their words were being published may have influenced the ways in which the Jesuit authors framed the information contained in their texts, a subject that will be further developed in chapter six. By examining Le Jeune's accounts of the myth, this chapter argues that the Jesuit focus on indigenous creation myths was simultaneously a strategy aimed at teaching Christianity to the Amerindians and an attempt to reassure or convince readers of the links between Old and New World beliefs, instead of merely instructing them on the unique nature of the latter. The differences between the two published versions of the myth suggest that the very fact of publication may have influenced the ways in which Jesuit missionaries framed the information contained in the Jesuit *Relations*.

As chapters three and four have already shown, the New World furnished much new information that needed to be explained in a way that was consistent with well-established truths, or recast in order to avoid undermining the Jesuits' mission project. The very existence of Amerindians, who seemed so culturally different from Europeans as to beg the question whether they shared a common origin with the inhabitants of the Old World, was perhaps the single most vexing of the intellectual challenges posed by Europe's developing awareness of the New World, and constituted what Normand Doiron has called "the biggest theological shock of the Christian era."[4] Because the Christian tradition suggests a common origin for all of mankind – God's creation of Adam and Eve – Europeans were left with the task of determining how Amerindians were related to the rest of known humanity. Failure to find such a link would imply that the Bible was wrong, surely an unthinkable outcome. As mentioned at earlier points in this book, one possible explanation, that Amerindians were animals instead of men and therefore did not by their very existence imply the possibility of a second act of divine creation of man, had already been taken off the table by papal pronouncements in 1493 and 1535.[5] Once Amerindians were deemed human, Old World thinkers were left to grapple with the problem of how they were related to the rest of Adam and Eve's descendants.

Commentators from across Europe provided a wide variety of theories to explain the presence of human beings in the New World, drawing both on biblical clues and on stories and legends from antiquity, and usually offering explanations that could be used to support their home country's ambitions in the New World or their own religious point of view.[6] The French parliamentary lawyer and poet Marc Lescarbot, who wrote his 1609 *Histoire de la Nouvelle France* after visiting the French settlement in Acadia himself, included a chapter that can serve as a useful indication of the kinds of theories that Europe entertained on the subject during the seventeenth century. Some of Lescarbot's contemporaries, he noted, held that Spaniards or other Europeans had populated the New World, or that the Amerindians were the descendants of Ham, a son of Noah whose own son was cursed by the famous ark-builder for reasons that are not entirely clear in the Bible. Lescarbot himself speculated on the basis of Noah's reportedly long life that the famous flood survivor could have built a second ark and sent it to the New World. Another possibility, as far as Lescarbot was concerned, was that as-yet unknown connections between the continents furnished humans with a means of arriving in the New World on foot at some point after the Creation, "for I hold that all the parts of terra firma are joined together, or at least, if there is some strait, like those of Anian and Magellan, it is something that men can easily cross."[7]

More than one hundred years later, Joseph-François Lafitau, himself a former French Jesuit missionary, weighed in with his own chapter on Amerindian origins, starting from the premise that the inhabitants of the New World were of the "race of Adam," and concluding that they were the descendents of "barbarians" who formerly occupied Greece. "My own opinion is, then, that the largest number of the American peoples came originally from those barbarians who occupied the continent and islands of Greece, whence, having, for many centuries, sent out colonies in every direction. They were all, or almost all, at last forced to go out to spread over different countries."[8] Although the various genealogies proposed by Europeans differed widely, most explanations offered up until the eighteenth century shared at least one noteworthy trait with Lescarbot's and Lafitau's comments on the subject: the assumption that the ancestors of North Americans were created in Eden, in the same single divine act of creation as Europeans. Because the question was primarily understood as a religious one in early modern Europe, intellectual attempts to determine the origin of the Amerindians were, at least until the eighteenth century, generally limited by theological considerations.

One theory that could have explained the absence of a clear biblical account of Amerindian origins was proposed during the sixteenth and seventeenth centuries: God might have created mankind more than once and in various places. This possibility was by no means a mainstream opinion, and certainly was not one that the New France Jesuits and their Catholic brethren were likely to look upon with favour. Indeed, the case of Huguenot writer Isaac de la Peyrère demonstrates the power that the traditional interpretation of the Bible as accounting for only one Creation had over the debate in the seventeenth century. In his 1655 *Prae-Adamitae*, La Peyrère interpreted Genesis as necessarily implying the existence of men who were not descendants of Adam. The story of Adam's sons Cain and Abel, for example, only made sense if there were other people around, he claimed. For if Cain was a farmer, did that not imply the existence of artisans to fabricate his tools? And if Abel was a shepherd, from whom was he guarding his flock if the entire population of the world consisted only of Adam's immediate family? La Peyrère's theory was not greeted with enthusiasm. The book was condemned both by the Parlement of Paris and by ecclesiastical authorities, and the author was arrested and threatened with a heresy trial before Spanish inquisitors. La Peyrère himself renounced his ideas before Pope Alexander VII and simultaneously converted from Calvinism to Catholicism. Although the publicly humiliated writer would privately continue to defend his ideas until his death, the harsh reaction to La Peyrère's hypothesis indicates the degree to which traditional interpretations of Genesis as accounting for a single divine act of creation – one that included the ancestors of Amerindians – dominated Catholic Europe's thinking on the subject during the seventeenth century. Explanations that could not be reconciled with settled doctrine were not widely acceptable, and certainly not among Jesuit missionaries.[9]

Given the high stakes of the question for Christianity, it should not be surprising that Jesuit missionaries in New France devoted considerable energy to attempting to teach their Amerindian interlocutors about Creation as described in Genesis. The *Relations* record frequent references to God's creation of the world by missionaries who sought to introduce their religion to potential converts. In 1637, for example, Le Jeune described the case of a Montagnais leader named Makheabichtichiou who wished to befriend Monsieur de Montmagny, the colony's governor at the time. The governor told him that friendship was reserved for those who took care to learn the Christian faith, prompting the Montagnais man to ardently seek lessons from the Jesuits. The Jesuits, of course, were only too happy to oblige: "We granted his wish, and in the evening, after having said our prayers, instead of sleeping we talked over the articles of our faith, doing the same during the day when we had time. I explained to him the creation of Heaven and earth, the fall of the rebellious Angels, how our first Father had been created."[10] After long conversation with Makheabichtichiou, Le Jeune doubled down on his lessons about the Creation, reportedly realizing that pointing to physical, natural proofs of God's existence might be more convincing as an initial introduction to the faith than biblical history that simply had to be believed. Le Jeune sought to prove the existence of a God on the basis of features of the natural world such as the tides, the rotation of the heavens, the formation of babies in their mothers' wombs, and other observable natural phenomena: "'Men,' said I to him, 'cause none of all these things, and yet they appear every day before our eyes. There must, then, be another and more powerful cause.'"[11] Le Jeune's lessons to his curious interlocutor included many topics of Christian doctrine, but it is significant that the list of subjects covered prominently features the creation of the world and of mankind, and that he apparently deemed what he took to be the visible signs of creation to be the ideal place to start.

Another instructive example was furnished the same year by Jérôme Lalemant in his report from the Huron mission. At the request of an unspecified reader, Lalemant provided the text of a prayer recited in the Huron language by convert Joseph Chiouatenhoua, along with a French translation. The prayer begins: "Lord God, at last, then, I know thee, Happily now I know thee. It is thou who hast made this earth that we behold, and this Heaven that we behold: thou hast made us who call ourselves men."[12] The prayer, which covers four pages in the Campeau edition, begins with the identification of God as the creator of everything that exists. This aspect of the Christian God's identity also is emphasized in Jesuit catechisms used to instruct potential converts in North America. One such document, published as an appendix to Samuel de Cham-

ARRIHOVAIEN- *ſtaçoüa Achriſteehaan.*	*DOCTRINE* *Chreſtienne.*

Achriſterronon ochien- da chè orrihoüaien- ſtécha.	Du nom Chreſtien, & de la doctrine Chre- ſtienne.

Escat Aienstacoüa.	Premiere Leçon.

Arrihoüaienſtechaens.	*Le Maiſtre.*

Sſa Acriſterronon chiont?

Estes vous Chre-ſtien?

Ateienſtechaens.

Le Diſciple.

Aau, daotan haatarrat Aatio.

Ouy, par la grace de Dieu.

M. Sinen Atoñas Achri-ſterronon?

M. Qui eſt celuy qu'on doit appeller Chreſtien?

D. Nihen de hotoain, chiachè hocarratat arri-hoüaienſtécha Achriſt-ehaan, ſtat onnè atoña-choña.

D. Celuy, lequel ayant eſté baptizé croit, & fait profeſſion de la Doctrine Chreſtienne.

M. Tout aotan nondée A-chriſtehaan arrihoüaienſtecha.

M. Qu'eſt-ce que la Doctrine Chreſtienne.

D. Nen arrihoüaienſte-choutan dè Aſſoñaien-

D. C'eſt celle que noſtre Seigneur Ieſus Chriſt

A ij

5.1 · First page of the Huron-language translation of the Ledesma catechism *Doctrine Chrestienne*, 1630, by Diego de Ledesma, translated by Jean de Brébeuf. This bilingual catechism was prepared by Brébeuf for use in New France. Questions and their prescribed answers appear on the left in Huron, and on the right in French.

plain's *Les Voyages de la Nouvelle France Occidentale* (1632), was written by the Spanish Jesuit Diego de Ledesma and translated into Huron by Brébeuf. It contains the following question, and the answer potential converts were expected to give to demonstrate their knowledge of Christian doctrine: "You say that you believe in God, what is God? [Answer:] It is the Creator of Heaven and earth, and the Universal Lord of all things."[13] As these and countless other examples attest, God's role as a creator of the visible world was a focal point of the Jesuits' efforts to communicate Christianity to potential converts.[14]

Not all Amerindians, of course, were as motivated to learn about Chrsitianity as Makheabichtichiou or Joseph Chiouatenhoua, and some reportedly resisted the lessons that Jesuit priests attempted to give them on the topic, posing objections that the missionaries dismissed out of hand. The Huron, to cite just one example, reportedly disputed on practical grounds the notion that they were created in the same time and place as their European visitors. Reported one missionary, "Besides, they had often admitted to us that they took us for liars, and did not believe in the least what we taught; and that what we said was not at all probable, – that there was no likelihood that they and we had the same God, Creator of their earth as well as of ours, and that we had all descended from the same father. 'Indeed,' said *Sononkhiaconc* one day, 'who would have brought us to this country, – how would we have crossed so many seas in little bark canoes? The least wind would have engulfed us, or we would at least have died of hunger at the end of 4 or 5 days. And then, if that were so, we would know how to make knives and clothes as well as you people.'"[15] The Jesuit response to these arguments was typical of the missionaries' expressed opinions about the state of Amerindian knowledge on weighty matters of religion. Father François-Joseph Le Mercier, in whose 1637 report from the Huron mission the above comments appear, curtly dismissed the Huron objections, suggesting to his readers that such questions were nonsense unworthy of being committed to paper: "I would waste too much paper if I were to undertake to set down here all their extravagances."[16] The logical holes that Amerindians apparently found in the priests' account were deemed not worthy to write down, and therefore could not, as suggested in chapter three, be counted as legitimate contributions to knowledge by Old World observers who were accustomed to truth being fixed in writing.

Although Amerindian objections to Christian knowledge were in at least some cases deemed too frivolous to be committed to paper, the Jesuits were less reluctant to write detailed accounts of Iroquoian and Algonquian creation stories, which presumably also were deemed to be false by Old World Christians who believed in the literal truth of Genesis. The *Relations* contain numerous accounts of Amerindian myths pertaining to the creation of the world and the arrival of mankind in it, including several versions of a Huron myth, an Algonquin myth, and two versions of a Montagnais myth. Although this chapter focuses on the Montagnais myth, its conclusions in many instances could also be applied to the Jesuits' treatment of the beliefs about creation of the other Amerindian groups they encountered.[17] As the rest of this chapter argues, Jesuit discussions of Amerindian origins were included in the *Relations* not, or not only, out of a desire to record for posterity the lessons they had learned while interacting with a unique and interesting culture. Instead, such passages presented to European readers the argument that Amerindians were, in fact, creations of God who had simply strayed somehow from the Old World and forgotten their roots, and that their existence therefore did not pose a challenge to biblical authority. The emphasis placed on creation stories by the Jesuits, it turns out, reflects not only an interest in documenting unfamiliar beliefs or a preoccupation with convincing Amerindians that they were created by God and thus were subject to his – and, by extension, the Jesuits' – authority, but also a desire to reassure Europeans that such was the case.

What has generally been perceived to be a Montagnais creation myth appears twice in the Jesuit *Relations*, in the instalments published in 1633 and 1634. The two versions of the myth essentially confirm each other, as might be expected given that they were both born of mission superior Paul Le Jeune's conversations with the Amerindians with whom he would spend the arduous winter of 1633–34. Both accounts of the Montagnais tale begin by briefly mentioning the possibility that a mythical figure named "Atahocan" was the Christian God in disguise, and then recount a story about "Messou," who repaired the world after a catastrophic flood. Messou goes hunting with his lynxes, which he kept instead of dogs. The animals fall into a lake and sink, and Messou searches everywhere for them. A bird flying overhead reports seeing the lynxes at the bottom of the lake. Messou enters the water to try to rescue his pets, but is thwarted by suddenly rising waters. The lake breaches its banks and inundates and drowns the whole world. Messou, stunned by this turn of events, abandons all thought of rescuing his lynxes, and turns his attention to re-establishing the world. He sends a raven to fetch some dirt in the hopes of using it to restore the land. When the raven fails to find any, Messou sends an otter to dive for a piece of earth, but the water proves too deep. Finally, a muskrat dives and brings some back, which Messou uses to restore the world to its normal state. Messou marries the muskrat and they repopulate the world with their children.[18]

The tale's account of the creation of land is by no means unique in the creation myths of cultures world-wide. The "Earth Diver," a mythical figure that dives into the water to retrieve dirt from the bottom and then uses it to create land, is a common feature of Iroquoian myths, and is among the most widespread religious ideas in Native North America and throughout the world. In an article on the myth, folklorist Alan Dundes provided a brief and useful survey of scholarship that has catalogued the presence throughout the world of tales involving animals diving for dirt or mud in order to make land. Wrote Dundes: "Anna Birgitta Rooth in her study of approximately 300 North American Indian creation myths found that, of her eight different types, earth-diver had the widest distribution. Earl W. Count who has studied the myth for a number of years considers the notion of a diver fetching material for making dry land 'easily among the most widespread single concepts held by man.'" Stith Thompson's *Motif Index of Folk Literature* reports that variants of the myth have been found in India, Siberia, Borneo, and California, among other far-flung places. And versions featuring Satan in the role of the diver have been found in Estonia, Finland, Lithuania, and Siberia.[19]

Stories that resemble the creation myth in the *Relations* exist among modern Algonquian groups that are related to the historical Montagnais, such as the East Cree. And Messou himself may correspond to the Naskapi trickster figure Mâsw, the East Cree Maasu, and others.[20] Many scholars, however, have failed to recognize a connection between such modern materials and the tale recorded by Le Jeune in the seventeenth century. Writing in the *Journal of American Folklore*, Frank G. Speck reported specifically asking his Montagnais interlocutors about Messou in the early nineteenth century, and finding no trace of the story or any like it among that group or related Algonquian groups. Scholars have attributed the perceived absence of the tale from modern accounts of Montagnais beliefs to a variety of factors. Hartley Burr Alexander suggested that the priest misunderstood the myth due to the "nebulous and confused" nature of Algonquian cosmogony compared to that of Iroquoian groups. Lucien Campeau pointed to the Jesuits' own imperfect mastery of the Montagnais language in the early 1630s when Le Jeune recorded the myth, which might have led him to so badly misunderstand it as to practically invent the version that appears in the *Relations*. Campeau, himself a Jesuit priest, also optimistically claimed that the myth and other aspects of Montagnais spirituality simply died out after the arrival of the missionaries who preached Christianity, due to the rapid implantation of Christianity.[21]

Perhaps at least in part because of the failure of such scholars to see a connection between the Montagnais tale in the *Relations* and the more recently collected stories of related groups, Le Jeune's versions of the myth have stood as the standard accounts of Montagnais beliefs about the creation of the world. Jean Louis Fontaine, himself of Montagnais-Innu extraction, quoted Le Jeune's first version of the myth at length in his book *Croyances et Rituels chez les Innus*. Nicholas P. Cushner and Emma Anderson both cited Le Jeune's version of the myth as indicative of Montagnais beliefs in their recent books, and philosopher and folklorist Hartley Burr Alexander cited Le Jeune's first account of the myth in his 1936 book on Amerindian mythology. Alfred G. Bailey, in turn, cited Alexander's work as evidence of Montagnais beliefs in his 1969 book on colonial contact in North America, in effect relying on the account offered by Le Jeune but lending it the weight of a twentieth-century source. Although this chain of citation may make it appear to the casual observer that the myth has more than one source, following the chain backward reveals that Le Jeune is the ultimate source of practically all accounts in modern scholarship – or at least all those uncovered in the course of the research for this book – of what the Montagnais believed at the time of contact with missionaries.[22] It is a testament to the degree to which the *Relations* have long been regarded as a first-rate source of information about Amerindian cultures that Le Jeune's account of the Montagnais myth so often has overshadowed other potential sources of information about that group's beliefs.

A closer look at the two versions of the tale in the *Relations* reveals that Le Jeune himself did not suggest that it represented original knowledge, and was instead skeptical of its elements that could not be recognized as harmonious with the Bible. Introducing the terrestrial repairman Messou in 1633, Le Jeune wrote: "You see that they have some traditions of the deluge, although mingled with fables. This is the way, as they say, that the world was lost."[23] In 1634, the priest again opened his account of the tale in similar terms: "As to the Messou, they hold that he restored the world, which was destroyed in the flood; whence it appears that they have some tradition of that great universal deluge which happened in the time of [Noah], but they have burdened this truth with a great many irrelevant fables."[24] In both *Relations*, Le Jeune went on to offer a detailed summary of Messou's restorative actions before closing by once again characterizing the tale's unique aspects as fables. Although Le Jeune implied that the actions of Messou reflected true, if distorted, knowledge of Genesis, other aspects of the myth were, for the missionary writer, an inferior record of Creation that was corrupted with silly stories, instead of unique and potentially legitimate knowledge of the world's earliest days.

The inferiority that Le Jeune saw in the Montagnais' version of the flood story was rooted in its oral nature. Le Jeune insisted on the fact that the story was transmitted and preserved orally by repeatedly using verbs like "*dire*" (to say) and "*raconter*" (to tell) in both versions, to explain how he came by the information that he was presenting. The second version of the myth in particular, we will soon see, is framed as a discussion between the skeptical priest and his Montagnais informant. Although the conversations that Le Jeune engaged in obviously yielded some information about Montagnais beliefs, that does not mean that the Montagnais story was regarded as a credible competitor to scripture. As Walter Mignolo has noted of the relative worth of written and oral knowledge to European visitors to the New World, "The celebration of the letter and its complicity with the book were not only a warranty of truth but also offered the foundations for western assumptions about the necessary relations between alphabetic writing and history. People without letters were thought of as people without history, and oral narratives were looked at as incoherent and inconsistent."[25] Knowledge and writing were intricately bound up in early modern European thought, and true knowledge like that contained in the Bible did not rely on word of mouth, and was therefore not susceptible to the same kind of imprecision and variation that seemed to mar Amerindian myths.

In contrast to the account of Creation in written scripture, the Montagnais tale existed only orally up until Le Jeune chose to write it down.

By insisting on this fact in his versions of the myth, then, the priest also was insisting on its incomplete and degraded nature. Though it was interesting enough to write down, it certainly could not have competed with Genesis, which had been in written form since long before Le Jeune's time. Le Jeune would make this point explicitly in his 1637 *Relation*, in a passage in which he reported telling a Montagnais shaman about the creation of Earth and man according to the Bible, the fall of man in the Garden of Eden, and the great flood. Of the Montagnais' knowledge of the flood story, Le Jeune wrote: "I told him that their nation had sprung from this family; that the first ones who came to their country did not know how to read or write, and that was the reason their children had remained in ignorance; that they had indeed preserved the account of this deluge, but through a long succession of years they had enveloped this truth in a thousand fables; that we could not be mistaken about this event, having the same belief as our ancestors, since we see their books."[26] By specifically claiming in both versions that Messou's story proved knowledge of the great biblical flood, and then insisting on the strictly oral nature of the tale, Le Jeune invited his readers to interpret it through that lens, as a fragment of Genesis that had been corrupted by fables and degraded by the absence of reading and writing in Amerindian cultures. The tale was to be read as an inferior version of an episode from Genesis, and not as a unique Montagnais account of the early history of the world. Attempting such a reading no doubt would have been confusing to Le Jeune's Christian readers in France. Given that Genesis explicitly says that all men aside from Noah and his family were killed in the flood,[27] readers would be left to speculate whether Messou was Noah, a member of Noah's family, or God – the only remaining possibilities – in the Montagnais' warped version of the biblical story. Each of these possibilities is worth briefly exploring in the context of Le Jeune's accounts of the Montagnais myth.

Le Jeune never explicitly equates Messou with Noah or a member of his family, but some of the details of his version of the myth might have led his readers to the conclusion that Messou was indeed a passenger on the ark. Like Noah, Messou employs a raven in his efforts to cope with the aftermath of the flood. The raven is the first of three animals Messou sends in search of a piece of earth, and Noah sends a raven forth from the ark after it settles in the mountains of Ararat. According to Genesis, "At the end of forty days, Noah opened the window of the ark that he had made and sent out the raven; and it went to and fro until the waters were dried up from the earth."[28] The goal of this action is not entirely clear, but after sending the raven out, Noah sends a dove to see if the earth was dry. Genesis seems to suggest that the raven had a role in verifying the post-diluvial inhabitability of the world. The ends to which Messou and Noah employed their ravens are related: both concern determining or ensuring the habitability of the earth. Read as a version of Noah's ordeal, the Montagnais belief that the raven's role was to search for a piece of dirt with which to remake dry land appears as an absurd literalization of the bird's limited role in reestablishing the world, since the Bible makes clear that God himself was responsible for making the earth dry.[29] Christian readers tempted by Le Jeune's comments to read Messou as Noah would find an explanation for these inconsistencies in Le Jeune's caveat in each of his two versions that the biblical flood story had been corrupted by fables. Despite the clues Le Jeune provided that Messou might have been Noah, the Montagnais figure is in some ways a wildly imperfect fit for that role. Messou does not have prior warning of the flood, as Noah did in Genesis.[30] Indeed, he appears to be caught completely by surprise by the rising water, which interrupts his search for his pets. In the 1633 *Relation*, Le Jeune wrote that "[h]e leaped into the water to rescue them; but immediately the lake overflowed, and increased so prodigiously that it inundated and drowned the whole earth. The Messou, very much astonished, gave up all thoughts of his lynxes, to meditate on creating the world anew."[31] The following year's *Relation* would again characterize Messou as being caught unawares by the flood.[32] In addition, Messou builds no ark, collects no animals, and apparently has no family that rides out the flood with him, all features of Noah's ordeal.

Reading Messou as a God figure is no less problematic. Readers could have been tempted to do so by the fact that Messou, in the Montagnais myth, is responsible for repairing the world, a task performed by God in Genesis. But many elements of Messou's story seem to disqualify him for the role. In the myth, Messou is present on Earth during the flood, and did not intentionally cause it or even know it was coming. His candidacy for God would have been further damaged by Le Jeune's repeated insistence that Messou merely *repaired* the world, as opposed to creating it. Accordingly, Le Jeune mockingly referred to Messou as "this great restorer" ("ce beau Réparateur") in his 1633 version of the myth and a year later ends his telling of the story by emphasizing the restorative, as opposed to creative, role of the mythical figure: "So this is the way in which the Messou restored all things."[33] By framing the Montagnais myth as a corrupted version of the biblical flood story, Le Jeune neutralized the threat that it might otherwise have posed to scripture-based knowledge of the world. Instead of representing unique knowledge about Creation, the story became, under Le Jeune's quill, a distortion of a later episode in Genesis to be mocked rather than feared as a potential competitor to Old World knowledge. For readers following the priest's cues, Messou's puzzling role in the tale could be interpreted as a conflation of the roles of God and Noah, since any other option would contradict the biblical account of a flood in which "everything on dry land in whose nostrils was the breath of life died."[34] Such apparent confusion would have been seen as yet more evidence that the Montagnais myth was taken from Genesis, but corrupted by fables because of faulty Amerindian preservation of knowledge. Just like the simultaneous richness and poverty that the *Relations* ascribed to Amerindian languages and discussed in chapter three, this dynamic would suggest a link between European Christians and the inhabitants of the New World, while preserving the need for missionary intervention.

Despite their similar contents and common focus on establishing links between the Christian tradition and Montagnais beliefs, Le Jeune's two accounts of Atahocan and Messou are strikingly different in the way they frame the tale. These differences suggest that the knowledge that their words were being published may have had an important influence on the missionaries' rhetorical strategies. The *Relations* that contain the two versions of the Montagnais myth straddle the moment in the history of the series in which Le Jeune and his colleagues seem to have become aware that their words were being published and circulated among France's reading public. As mentioned in chapter one, the Jesuits' annual reports from New France were born of a long letter-writing tradition of the Society of Jesus. Although Le Jeune apparently believed himself to be participating in this longstanding practice when he inaugurated the series in 1632, the New France *Relations* were published beginning with the first instalment in the series, as were many other mission reports from around the world. According to Lucien Campeau, it is not clear if Le Jeune knew in 1633 that his 1632 *Brève Relation* had been published. If he did know, that information would only have arrived in New France when it was too late to rewrite the 1633 instalment with a wide readership in mind. Accordingly, writes Campeau, "[i]n 1633, he still writes, without affectation, a letter that is not intended for publication."[35]

Perhaps not coincidentally, Le Jeune adopted a more reader-friendly format for his 1634 *Relation*, organizing the report into thematic chapters instead of a long, rambling letter. The change in format suggests that the missionary author understood, upon learning that his work was being published, that the *Relations* had a broader purpose than originally thought. Le Jeune himself indicates in his 1633 *Relation* that he was already realizing the limitations of the letter format: "But it is about time for me to reflect that I am no longer writing a letter, but a book, I have made it so long. It was not my intention to write so much; the pages have insensibly multiplied and I am so situated that I must send this scrawl, as I am unable to rewrite it and to make a clean copy of it, such as I think ought to be presented to Your Reverence. I shall write another time more accurately, and with more assurance."[36] Coming at the end of Le Jeune's 1633 *Relation*, apparently as he was finishing it, this sentiment may reflect Le Jeune's new awareness of a larger audience for his text as much as it reflects his own impressions of his text. The realization that his words were reaching readers other than members of his own religious order would leave clear marks on subsequent instalments in the series.[37] Beginning with the text that contained his second account of the Montagnais myth, then, Le Jeune was no longer writing an internal Jesuit memorandum, but a book designed to educate the public and convince them to contribute to the mission. If the 1633 text was a simple report for internal use only, the 1634 text was simultaneously an internal report and a text crafted with a wide readership in mind.

It is interesting to note that although the *Relations* of 1633 and 1634 are fundamentally different, both in their organization and in the role that the New France superior envisioned for them, the 1634 *Relation* was still presented to readers as if it were a strictly internal report, an artifice that would be preserved for the duration of the series. Like the 1633 *Relation*, which apparently was not prepared with publication in mind, the 1634 instalment opens and closes with direct references to the "Reverend Father" who served as the Jesuit provincial in Paris. And in both *Relations*, Le Jeune occasionally addressed his official correspondent directly,

RELATION

DE CE QVI S'EST PASSE'
EN LA
NOVVELLE FRANCE
EN L'ANNE'E 1635.

Enuoyée au
R. PERE PROVINCIAL
de la Compagnie de IESVS
en la Prouince de France.

Par le P. Paul le Ieune de la mesme Compagnie,
Superieur de la residence de Kebec.

A PARIS.

Chez SEBASTIEN CRAMOISY, Imprimeur
ordinaire du Roy, ruë sainct Iacques,
aux Cicognes.

M. DC. XXXVI.
AVEC PRIVILEGE DV ROY.

5.2 · Frontispiece of Paul Le Jeune's 1635 *Relation*, the full title
of which reads, as translated by Thwaites, "Relation of What
Occurred in New France in the Year 1635 Sent to the Reverend
Father Provincial of the Society of Jesus in the Province of
France. By the Father Paul Le Jeune of the same Society, Superior
of the residence of Quebec." The text was published in Paris
by Sebastien Cramoisy in 1636. Most instalments in the series
bore titles that similarly foregrounded the role of the texts as
correspondence between two officials in the Society of Jesus.

as "Your Reverence."[38] The official sender and receiver of the texts also are explicitly mentioned in the full title of each of the two *Relations*, which is characteristic of the series. The 1635 text, to cite just one typical example, bore the following full title: "Relation of What Occurred in New France in the Year 1635 Sent to the Reverend Father Provincial of the Society of Jesus in the Province of France. By the Father Paul Le Jeune of the same Society, Superior of the residence of Quebec."[39] Suggesting, as it does, official communication between two specific members of the Society of Jesus, the title would have given readers the impression that they were reading internal, private correspondence. Despite Le Jeune's new awareness that his words were public and the corresponding shift to a more reader-friendly format, it is clear from these details that Jesuits in New France and the Paris authorities charged with publishing the *Relations* sought to encourage their readers to continue to perceive the texts as internal, official communiqués, rather than texts destined not only for Jesuit readers, but also for France's reading public. This framing of the *Relations* as internal reports instead of as carefully crafted accounts intended to please a wide readership could be one reason they have long been treated more as a rich source of historical data than as texts.

Despite the pretense that the 1634 *Relation* was still primarily an internal memorandum, Le Jeune's new awareness of his audience as he was composing the 1634 text seems to have had important consequences for his treatment of the Montagnais myth and no doubt for myriad other topics. Indeed, the Jesuits were not disinterested or neutral observers of Amerindian customs and lore, particularly once they learned that their texts had a role in attracting spiritual and material support for the mission. In light of the fundamental differences between the texts that contain them, it is worth examining in detail each of Le Jeune's two accounts of the myth for clues about how the knowledge that his words were being published may have influenced his presentation of the story.

Le Jeune began his first discussion of Montagnais beliefs about their own origins in the 1633 *Relation* with a refutation of the common European claim that Amerindians had no knowledge of God. Wrote Le Jeune, "I confess that the Savages have no public or common prayer, nor any form of worship usually rendered to one whom they hold as God, and their knowledge is [but shadows]. But it cannot be denied that they recognize some nature superior to the nature of man."[40] This assertion sets the tone for the account of Montagnais beliefs that follows by suggesting that it demonstrated at least some knowledge of a Supreme Being, even if it was "but shadows" in comparison to Christian doctrine preserved in writing. Le Jeune's introduction of "Atahocan" makes the message explicit: "They say that there is a certain one whom they call *atahocan*, who made all things. Talking one day of God, in a cabin, they asked me what this God was. I told them that It was he who could do everything, and who had made the Sky and earth. They began to say one to the other, '*Atahocan, Atahocan*, it is *Atahocan*.'"[41] Thus establishing that the Montagnais knew the Creator and that they called him Atahocan, Le Jeune moved on to muddy the waters by introducing the other figure, Messou, who also could have been the Christian God in disguise and whose story bore at least some resemblance to Noah's ordeal during the biblical flood. As mentioned earlier, Le Jeune reported that Messou repaired the world after a flood destroyed it. Taken together, the stories of Atahocan and Messou indicate that the Montagnais were aware of a Creator, Le Jeune claims: "You see by these stories that the Savages have some idea of a God."[42] By suggesting that the Montagnais and the Jesuits could each see aspects of their own beliefs in the beliefs of the other, Le Jeune drew a clear link between the two cultures, suggesting that they must have shared a common origin, even if the priest did not offer any specific theory on how the descendents of Adam had come to populate the New World. Conversion, then, would not require starting from scratch, but only correcting the Montagnais' biblical knowledge, which had become corrupted with fables.

Although the Montagnais' knowledge may have been encouraging, its flaws appeared serious. The existence of two figures who are positioned in the 1633 *Relation* as candidates for the office of God would have suggested to the Jesuits and their readers that the Montagnais had mistakenly fragmented the Judeo-Christian deity, and assigned its various roles to different figures. Such a fracture would surely indicate that the Montagnais, though they had some knowledge of God, were not wholly acquainted with the truth. In fact, Le Jeune found the story too flawed to bother writing down all its details, despite the promise it showed for the potential of the Montagnais to be converted. Wrote the missionary, "It would be a long story to recount how he reestablished everything; how he took vengeance on the monsters that had taken his hunters, transforming himself into a thousand kinds of animals to circumvent them. In short, this great Restorer, having married a little muskrat, had children who repeopled the world."[43] The dismissive way in which Le Jeune ends the story suggests that he knew more details about it than he cared to record. And his mocking reference to Messou as a "great restorer" signals his general disdain for the tale, the only value of which was the indication it gave that the Montagnais had some knowledge of God, even if they were laughably wrong about the details. For the priest, there was no point in discussing the minute details of the myth that did not demonstrate rudimentary knowledge of the biblical Creator.

Le Jeune's 1633 decision to withhold details of the myth that he deemed irrelevant stands in stark contrast to the reasons he gave for telling the story again in 1634. Le Jeune justified telling the myth a second time, just one year after his first account of it, by claiming to want to correct and complete the record on Montagnais beliefs. Wrote Le Jeune, "I touched upon this fable last year, but, desiring to recapitulate all I know about their beliefs, I have repeated many things."[44] The ways that Le Jeune went about the summarizing and correcting that he claimed motivated him to repeat the story are revealing in light of the fundamental change in the nature of the texts that occurred between 1633 and 1634. Despite his apparent change of opinion regarding the importance of completeness in documenting Montagnais beliefs, the version of the story of Messou recounted by Le Jeune in 1634 for the most part mirrors his earlier version, and includes only a few new details. The reader learns that Messou's wife was responsible for unleashing death in the world, and that Messou was the "big brother" of all animal spirits. It is unclear if these are the same details that Le Jeune purposely omitted in his first version of the story or if he only learned them in the intervening year. In either case, the content of the two versions is different only in a few details about Messou that have nothing to do with his restoration of the world after a flood.

Despite the nearly identical content of the two versions of the myth, they were deployed to divergent ends in each of the two *Relations*. The 1633 version indicates that the purpose of telling the story was to rebut claims that the Montagnais were not aware of God, and indeed the tale is bookended with comments indicating that the stories of Atahocan and Messou were proof of imperfect knowledge thereof. Le Jeune's second version of the myth, in contrast, actually suggests an absence of knowledge or belief about the creation of the world. Le Jeune opens his second account of the myth by claiming to have learned in the intervening year that Atohocan was not as important to Montagnais mythology as he previously thought: "I have questioned upon this subject the famous Sorcerer and the old man with whom I passed the Winter; they answered that they did not know who was the first Author of the world, – that it was perhaps Atahocham, but that was not certain; that they only spoke of Atahocam as one speaks of a thing so far distant that nothing sure can be known about it."[45] Le Jeune's report in 1633 of the Montagnais' enthusiastic identification of Atahocan as the Creator is replaced in 1634 by a far more tentative acknowledgment of that possibility, and an assertion that the Montagnais had no certain knowledge of the "first author" of the world. And the missionary also noted the similarity between the name of this figure that he had believed to be a deity and the Montagnais word *nitatahokan*, which meant, according to Le Jeune, "I relate a fable, I am telling an old story invented for amusement."[46] Indeed, seventeenth-century Montagnais-French dictionaries prepared by the Jesuits contain words similar to "Atahocan" that refer to the act of telling stories, but not to a god-figure, suggesting that Le Jeune may have misunderstood his interlocutor's enthusiastic exclamation "Atahocan!" in the conversation recounted in the 1633 *Relation*.[47] In any case, although he suggested in 1633 that both Atahocan and Messou proved that the Montagnais knew something about God, Le Jeune went out of his way to avoid that implication just one year later.

It would be unfair to wholly discount Le Jeune's explanation for these changes: that he learned more about the tale during a long winter spent in the company of a nomadic Montagnais group. But it seems unlikely that increased knowledge is solely responsible for the differences between the two versions, particularly since those differences are mostly rhetorical. Both accounts of the myth cast it as biblical knowledge corrupted by fables, and the actions of Messou that are described in each version are practically identical. And yet, the second version of the Montagnais beliefs paints a bleaker picture of the spiritual situation in New France. In 1633, Le Jeune's account suggested that missionaries merely needed to flesh out the Montagnais' understanding of God and teach them how to honour him. The 1634 version of the tale implied a void at the position of God and therefore a more urgent pedagogical challenge for the missionaries and their financial and political backers in France. This may have not only spurred supporters in the Old Country to action, but also helped to excuse the disappointing results in the earliest years of the missionaries' efforts, discussed in chapter two, to convert Amerindians to Christianity. Tellingly, the word "God" – "Dieu" – does not even appear in the second account of Montagnais beliefs about Atahocan and Messou. In both texts, the need to instruct the Montagnais on Christianity is implied. But in the second version of the myth – the one Le Jeune knew would be read by potential donors in France – the superior trades his glass-half-full rhetoric for a glass-half-empty analysis, and downplays any knowledge the Montagnais might already have had, giving stronger justification and greater urgency to the missionary project.

In addition to being deployed to make divergent arguments in 1633 and 1634, the story is framed differently in each *Relation*, particularly with regard to the process by which Le Jeune acquired the information. The act of posing questions is central to modern fieldwork methodology, which the Jesuits are sometimes considered to have anticipated in some ways, and, as should be clear from the passage examined above, such interrogation played a key role in the Jesuits' engagement with Amerindian cultures. But questioning is not always a matter of obtaining information. To borrow a distinction from Hans Robert Jauss, "impudent" questions "look beyond the horizon of the known and the secure" to obtain new information. "Didactic" questions, on the other hand, seek "a solid answer" and serve "to transmit some doctrine or, then again, to undermine it."[48] Was the questioning that produced the materials recorded in the *Relations* akin to that of an anthropologist seeking facts about an unknown culture, or was it more didactic in nature, seeking to make a convincing argument about religious belief? Although Le Jeune's interrogation of his informant in the 1634 *Relation* does appear to bring some new information to light – Atahocan was not, it turns out, a god figure or even a character in the story – it is also possible to interpret such questioning in light of Catholic and Jesuit pedagogical traditions. The Jesuit missionaries who wrote the *Relations* were, after all, pedagogues, trained to impart their knowledge to students in Europe's Jesuit colleges, and attempting to do the same with the Amerindian potential converts who inhabited New France.

The logic of the catechism – "the core of all primary and religious education in the early modern period"[49] and a tool that Jesuit missionaries in New France put to work in their efforts to teach doctrine to potential converts – is useful in thinking about the questioning of informants and potential converts that was reported in the *Relations*. As will be familiar to modern generations of former Catholic school students whose knowledge of doctrine was tested by the Baltimore Catechism and its successor or any of the French-language catechisms developed in Quebec,[50] such texts resemble written conversations in that they are made up of a series of questions to be posed by a religious instructor, and corresponding answers to be given by the student. The Ledesma catechism that was, as mentioned earlier, translated into Huron and used in New France contained twenty "lessons" in the form of questions to be posed by the catechist and the correct answers that all Huron interlocutors were expected to provide, on topics including the characteristics of God, the veneration of saints and relics, the holy sacraments, and other aspects of Catholic faith. In contrast to the kind of questioning that might be performed by an anthropologist or folklorist attempting to elicit information from an interlocutor, responses to a catechist's questions are pre-determined. Asking questions is not, in the missionary context, only about seeking information, but rather about inviting the respondent to demonstrate mastery or to reveal insufficient knowledge in matters of religion. Deviation from the script is not acceptable.

Even before they began using catechistic questioning in the mission setting, the New France Jesuits would have been familiar with the use of questions as a pedagogical tool, and not only as a means of obtaining information. As former students and teachers in France's Jesuit colleges, the missionaries were formed by an educational tradition that emphasized questioning and argumentation. The famous Jesuit educational guide *Ratio Studiorum* emphasized the use of "disputations," in which students were required to defend points of doctrine from objections posed by other students. As the twentieth-century Jesuit scholar George E. Ganss has described them, such activities not only helped students grasp newly acquired knowledge, but prepared them to defend their beliefs from objections raised by non-believers and, perhaps especially, Protestants.[51] Although such exercises followed no particular script, they were nonetheless intended to hone students' skills in defending doctrine from the challenges posed by their non-Catholic interlocutors. As in the case of the catechism, questioning in this context – in which the Jesuits learned how to discuss religion with non-believers – was not about probing the unknown, but about testing and defending the accuracy of existing knowledge.

Le Jeune's two versions of the Montagnais tale are revealingly different in the way they describe the priest's role in learning it and writing it down, particularly with regard to the act of questioning. The 1633 version of the myth is presented as an aside. While on the topic of his efforts to describe God to a Montagnais interlocutor, Le Jeune takes the opportunity to describe the general beliefs of that group about the existence of beings superior to man. As noted above, a Montagnais man reportedly asked him what God was, and upon hearing Le Jeune's explanation exclaimed "*Atahocan, Atahocan*, it is *Atahocan.*"[52] Le Jeune then turns without segue to the story of Messou, which he summarizes without explaining the context in which he learned it. In narrating the story he learned from his interlocutors, Le Jeune appears to be a passive recipient of Montagnais knowledge, writing down the information on Montagnais spirituality that he learned only accidentally, in conversation, and, in the case of Atahocan, as a consequence of a question posed by a curious Montagnais interlocutor.

One year later, in the version of the myth that was prepared with the knowledge that it would be published, Le Jeune no longer omits from his account the context in which he learned the tale. Instead, he depicts himself in conversation with a Montagnais informant. The chapter containing the myth opens with Le Jeune's report, cited above, that he interrogated a Montagnais leader about Atahocan, who reportedly answered by saying he did not know who was the "first author" of the world. At the end of the relatively short passage, Le Jeune asks his interlocutor for more information about Messou's relationship to other spiritual beings, and receives a claim of ignorance in response. This emphasis on questioning, and on the unsatisfying responses elicited by questions, casts Le Jeune as a religious examiner, of the sort that would have been familiar to European readers, and particularly those exposed to catechistic teaching either in Jesuit schools or elsewhere. Interpreted as didactic questioning akin to the pedagogical strategies that the Jesuits and other Catholic teachers often employed, Le Jeune's queries do as much to reveal inadequate knowledge of the creation of the world as to elicit information about the particular beliefs of the Montagnais. The message is clear: the Montagnais did not know much about the creation of the world, because they were unable to respond to even basic questions that the priest posed. Thanks to the different role questioning takes on in the second account, it is presented not as the dutiful transcription of a lesson that the missionaries received on Amerindian religion, but as a missionary's active examination of his interlocutor's religious beliefs that displayed a lack of knowledge on the part of the Montagnais and therefore underscored the need for missionary intervention.

Although the Jesuit *Relations* sometimes have been taken by modern scholars to offer a straightforward account of Montagnais beliefs about the creation of the world, it is clear now that this conclusion is not so easy to draw. The Jesuits' own bias toward a monogenetic conception of human history, their role in transmitting specific messages both to Amerindians in New France and to readers at home in the Old World, and the rhetorical features of their accounts of the myth suggest that the missionary authors sought to undermine the tale as legitimate religious knowledge as much as preserve it in writing. Perhaps not coincidentally, at least some of the scholars who have cited the Jesuit *Relations* as a source on the religious beliefs of the Montagnais – Alexander and Fontaine among them – have cited the first, 1633 account of the myth, the version in which Atahocan is specifically identified as the Creator.[53] As this chapter has argued, the story is framed in both years less as a unique creation myth than as proof of flawed knowledge of the biblical flood. Although the 1633 *Relation* initially framed Atahocan and Messou as proof of knowledge of God, the second telling of the myth downplays the importance of Atahocan – and even suggests that there was no such character in the first place – and demotes Messou to a mere repairman who was caught up in Noah's flood. The fortuitous repetition of the story immediately before and after Le Jeune learned that his texts had a public as well as a private function suggests that the Jesuit authors framed their accounts of Amerindian cultures for maximum effect among European readers once they became aware that their words were being published. What is taken as definite knowledge of God in the first version is cast instead in the second version as uncertainty about Creation, and knowledge only of a later episode from Genesis, making the need for missionary instruction all the more urgent. As the case of the Montagnais myth demonstrates, even passages of the *Relations* that superficially appear to record traditional knowledge may undermine that knowledge at least as much as they preserve it. Put another way, the accounts of the Montagnais myth in the Jesuit *Relations* – and other legends, beliefs, and cultural practices, for that matter – were concerned at least as much with conveying a specific argument to seventeenth-century French readers about the relationship between Worlds Old and New as they were with preserving and transmitting knowledge about the Amerindian groups that Jesuits encountered in the New World.

On 28 May 2007, the Creation Museum in Petersburg, Kentucky, opened its doors to the public. With animatronic dinosaurs, collections of fossils, and realistically recreated pre-historic plant life, the museum in some ways resembles a more traditional natural history museum. But in the Creation Museum's displays, dinosaurs frolic near human children, the Grand Canyon was carved into the face of the Earth in a matter of mere days during Noah's flood, and dinosaurs, like all other animals, were created 6,000 years ago on the sixth day of Creation. In presenting these and other subjects, the $27-million museum interprets evidence that would seem to cast doubt on a literal reading of Genesis in such a way that the threat is neutralized. According to the *New York Times*'s account of the project, "It is a measure of the museum's daring that dinosaurs and fossils – once considered major challenges to belief in the Bible's creation story – are here so central, appearing not as tests of faith ... but as creatures no different from the giraffes and cats that still walk the earth."[54] Like the Jesuit missionaries to New France almost four hundred years before them, the modern young-Earth creationists who are behind the museum seek to dismiss challenges to biblical truth by reconciling potentially damaging evidence with the scriptural accounts that it appears to contradict. As the *Times*'s reporter astutely pointed out, that move is probably more useful in reassuring believers who visit the museum than in changing the minds of those who think differently.

Not only is the very existence of the Creation Museum evidence of the durability of the tactics for coping with challenges to settled and deeply held knowledge that this chapter has explored, it also serves nicely to illustrate a larger point that this book attempts to make about ethnography in the Jesuit *Relations*. The Creation Museum contains fossils and other objects of legitimate scientific interest. And yet many scientists understandably view the entire enterprise as an affront to science. Upon visiting the museum on opening day, Lawrence Krauss, a Case Western Reserve University physicist, was dismissive of the museum's attempt to bridge science and religion. "It's really impressive – and it gives the impression that they're talking about science at some point. I'd give it a four for technology, five for propaganda. As for content, I'd give it a negative five," he told the Associated Press.[55] Like the fossils in the Creation Museum, the descriptions of Amerindian creation myths in the pages of the Jesuit *Relations* appear in a context that recasts them as support for the version of the history of the world found in Genesis. The Jesuits, like the curators of the Creation Museum, collected information only in order to explain it in a way consistent with doctrine. Although fossils on display at the Creation Museum theoretically could be removed from that context, studied, and used to advance a scientific rather than a religious understanding of the world, the "facts" in the *Relations* remain forever tied to their source through footnotes, bibliographies, and the glowing praise of those who mine the texts for ethnographic data. Attempts to de-contextualize those facts and put them to work in modern studies of Amerindian cultures may not, as this chapter has shown, result in a better understanding of Amerindian cultures, and risk suggesting that the Jesuits were more neutral and careful ethnographers than they actually were. The prestige of the Jesuits as able ethnographers can only grow each time a vivid description of Amerindian life, custom, or belief, cleansed of signs of how the priests understood it, is attributed to the *Relations*.

CHAPTER SIX

Travelling Texts:
Toward a Decentred Reading of
Jesuit Mission Ethnography

The Jesuit *Relations* from New France have long been understood to have been the products of a daring voyage. As the common conception of the texts would have it, French missionaries departed the Old World to brave the perils of the open ocean and settle among Iroquoian and Algonquian potential converts in what is today eastern Canada, risking their lives at every step of the process. The Jesuit superior in New France compiled the *Relations* on the basis of the letters and journals of missionaries who were scattered throughout the Canadian wilderness, removing irrelevant or tedious details, reorganizing the raw material, and writing connective sentences to make a coherent whole of the various parts.[1] The texts then were sent to France on one of the merchant ships that departed the colony each autumn, where they were edited a second time before being published and widely read from 1632 to 1673.[2] Although accurate within its limits, this common understanding of the texts as vehicles that transported to Europe new information about the world outside its borders does not fully reflect how news circulated between the colony and the Old Country during the Jesuits' tenure in New France. Just as important to the ethnographic qualities of the texts was, this chapter argues, information that moved in the opposite direction, from Europe to the colony, in the form of letters from readers and published versions of the *Relations* themselves.

Until now, this book has focused on Jesuit teaching and learning in New France, and on the lessons about Amerindian customs and nature that the missionary authors also furnished to their readers in the Old World. The focus of this chapter is the end point of the process, traced in chapter two, that was started when the Jesuits took up residence in New France and began writing about their experiences. The production and circulation of the *Relations* themselves is an aspect of their role in collecting and preserving information about the Amerindian groups of the New World that has not received the attention that it deserves in either literary or ethnohistorical scholarship. And yet, understanding the editorial processes that shaped the *Relations* is absolutely critical to a clear understanding of Jesuit mission ethnography because in those processes – as in the missionaries' interactions with Amerindian groups – the Jesuits were students as much as they were masters. This chapter examines the lessons that the priests received from Europe in various forms, including letters from readers and benefactors as well as the edited and published versions of the *Relations* themselves, and seeks to discern how the place of the *Relations* in a yearly bi-directional exchange of information between the colony and France may shed light on the relationship of the texts both to the textual genre of travel writing and to ethnography.

If the missionaries' annual published texts often have been recognized as valuable precursors to scholarly ethnographic accounts, it is surely due at least in part to the relationship between early accounts of travel and encounter and the modern academic discipline of anthropology. Indeed, as Johannes Fabian has remarked, anthropology can be thought of as having grown out of the earlier tradition of observing and then writing about unknown cultures that was inaugurated and then developed by travellers and explorers such as the Jesuit missionaries in New France. Anthropology, wrote Fabian, "acquired its scientific and academic status by climbing on the shoulders of adventurers and using their travelogues, which for centuries had been the appropriate literary genre in which to report knowledge of the Other."[3] Indeed, it is perhaps not surprising that modern anthropology would see in travel writing an early model for its own project – as well as a source of data. Since the professional-ization of the discipline in the early twentieth century, anthropologists have staked their claim to authority at least in part on their experience of and presence among the cultures studied. Wrote James Clifford in de-scribing the frontispiece of Malinowski's *Argonauts of the Western Pacific*, a foundational work in the academic discipline of anthropology, "The predominant mode of modern fieldwork authority is signaled: 'You are there ... because I was there.'" Personal experience has remained an important aspect of ethnographic authority, even if the old ideal of the anthropologist as an objective and highly trained collector of information has lost ground in recent decades to what Clifford has called "discursive paradigms of dialogue and polyphony."[4]

Similarly, travel accounts were generally believable – and are today recognizable as a potential source of data for ethnohistorical studies – at least in part because they often draw on the same guarantor of authority upon which anthropology has relied for much of its history: first-hand experience. As Mary Baine Campbell has observed, "Neither power nor talent gives a travel writer his or her authority, which comes only and crucially from experience."[5] Like twentieth-century anthropologists, the Jesuits were credible – and generally remain so today – because they were *there*, and knew things from experience that those who had stayed at home in France did not and could not know without relying on the knowledge carried eastward by the Jesuits' texts. This similarity to modern professional anthropology and the roots of that discipline in texts such as the *Relations* go a long way toward explaining the popularity of early travel accounts in ethnohistorical scholarship, and indeed license their use in such work, albeit with the usual caveats about the more or less obvious biases of proto-ethnographers who were also – and primarily, in most cases – missionaries, merchants, or treasure-hunters.[6] Indeed, as each of the previous chapters of this book has shown, the value of the texts as a source of information on the Amerindian cultures that the Jesuits encountered is well established among social scientists of various disciplines. And yet, a closer look at the relationship between the Jesuit *Relations* and the travel-writing genre to which they often are assigned suggests that the information about Amerindian groups contained in the texts is not, or not only, rooted in the kind of experience that continues today to serve as a guarantor of ethnographic authority. In other words, the mechanism that confers authority on the Jesuits' texts and makes them recognizable as early precursors of academic anthropology – the authors' presence among and unrivalled experience of the cultures that they wrote about – was not the only factor at work in determining the contents of the texts. This chapter examines how the *Relations* were composed and circulated, with particular emphasis on the role played by correspondents and editors at home in France.

It is useful to begin with some general remarks on travel accounts as a genre. To borrow a phrase from Mary Baine Campbell, travel writing is "a genre composed of other genres." Texts as different from each other as the journals of explorers and traders, missionary reports, shipboard logs, diaries, letters, and botanical treatises are often grouped under the heading "travel writing."[7] Although extremely diverse in its forms, the genre typically has been understood at least since the seventeenth century to have a clear relationship to the physical movement of the voyager. Upon leaving home, the traveller experiences a rupture, an opening of literal and figurative distance between him or herself and the home, populated by those who will stay home and therefore will not see what the traveller sees, nor experience the things that he or she experiences.[8] As a number of theorists have remarked, travel – as opposed to wandering, exile, and other forms of physical displacement – is organized around the concept of gain, whether the goal is spiritual, intellectual, or material enrichment.[9] The voyage therefore is concluded only when the voyager takes account of what has been gained or lost in the journey, and of how his or her relationship to home has changed, thereby closing the distance between the traveller and the home that was opened by the traveller's departure and experience of a distant and strange place. The goal of acquiring something beneficial makes all voyages essentially circular, since, as Georges Van Den Abbeele has pointed out, no loss or gain can be registered without a fixed, unchanged point against which to measure it, whether the traveller's home or a substitute.[10] The "home" in relation to which the voyage is defined and evaluated does not necessarily correspond to the actual place of residence, but in most conventional voyages it is indeed the homeland, hometown, or home base that serves as the fixed point against which a journey's success or failure is measured.

And yet, the home to which the traveller returns logically cannot be identical to the point of departure. According to Van Den Abbeele, "the point of return as repetition of the point of departure cannot take place without a difference in that repetition: the detour constitutive of the voyage itself. Were the point of departure and the point of return to remain exactly the same, that is, were they the same point, there could be no travel."[11] Aside from whatever social or physical changes might have occurred during the voyager's absence, the home is changed irrevocably in his or her eyes by all that was seen and experienced during the journey. The point of origin and return of any voyage is therefore caught in the tension between the need to be recognizable upon the traveller's return to it – for without a return home to evaluate what was gained or lost, the voyage becomes exile, wandering, or another form of displacement – and the inevitability that it is changed in the eyes of the traveller, who has experienced and seen things that cast the questions, problems, and truths of the homeland in a new and perhaps revealing light. Returning home is therefore not, for the traveller, a mere matter of returning to the geographic point of departure, but also of renegotiating a relationship to that place, of reconciling the home of departure with the home of return – populated by friends, family, and financial backers who did *not* travel.

As Michael Harbsmeier has observed, recounting the voyage to those who stayed at home is one way of effecting this reconciliation: "Returning home after a long absence can generally be seen as a transition asking for some kind of *rite de passage* through which the traveller is reintegrated into the community of those who stayed at home. Telling about what happened out there is thus tantamount to reaffirming the traveller's membership of the group with which he again can feel at home."[12] By imparting the wisdom accrued over the course of the voyage to those who stayed behind, the traveller permits them to glimpse the things he or she glimpsed, and thereby to close the figurative distance between traveller and home opened up during the voyage.[13] Reflecting this function of travel writing, such texts typically were organized in the seventeenth century in such a way as to facilitate a reader's repetition of the voyage. Seventeenth-century texts reflecting on the genre called on authors to use the voyage itself as a model for their *récits*. According to Normand Doiron, "The rules to which voyagers are recommended to conform their itineraries concern writing just as much. The route followed in nature will serve in a second stage to define the natural order of classical discourse. The world and the book are then included in the same space."[14] Accounting chronologically for his or her movements and experiences, the traveller transforms the rupture of departure and the potentially turbulent reintegration upon return home into a smooth, unbroken line "that can be drawn on the map," allowing those who stayed at home to repeat the voyage by reading the traveller's tale, and providing the knowledge that they would need to update their understanding of the world to match that of the traveller.[15] And indeed, if one purpose of the travel account is to effect a rapprochement between the traveller and those who stayed at home, the vicarious journey offered by the travel account would surely be superior even to an actual voyage, since there could be no guarantee that a second traveller's experience of the treacherous Atlantic crossing and poorly known Amerindian groups would be sufficiently similar to that of the first traveller to bind them together with shared knowledge.

At least superficially, the Jesuit *Relations* seem to be a good fit for this varied genre rooted in Eurocentric travel. Like the genre itself the texts are, as has already been shown in this book, far from homogenous, with some instalments taking the form of long chronological narratives or collections of short letters instead of the usual book organized into thematic chapters. Indeed, the Jesuits' reports were framed from the beginning as belonging to this widely varied assortment of texts inspired by experience of faraway places. It is worth briefly returning to the full title of the 1635 *Relation*, cited in the previous chapter: "Relation of What Occurred in New France in the Year 1635 Sent to the Reverend Father Provincial of the Society of Jesus in the Province of France. By the Father Paul Le Jeune of the same Society, Superior of the residence of Quebec."[16] The title, and the minor variations that appeared on the frontispieces of most of the other volumes in the series, labels the texts as a contribution to a literary genre inspired by travel that thrived in early modern France, with approximately 1,500 texts in print by the end of the seventeenth century.[17] The title also makes clear the direction in which the voyage in question was understood to operate: a European had gone to the New World, and was offering readers in the Old World an account of that experience. In light of the texts' role in giving the reading public a carefully selected glimpse of Jesuit activities in the New World and attracting spiritual and material support for the mission, discussed in chapter one, it is not particularly surprising that the authors or their editors in France would choose to frame the texts this way, as firsthand accounts of Old World travellers who had unique knowledge because they had journeyed far from home. And perhaps naturally, given the texts' prominence and the implications of their very titles, they often have been understood as key texts in the development of seventeenth-century travel writing. Normand Doiron, for example, credited the first of the *Relations* – along with Gabriel Sagard's *Le Grand Voyage du Pays des Hurons* and Samuel de Champlain's *Les Voyages de la Nouvelle France Occidentale* – with inaugurating the genre in seventeenth-century France.[18]

And yet, the texts also diverge in important ways from typical travellers' texts. Their organization, with a few exceptions, into thematic chapters instead of in the typical chronological fashion could be explained by the fact that there was not, in fact, a voyage in the sense outlined above to be recounted. Once established in New France, the Jesuits seldom returned to Europe. Instead, the New France missionaries, like their brethren around the world, sent their reports of each year's events to their Old World superiors, fulfilling the prescription of Ignatius Loyola himself – discussed in the first chapter of this book – that all members of the Society of Jesus be kept informed of their colleagues' work through the regular circulation of letters. It is not an exaggeration, to borrow an expression from Marie-Christine Pioffet, to say that the Jesuit texts are more *relations de séjour* than *relations de voyage* as far as the Jesuits' own physical movements are concerned.[19] Year after year, the Jesuit missionaries stayed in the colony as their texts were appearing in France, going to Europe only when bureaucratic duty or material necessity demanded it, and usually returning to the colony at the earliest opportunity.

Le Jeune's visits to France in 1641 and 1643 to request aid against Iroquois aggressors, for example, occasioned not the nostalgic musings of a traveller returned home after a long absence, but the priest's longing for a departure at the earliest opportunity to New France, which he apparently considered his home. Wrote Le Jeune in the introductory letter to his 1641 *Relation*, "I hope that, as soon as I have executed my mission, Your Reverence will give me my Passport, that I may return to the New World and die in a new country, or among these good Neophytes who have ravished my heart by their Piety and their devotion."[20] Le Jeune's verb choice – "return" (*retourner*) – indicates that the departure from France that he was hoping for was not, to his mind, the start of a new voyage, but a return to a home he had only grudgingly left in the first place. And his mention of the possibility of dying in a "new country" instead of among the Amerindians he already knew suggests that his nostalgia for his adopted homeland extended to parts of it that were not yet entirely familiar to him.

It seems that Le Jeune's attitude was shared by his colleagues, many of whom expressed a desire to finish their lives in the colony instead of returning to the country they once called home. Being a Jesuit mission-ary in New France ideally meant living out one's days in the New World. In fact, Le Jeune boasted in his 1634 *Relation* that Jesuits in France were clamouring to make one-way trips to the colony: "I would like to have now only five or six of our Fathers in each of these nations; and yet I would not dare to ask for them, although for one that we desire ten would volunteer, all ready to die in these countries."[21] Not only did Le Jeune and his associates return to France in only the rarest of instances, it seems that a return trip to France was not part of the missionary en-terprise as they envisioned it, a fact that explains the missionary-authors' oft-expressed desire to die in New France.[22] As Carole Blackburn has noted, the value of such a death was not only in maximizing the amount of time each missionary spent working toward the Christianization of the Amerindians. Wrote Blackburn, "Many Jesuits thought that martyrdom was necessary in order to plant the faith in New France ... the 'Blood of the Martyrs' was 'the seed and germ of Christians,' not least because the Jesuits believed that their willingness to die would impress people with the truth of their teaching."[23] As defined above, "travel" – with its im-plication of circular movement between the home and an exotic destina-tion – is a concept that simply does not apply to the typical New France Jesuit's expectations or experience.

Although the missionaries may have more closely resembled perma-nently relocated Europeans than typical travellers, the *Relations* might yet be understood as travel writing, albeit perhaps not in the way implied by their full titles and privileged status as a source for ethnohistorians. The texts, after all, carried information to Europe that helped the West adjust its knowledge and beliefs to account for the example of people beyond its borders, thus fulfilling one role of the typical traveller's tale as described above: providing vicarious knowledge to readers who had stayed at home. The other major function of travel writing discussed earlier – the recon-ciliation of the author with the home – could not have occurred upon the texts' arrival in France and publication there, since the priests were not present to update their relationship to the once-familiar place in light of their own experiences and perceived changes in the homeland. And yet, this reconciliation may have been made possible by the regular trans-Atlantic movements of information in the opposite direction, from Europe to the colony. Feedback from the Old Country took multiple forms. Letters from other Jesuits, from lay readers, and from powerful benefactors arrived in the colony each year. Such letters sometimes contained comments, questions, and criticisms that left clear signs of their influence in subsequent instalments of the published series. The missionaries also frequently received gifts of books, which were housed in the library of the Jesuit college in Quebec, and which may have served to keep the priests abreast of the latest intellectual developments in Europe.

Perhaps the most intriguing of these books, at least for the purposes of the present study, were the published versions of the New France *Relations* themselves. The manuscripts prepared in New France were in at least some cases, as we will soon see, changed in significant ways by editors in Paris. Like other aspects of mission ethnography examined in this book, the preparation and circulation of the *Relations* was part of a broader, multi-directional exchange, reflecting the Jesuit missionaries' simultaneous efforts to learn from, and teach their own beliefs and perceptions to, both Amerindians and Europeans. Accounting for westward movements of information associated with the *Relations* in the forms of the texts themselves and letters from readers can bring nuance to the texts' status as early forerunners of ethnography, as well as to the place within the genre of travel writing to which they have often been assigned. It is worth examining in detail some of these forms of feedback.

The most obvious way the Old World talked back to the New France Jesuits was through the countless letters from authorities and readers in Europe that arrived in New France over the course of the Society's tenure there. Such letters often were the subject of gushing gratitude on the part of the Jesuit authors, receiving top billing in the prefatory letters to many of the *Relations*. The 1644 *Relation* specifically mentions that such letters arrived on a yearly basis.[24] And news from the Old Country plainly was on the missionary authors' minds as they composed their annual texts. In a ruminative letter to the Paris provincial that serves as a preface to the 1637 text, for example, Paul Le Jeune reflected on the factors that would inform his report, and drew a direct parallel between ships bearing news from France and canoes carrying the reports of missionaries in the field:

When I took my pen in hand to begin the Relation of what
occurred this year in some places in new France where our Society
makes its dwelling, my mind was almost void of ideas, if not quite
bewildered. I found myself overcome by a feeling of wonder which

left my soul only the strength necessary to cast my eyes upon the
greatness of God, and to adore his guidance. Then, recovering
myself, I reflected upon the various tidings written to me from
your Europe, and from some parts of our America. I learned
through my eyes and my ears how France was on fire for us, and
how the upper countries of the Savages were nothing but ice ...
I learned through a great many letters that people of high rank and
most signal virtue were contending for us in heaven and upon the
earth; and it was made evident to me, on a bit of bark or paper,
that the Demons were let loose and were powerfully opposing
our plans ... Such were the news I received on the arrival of the
ships from France, and the bark canoes from the Algonquins
and Hurons.[25]

As he sat down to write his annual report, Le Jeune reported that he had
not only events in the mission on his mind, but also the feedback that he
had received from France. And he rhetorically equated the two sources of
information: both were sent to the mission superior on boats from distant places. The contrasting views of the missionary enterprise that were
reported by the passengers on both kinds of boats – the fiery passion of
France and the icy disdain of Amerindians – reflect the imperatives that,
as this book has argued in each of its chapters, influenced the *Relations*:
readers had to be pleased, and the spiritual situation of New France had
to be accounted for.

Letters received from France not only served to heighten the missionary
writers' awareness of their audience, but also sometimes contained queries, complaints, and suggestions from readers at home in France. And it
is clear that the Jesuits were at least sometimes sensitive to such feedback.
Questions and criticisms from readers could be used to justify amplification or silence on any given subject. The missionary Jérôme Lalemant, for
example, prefaced his return in 1639 to the already well-commented subject of the geography of Huron territory by pointing to the expressed desires of readers to know more. "It is not my intention to repeat here what
can be found in the preceding *Relations*, or in other Books which have
already treated of this subject, but only to supply the lack of certain par-
ticulars, regarding which I have discovered that some information is desired."[26] At least some of the rich detail about the territory of the Huron

that is contained in the *Relations*, then, must be attributed to something other than the missionaries' own precocious ethnographic instincts or rigour. Specific questions from readers, and the Jesuit authors' desire to please and instruct, produced a more detailed account of the subject than the missionaries might otherwise have provided on their own. Ten years later, Lalemant again responded to particular readers' questions, this time addressing the missionaries' pedagogical strategies among New France's Amerindian groups,[27] and other examples of reader-prompted amplification on subjects that might otherwise have received less detailed treatment can be found throughout the annual texts.

Feedback from readers not only influenced what the missionary writers chose to include in the *Relations*, but also could prompt them to omit details that they otherwise might have included. The 1637 *Relation* was among the longest and most detailed of the series, making it particularly valuable for modern scholars seeking to understand the mission and the Amerindian groups of New France. It seems, however, that the text's richly detailed portrait of Amerindian life was not universally appreciated in its own time. Gaston d'Orléans, King Louis XIII's brother and benefactor of the Jesuit college in Blois, apparently found it too ponderous and repetitive, complaining to Society officials in France that these aspects of the *Relation* diminished its authority. Coming from such a highly placed and influential reader, these complaints were taken seriously. Jesuit Governor General Mutius Vitelleschi reported the criticism to Paris Provincial Etienne Binet in a 1638 letter written in Latin, urging that "serious care" be taken to remedy the perceived problem.[28]

Perhaps not surprisingly, the following year's text reflects a new concern with succinctness. Whereas the 1637 *Relation* approached 600 pages in length, its successor weighed in at less than 150 pages.[29] Wrote Le Jeune in his opening letter in the 1638 *Relation*, "People are already so full of the customs of our Savages, and of our labors for them, that I fear disgust; hence I shall say little of many things – omitting whole chapters, lest I be accused of tediousness."[30] In addition to the promise to avoid long-windedness with which he opened the *Relation*, the missionary's newfound appreciation for brevity manifests itself repeatedly throughout the text. The report is riddled with comments emphasizing a new concern to be succinct: Le Jeune pledges to be more selective in recounting the baptism of Amerindians, he reports leaving out "an infinity" of good sentiments that God gives the Amerindians, and he congratulates himself at the end of the text for having adhered to his own promise to be brief. Wrote Le Jeune, "I do not think I have infringed upon the resolution I made to be brief, since I omit many things lest I be tedious."[31] Although it is impossible to know for certain whether Le Jeune received word of Gaston d'Orléans' criticism and crafted the 1638 text accordingly, or if those changes were made by editors in France, the contrast between the 1637 and 1638 *Relations* makes it clear that feedback from readers in France could lead to omissions from the annual *Relations* as well as amplification.

Another potentially influential form of information sent from the Old Country to the colony seems to have been entirely overlooked by scholars who study the *Relations*. The library at the Jesuit college in Quebec was the first and largest in colonial New France, and predated the collection at Harvard College. Hundreds of books, on topics including architecture, history, medicine, mathematics, philosophy, and religion, were sent to the Jesuits in New France by readers and benefactors beginning with the Society's re-entry into the mission field in 1632 and ending with the British Conquest in the following century. On the shelves could be found works as diverse as Cicero's *De Oratore*, the anatomical works of Ambroise Paré, and issues of the popular French periodical *Le Mercure Galant*. Regrettably, the full extent of the library's collection remains unknown, because it was pillaged and its contents dispersed when the conquering English requisitioned the college in 1759.[32] Two partial catalogues are known to have been produced in the early eighteenth century, but neither has been found. Fortunately, Antonio Drolet, Claude Pariseau, and Pierre-Emile Filion have managed to at least partially reconstruct the library's holdings in recent decades. Those researchers combed through the collections of other Canadian libraries to locate and catalogue volumes that bear inscriptions indicating that they originally belonged to the Jesuit college library, and eventually identified 750 such books.[33]

Although the library's full catalogue has been lost, the available clues suggest that it had a complete, or nearly complete, set of the published Jesuit *Relations*.[34] Among the books from the Jesuit college library that have been recovered are thirteen of the forty-one published New France *Relations*. Other volumes in the series that originally belonged to the New France Jesuits are known to have been destroyed in the nineteenth

century. Between six and ten first editions of the *Relations* were lost in a
fire at the library of the Québec Parlement in 1849, some or all of which
theoretically could have belonged originally to the seventeenth-century
Jesuit library, although it is impossible to know for sure. That a second,
more devastating fire at the Parlement in 1854 destroyed *Relations* from
the Jesuit library is nearly certain. The fire took a heavy toll on the Parlement's *Histoire de l'Amérique* collection, which included what may have
been the only full set of the Jesuit *Relations* in a single collection at the
time, including thirty volumes that reportedly had once belonged to the
Jesuit college library. Only eight volumes of the *Relations* survived the
second fire, meaning that many volumes from the former Jesuit library
must have been destroyed.[35] Although the current state of knowledge on
the Jesuit college library and what happened to its collection in the wake
of the conquest unfortunately does not allow for a volume-by-volume
accounting of its holdings of the Jesuit *Relations*, it is clear that some and
perhaps all of the texts were sent back to the missionaries in New France
after being edited and published in Paris, giving the missionary authors
an opportunity to observe how their words had been changed by Old
World editors.

Notations in some of the books that are known to have been held in
the Jesuit college library suggest that it was not uncommon for newly
published works to be received by the Jesuits in New France soon after
their publication, including, in at least some cases, the annual *Relations*.[36]
St. Augustine's *Concordantia*, for example, arrived in the library just thirteen months after its publication in 1656, and religious works by San-
roman and Mascarenhas were sent to New France in similarly timely
fashion after their publication. In an article examining the medical holdings of the college library, Antonio Drolet identified fifteen texts that
arrived within a few years of publication.[37] Although those tasked with
maintaining the college's library do not seem to have inscribed the arrival
date in new books frequently enough to provide much certainty about
the typical interval between publication of new books and their reception
in the colony, a streamlined procurement process for many of the books
that ended up in the college library may have allowed the *Relations* to
be sent to the colony immediately after publication. Many of the books
that scholars have identified as having belonged to the New France Jesuits bear inscriptions indicating that they were gifts from Parisian printer

Sébastien Cramoisy, the publisher of the *Relations*. In fact, if the provenance of the recovered texts is any guide, Cramoisy was the college library's most important source of books during the seventeenth century, the period during which about two-thirds of the library's collection seems to have arrived in the colony.[38] It is not difficult to imagine that as long as the printer was frequently sending books to the New France Jesuits, he may have routinely included the small and inexpensive annual *Relations*.

Indeed, the *Relations* themselves contain comments that indicate clearly that at least some of the Jesuit missionaries' own texts found their way back to New France less than a year after publication, and that the missionaries drew lessons from the published versions of their texts. As mentioned in the previous chapter of this book, the published 1632 text arrived in New France in time to alert mission superior Paul Le Jeune that his next report would be printed for public consumption. More than one scholar has attributed the shifts of tone and organization in subsequent volumes to Le Jeune's realization that his first text had been published.[39] And a contemporaneous handwritten copy of the 1634 *Relation* reveals that Le Jeune included a note – ultimately deleted by the editor or printer – urging care in the typesetting of two prayers in an Amerindian language: "If these two short prayers are printed, I beg the printer to take care with the savage words. Those included in last year's *Relation* were corrupted and filled with printing errors."[40] Aside from indicating that Le Jeune had received and carefully reviewed a copy of his 1633 text in time to complain about it in the following year's *Relation*, this comment suggests that the missionaries in New France had no expectation that their manuscripts would survive intact the editorial process in France. Le Jeune does not ask the printer to be careful *when* typesetting Amerindian words, but only *if*, suggesting that he knew that his texts, like any traveller, were bound to be changed in ways that were perhaps not entirely predictable to him by their experience of a foreign place. Indeed, as explained in chapter one, members' reports originally were intended for circulation within the order from the very inception of the Society of Jesus, a process for which the Society's authorities in Europe – and not individual priests in the field – were responsible. It surely came as no surprise to the New France Jesuits, then, that their texts could be edited, but that does not necessarily mean that they would have been incurious about the changes editors wrought.

In 1638, Le Jeune again offered a hint that he had the read the previous year's published text before assembling its successor. Unlike all of its predecessors and all of the *Relations* that would follow it, the 1637 New France *Relation* was published by Rouenais printer Jean le Boullenger instead of Sébastien Cramoisy. The reason for the change is not clear, and the Society switched back to Cramoisy after only one year, perhaps at least in part due to the typographical mistakes that Le Jeune found so vexing in the new printer's work.[41] Wrote Le Jeune,

> I shall have this consolation this year, that, in saying little, few faults will slip under the roller of the press. The Relation of last year is full of them. I must mention one of them, in order to induce the Printer to take some pride in his work. In chapter 8, on page 145, – where some quarrel I had with a sorcerer is in question, – the Printer makes me, in place of employing exorcisms against the devil, use a sword. This is what I wrote in the original: "In fact, I intended to employ a sort of exorcism;" the printer made it: "In fact, I intended to use a sword hereafter." I must confess that this pretty witticism made me laugh. When one speaks from so great a distance, [one does not make one's thoughts so well understood]. Writing is a mute language, which [changes as easily as] it is easy to take one Character for another; a child is made to say whatever one wishes, when its father is absent.[42]

Le Jeune's criticism of the text, including precise corrections that cited chapter and page number, suggests that he was not relying solely on descriptions of the book provided by those who had seen it in Europe, and must have possessed and carefully reviewed a copy. And the way Le Jeune characterized his text and what happened to it in Paris suggests that he understood that his own intent was not necessarily the final word in the texts' contents. The desires of others – and not just the typesetter's errors – also played a role. In the final two sentences of the passage, Le Jeune first portrays himself attempting from a distance to convey his thoughts, as an active creator of meaning in the text. But he follows this formulation by shifting agency to an unknown "one" who caused the *Relation* to say what he or she wanted, instead of the what the distant father – Le Jeune – had intended. The final result, the passage implies, is simultaneously a reflection of Le Jeune's words, and also a reflection of the desires of those who edited the text in Paris.

Although the Jesuit *Relations* superficially appear to have served to communicate to Europe the missionaries' assessments of events and conditions in distant New France, it is now possible to conceive of another important function of the texts, one linked to their apparent collection in the Jesuit college library shortly after publication. Christine Montalbetti has traced the relationship between such collections of texts and travel writing in her excellent 1997 book *Le Voyage, le Monde, et la Bibliothèque.* According to Montalbetti, the library – or the body of existing texts about a distant and poorly known place – exercises a two-part influence over new interventions. First, those previous texts cause any new attempt to describe the place and people in question to run the risk of merely repeating what is already well established, rather than adding substantially to knowledge of the world outside of Europe. In order to constitute a legitimate contribution to knowledge of the world beyond the home – to be worthy of committing to paper and publishing – new travel books could not simply repeat what had already been said. At the same time, new texts at least had to resemble – in form and content – what had already been published, in order to be recognized and taken seriously as credible and worthy contributions. In other words, texts that too radically repudiated or contradicted all that was previously published would risk not being taken seriously by readers who already knew what to expect from their previous reading experiences. In these two ways, to borrow an image from Montalbetti, the library acts as a kind of filter between the world and the pen of the travel writer, eliminating the need to say some things that have already been said but also forcing the things that are said to conform to certain expectations.[43]

Signs that the *Relations* that made their way back to New France influenced subsequent instalments in the ways described by Montalbetti's theoretical model can be found in the Jesuits' own justifications for the inclusion or exclusion of particular details of their experience in New France. Lalemant's 1639 indication, cited above, that he was responding to readers' desires in returning to the topic of the geography of Huron country was accompanied by the caveat that he did not intend to repeat what had been published previously. And the Jesuit Barthélemy Vimont in 1645 justified his own silence on certain topics by pointing to the

voluminous record already offered in previous *Relations*: "We will not
say anything in particular of the various residences, or of the various
Missions of our Society, for fear of repetition; the new events that occur
are so similar to those which have already been written of, that the fear of
causing distaste will make us more and more concise, – so much so that,
in this Relation, we will mention only some sentiments and some actions
of the most fervent Christians, without specifying whether they belong to
Montreal, to Saint Joseph, or to Tadousac."[44] With more than a decade's
worth of *Relations* already published, there was apparently no need to go
on at length about matters already covered. This care to avoid repetition
is expressed often in the *Relations*, and goes a long way toward explaining
why the texts corresponding to the earliest decades of the mission are so
much longer and more detailed than the texts from later decades.[45] Each
Relation was not, it seems, conceived as an individual book, but rather as
part of a larger whole intended to be coherent and succinct – or at least
to avoid saying the same thing too many times. Each new *Relation* would
have to be sufficiently different from those already published to be worth
committing to paper, and yet not so different as to strain credibility or
invalidate previous years' work.

The texts' long-lauded role in collecting and transmitting ethnographic
details about the Amerindian groups that missionaries encountered in
the New World must be re-examined in light of the facts traced above:
the texts completed a round-trip voyage of their own, beginning and
ending in the colony, and then at least sometimes served as a reference
for the Jesuit authors as they prepared the *Relations* for subsequent years.
Although modern ethnohistorians are sometimes sensitive to the various
factors that make the *Relations* a complicated source – the missionary
authors were, after all, primarily interested in converting the people they
encountered, and did not have the benefit of a modern theory of ethnography to guide their writing – the fact that the missionaries could
and did consult the published versions of their texts so far has not been
considered as one of those complicating factors. That could be because
it often has been assumed, and sometimes directly asserted, that editors
in Paris did not change the texts – or at least did not change them in any
significant way – prior to publication. In his book-length study of the
Relations, Jesuit scholar Léon Pouliot barely mentioned the role of Paris
editors in his account of the editorial process. In another well-known
introduction to the texts, historian Allan Greer noted that changes could

be made by editors in Paris, but stopped short of commenting on how extensive such changes may have been. Lawrence Wroth's article on the *Relations* – still one of the most detailed accounts available, despite being almost eighty years old – allowed that the texts were edited "with current European conditions in mind," but nonetheless affirmed that they maintain the integrity of firsthand accounts. Sara Melzer, to her credit, wrote that the Parisian editors were more concerned with "projecting the proper image than in historical accuracy," but did not examine changes made during the process. Campeau acknowledged the changes made by editors, but attributed them to nothing more than an editor's dislike of extraneous detail.[46] Although the possibility that editors in Paris could have made changes to the texts sometimes is acknowledged, no one has yet attempted to account for what those changes, and the authors' opportunity to notice them, might mean for Jesuit mission ethnography. Might the fact that the Jesuit authors at least sometimes had an opportunity to review their published texts prior to composing more *Relations* have influenced what they chose to include, and what was left out?

Opportunities to answer that question regrettably are rare, at least partly due to the unavailability of original manuscripts of the *Relations* that could be compared to the published versions to see what was cut out by editors in Paris. It remains unknown with any certainty what became of the manuscripts that the New France missionaries sent to France each year, although Campeau speculates plausibly that they were in no condition to be saved after the treacherous Atlantic crossing and after being marked up in preparation for printing.[47] Fortunately, several of the texts, along with contemporaneous handwritten copies, offer clues about how the *Relations* were changed by editors in Paris. Two cases – the 1632 and 1663 *Relations* – show that Parisian editors may have at least sometimes added substantial material to the texts before printing them. And three other cases show that material also could be deleted, sometimes substantially altering the message conveyed in the texts. Pierre Biard's 1616 *Relation* – an early precursor to the annual series that would begin in 1632 – bears clear marks of an editor's intervention, and comparison of that text to the missionary author's subsequent summary of his experience in New France suggests that he may have adjusted his writing based on the changes made to his published text. Two variant editions of the 1633 *Relation* show that editors could sometimes add material between printings of the texts. And a handwritten copy of the 1634 *Relation* similarly reveals clues about how editors intervened in the texts after receiving the manuscript reports from the missionaries in New France. Although broad conclusions about, and rhetorical analysis of, how the texts were shaped by editors in France will remain impossible unless the original manuscripts come to light, the changes discussed in the following pages show that the Jesuit authors may have found the published versions of their texts substantially different from the manuscripts they sent to France. Even though deep analysis of this process is not possible at present, the certainty that the examples below afford that editors sometimes intervened in the texts in substantial ways has, as will soon be clear, important implications for the ethnographic qualities of the *Relations*.

The two versions of Le Jeune's 1632 *Relation* offer what is perhaps the most intriguing of the opportunities to assess the role of editors in Paris, but also affords the least certainty of the examples mentioned above. Both versions of the text take the form of a long letter. The manuscript letter, dated August 16, 1632, apparently was composed for the purpose of informing Church authorities in Rome of progress in the mission. The published *Relation* is dated August 28 of the same year, apparently the date on which its source, a letter to Parisian provincial Barthélemi Jacquinot, was written. Despite their roughly contemporaneous composition and the fact that they would have been sent to Europe at the same time, the one scholar who has compared them concluded, on grounds that are not clear, that the two texts each had their "own originality." Comparing the two texts, Campeau finds reason to believe that the editors who prepared the second letter for publication as a *Relation* changed the text only minimally, if at all. The published version of the text, he notes, reports on the same events as the Rome-intended manuscript, and the material is organized in similar fashion in both texts. According to Campeau, "It appears therefore that the integrity of the manuscripts was then the object of great respect and the initiative of the editor was minimal."[48] Although the similar content and organization of the two texts might well support the conclusion that editors in Paris saw no reason to change the manuscript (which regrettably has been lost) upon which the published text is based, other aspects of the two texts that might support the opposite conclusion are glossed over in this theory.

Despite their different wording in most places and one scholar's conclusion that the two texts were independently written, the texts themselves contain clues that they may share a common origin. In the manuscript letter, for example, Le Jeune described his first glimpse of Amerindians, and their apparent eagerness to interact with the Frenchmen who had just arrived in the New World. Wrote Le Jeune,

> As soon as they saw our vessel, they lighted fires, and two of them came on board in a little canoe very neatly made of bark. The next day [twelve of them came with their captain.] When I saw them enter our Captain's room, where I happened to be, it seemed to me that I was looking at those maskers who run about in Carnival time.[49]

The passage is repeated nearly word for word in the published 1632 *Relation*:

> As soon as they saw our vessel, they lighted fires, and two of them came on board in a little canoe very neatly made of bark. The next day a Sagamore, with ten or twelve Savages, came to see us. When I saw them enter our Captain's room, where I happened to be, it seemed to me that I was looking at those maskers who run about in France in Carnival time.[50]

With the exception of minor changes in spelling and punctuation, and the addition or deletion of a few words, the two passages are identical. And one does not have to look very hard in the two texts to find numerous other examples of passages that differ from each other in similarly minor ways. The word-for-word repetition in the published text of passages from the manuscript letter suggests that the two texts may not be as independent as they initially appear. One possible conclusion is that Le Jeune consulted and borrowed from his first letter while composing a second, more detailed letter for a different audience. Another possibility is that Le Jeune sent to Europe two identical letters, and that the differences between the passages above and the texts that contain them are attributable not to Le Jeune, but to editors in Paris who knew what Le Jeune did not know: that the text would be published, and therefore needed to be made appealing to a wider audience.

The possibility that the difference between the two texts is entirely due to the intervention of Parisian editors is tantalizing indeed, if unfortunately impossible to prove unless and until a manuscript of the Paris letter is discovered. Despite sharing subject matter, organization, and numerous sentences nearly word-for-word, the texts are in other ways quite different. Fully accounting for these differences would be an undertaking beyond the scope of the present chapter, but perhaps the most striking and important of these differences is that the published text is approximately twice as long as the manuscript. Key events, such as the perilous crossing of the Atlantic Ocean to reach the New World, are narrated in more detail and at greater length in the published text than in the manuscript. If the surviving manuscript letter is, in fact, representative of what Le Jeune sent to Paris, the published version of his text – longer, more detailed, and perhaps tailored for a reading public – would have been surprising indeed to its author, and would have suggested a need to more fully develop future texts in the series, in order to better appeal to readers. If this possibility must regrettably remain speculative for now, it is nonetheless useful as a plausible alternative to Campeau's theory about the relationship between the two texts. At a minimum, it can be said that the existence of two versions of the 1632 *Relation* does not support the theory that Parisian editors left manuscripts from New France largely unchanged.

Indeed, other texts in the series suggest that it may not be so far-fetched to believe that editors in Paris could have substantially added to and embellished the 1632 *Relation*. If they did, it would not be the last time new material was added in Paris. For example, editors in Paris added the entire final chapter of the 1663 *Relation*, drawing on a travel account that arrived in Paris during the printing process. The chapter itself indicates that the editors, and not the mission superior, were responsible for its content. The chapter opens thus: "While this Relation was being printed, there fell into our hands the account of a journey performed by a person of merit expressly to reconnoiter the country of New France, from the entrance of the Gulf of Saint Lawrence up to Montreal. Some persons have thought it fitting to make an extract from this narrative, and publish it in this Relation. Following is what the traveler writes."[51] The 1654 *Relation* similarly contained material that had arrived in France separately from the manuscript, and was added by editors there.[52] And, as mentioned in chapter one, it appears that Paul Le Jeune crafted a number of the *Relations*, and added content to others, after his return to Paris. Indeed, Léon Pouliot has concluded that between 1650 and 1662, only the 1659 *Relation* did not include a large block of text composed by Le Jeune in Paris.[53]

The three other cases mentioned above show that in addition to adding material to the *Relations*, Parisian editors also sometimes deleted passages or entire chapters penned by the missionaries in New France. Pierre Biard, a member of the Society's mission in Acadia (what is today Nova Scotia and northern Maine), wrote an early precursor to the annual series of New France *Relations* that would start in 1632. Biard's 1616 *Relation de la Nouvelle France* went through an editorial process in France that resembled the treatment of the texts that were published annually for forty years, and contains several editor-introduced oddities as a result. Chapters eleven and twenty-two are missing in the text, and promises of more information that go unfulfilled at the end of the preceding chapters indicate that simple numbering errors were not to blame for their absence. In addition, chapter twenty-one ends with an account of the Jesuits' vigorous efforts to defend themselves against an accusation that is not explicitly mentioned in the published text, indicating that a portion of that chapter also was omitted from the printed version. Drawing on contemporaneous documents, Lucien Campeau has made the case that the accusation in question was a colonial agent's assertion that one of the missionaries had admitted that the Society favoured the assassination of King Henry IV, a charge that Jesuits had been combatting in France since 1610. That theory also explains the omission of chapters eleven and twenty-two, in which the subject of conflict with colonial authorities likely would have required frequent mention of the same accusation. That Biard himself was made aware of these changes and accordingly adjusted his future writing is indicated by the Latin summary of the *Relation* that he subsequently prepared. That text, like the edited version of the *Relation*, avoids all mention of the accusation that the Society was in favour of the assassination of the king.[54] Not only did editors in France make substantial changes to the text, those changes appear to have influenced the author's succeeding accounts of his time in New France.

Two other *Relations* provide even clearer clues about how editors in France altered the texts prior to publication. The first is Paul Le Jeune's 1633 *Relation*, which, like many of the texts, was printed several times in Paris, apparently to keep up with readers' demand. In what apparently was the first printing of the *Relation*, Le Jeune recounts his own happiness at receiving the many supportive and encouraging letters that had been carried to New France in the care of the missionary Jean de Brébeuf, freshly arrived in the colony. He goes on to enumerate people for whom he was praying for God's blessing: "But I entreat him to apply one single drop of what he drank, especially to those who have helped us so much, to the associates of the Company of New France, of whom God wishes to make use for his glory, to Your Reverence, to all your Province, and to all those who cooperate in the salvation of so many poor lost souls; a little drop of this divine cup will enrich us all; and as my prayers are too weak to obtain so great a blessing, I beg Your Reverence to interpose yours, and those also of so many saintly souls who are under your charge. But let us pass on."[55] In the following paragraph, Le Jeune writes that he had learned of the recent arrival of Samuel de Champlain, and had gone to visit him at his fort. Le Jeune reported that he took advantage of the moment to thank Champlain for his good treatment of the Jesuits whom he had transported to the colony. Wrote Le Jeune, "I thanked Monsieur de Champlain, as well as I could, for the kindness shown by him to our Fathers, for it was very great, as Father Brébeuf has testified to me."[56]

In a second printing of the *Relation* that appeared shortly after the first, Le Jeune's expressions of gratitude to various figures is substantially changed. The first passage above ends after "his glory," eliminating Le Jeune's praise of the Jesuit provincial and miscellaneous unnamed others who served the cause of converting the Amerindians and his request for prayers to support the cause. The second passage, in which Le Jeune reports having thanked Champlain for his good treatment of the Jesuits, is eliminated entirely. These deletions apparently served to make room for praise of Cardinal Richelieu, who had only been mentioned in passing in the first printing for having intervened in a dispute between the trading company and a rival merchant group. Wrote an anonymous editor in Paris, "It occurs to me sometimes that this great man, who, by his admirable wisdom and peerless conduct of business, has acquired such renown on earth, is preparing for a very brilliant crown of glory in heaven, for the care that he shows himself to have for the conversion of so many souls that faithlessness causes to be lost in these wild lands. I pray affectionately for him every day, and our company, having by his means occasion to glorify God in this so noble initiative, will have for him an eternal obligation."[57] In this second version of the passage, expressions of gratitude to a

Jesuit official, a local authority figure in New France, and unnamed supporters in France make way for flattery of a powerful political figure in the Old Country. Cardinal Richelieu's involvement with the Compagnie des 100 Associés, which enjoyed a monopoly on trade in the colony at the time, made him an influential figure over affairs there, and one with whom the Jesuits would have been wise to maintain good relations. The changes made by an anonymous editor in Paris between printings of the 1633 *Relation* suggest that such political considerations could lead to the texts being altered in Paris. And the use of the first person in the inserted passage obscures the intervention of an editor, making it sound as if Le Jeune himself had written glowing praise of the cardinal.

The case of Paul Le Jeune's 1634 *Relation* provides more clues about how editors in France altered the *Relations* prior to publication, indicating that such changes could affect portraits of the Amerindians themselves, instead of merely reflecting colonial political necessity. The *Bibliothèque Nationale de France* houses a handwritten contemporaneous copy of the text, which preserves some elements of the original manuscript that did not survive the editorial process. These deletions are not included in Reuben Gold Thwaites' popular early-twentieth-century edition of the *Relations*. This omission perhaps explains why so few scholars seem to be aware of the handwritten copy and the ways in which it differs from the published version of the 1634 text. The more recent and superior, although less widely used, edition – *Monumenta Novae Franciae* – includes the deleted material in brackets, and catalogues hundreds of differences between the two versions. Although at least one scholar has asserted that this manuscript was the basis for Sébastien Cramoisy's published edition, it appears to be nearly certain that the Cramoisy version and the manuscript were independently produced copies of a single, earlier version of the text, which itself may or may not have been the original sent from New France. The vast majority of the differences between the published and manuscript versions of the texts are typographical errors, grammatical mistakes, and variations in spelling. But the manuscript also includes material that is absent from the printed *Relation*, indicating that it is not simply a handmade copy of the published text. And there are at least five places in the manuscript where the copyist apparently accidentally skipped a line of the source text, resulting in a temporary loss of coherence. Since the sentences concerned are intact in the published version of the text, it can be concluded that the published version of the text was based on a manuscript other than the one that has survived. In short, neither text is the source of the other, but rather both appear to be independently made copies of yet another version of the text – perhaps the original manuscript sent to France by the missionaries – making it possible to find in the manuscript elements of Le Jeune's original text that were omitted from the Cramoisy edition.[58]

Several passages that apparently were deleted prior to publication reveal that the editors made substantial changes. The *Relation*'s chapter on Montagnais food, for example, was cut short by several paragraphs in the published version of the text. As published, the chapter ends with a paragraph detailing hardships that the Montagnais endured due to their reliance on hunting for food in winter. Wrote Le Jeune, "Now, if the hunt for all these animals does not succeed (which with them occurs only too often) they suffer greatly."[59] Due to the frequency with which hunts came up empty, the Montagnais reportedly were reduced to a seasonal scramble for sustenance, and to long periods of famine punctuated by infrequent feasts when they were lucky enough to be able to procure meat. In the published *Relation*, the priest's treatment of the subject of Montagnais food concludes with a characterization of the Amerindian group as vulnerable and helpless, oscillating between feast and famine due to the scarcity of food in the winter.

The deleted material preserved in the handwritten copy, however, shows that the chapter originally ended on a very different note. Le Jeune recounts his inability to hide his disgust upon trying the smoked meat and fish that the Montagnais apparently held to be a delicacy. Such meat was as hard as wood, he complained, and gave him the impression of chewing on hemp or a similarly rugged fiber. When heated and rubbed between two stones, as was apparently an especially esteemed method of preparing the dish, the meat became even dirtier than it was to begin with. Le Jeune partook of the Montagnais' *boucan* only twice, and his disgust did not go unnoticed by his hosts: "The first, I could barely eat it, for which, having inadvertently shown it, not knowing that it was their nectar, I was reprimanded, for they told me I was arrogant, that I had no spirit, that I did not know what was good, that it was a feast fit for a king. These are the caresses of the Savages. One must take them as given, without becoming angry."[60] In contrast to the published version of the chapter, the manuscript version ends with the missionary cast as vulnerable and weak, forced to endure insult without defending himself because he had no choice but to rely on his Montagnais hosts for shelter and sustenance, disgusting though it may have been. The two versions of the chapter's conclusion could be read as a dialogue between New France missionary and Old World editor over the nature of Jesuit power. As discussed in chapter two, Jesuit missionaries in New France had a strategic incentive to emphasize their own weakness relative to potential converts – particularly in the early years of the mission – in order to justify slow progress in converting souls to Catholicism, and this is indeed what the manuscript version of the chapter does. Jesuit authorities in Europe, in contrast, would have had an interest in portraying the Jesuits as strong in comparison to Amerindians in order to represent the mission in the best light possible to readers and potential donors, and also to fend off challenges to the Jesuits' authority and capabilities that were launched by the missionaries' enemies and rivals in France. It is perhaps not surprising, then, that the chapter was edited in France to remove a passage in which a Jesuit missionary appeared particularly weak and vulnerable.

Another intriguing difference between the published 1634 *Relation* and the handwritten copy comes in the tenth chapter, on Montagnais clothing and fashion. Le Jeune begins by briefly mentioning Aristotelian ideas about three stages through which mankind passes in pursuit of perfection. As Le Jeune summarized, humans in the first stage are concerned only with survival. In the second, they begin to combine utility with an aesthetic sensibility before finally arriving at the third stage, in which the pursuit of knowledge becomes a top priority. Amerindians, Le Jeune asserts in the published text, were stuck in the first stage: "Their only thought is to live, they eat so as not to die; they cover themselves to keep off the cold, and not for the sake of appearance. Grace, politeness, the knowledge of the arts, natural sciences, and much less supernatural truths, have as yet no place in this hemisphere, or at least in these countries. These people do not think there is any other science in the world, except that of eating and [living]; and in this lies all their Philosophy."[61] Le Jeune follows this assessment with examples of how the Montagnais' utilitarian orientation was reflected in their sartorial choices. In the winter, wrote the priest, "anything is good, provided it is warm. They are dressed properly when they are dressed comfortably."[62] Questions such as fashion, fit, and colour did not, according to the published version of the chapter, enter into Montagnais thinking on the subject of clothing, and men and women did not dress differently. As published, the chapter generally supports its opening remarks about the strictly functional quality of Montagnais clothing, and that group's interest in survival to the exclusion of aesthetics.

Two passages that were deleted prior to publication, however, undermine the chapter's premise by suggesting that the Montagnais were not concerned only with survival in their choice of attire. The first deletion preserved in the handwritten copy spans five paragraphs, and describes the Amerindian group's tattooing practices, face and hair painting, piercing, and jewellery. From the beginning, it is clear that the lack of interest in fashion that Le Jeune appeared to ascribe to the Montagnais in the published *Relation* was not the whole story. Describing the group's tattoos, the deleted passage reads, "But let us consider them dressed and adorned according to their style. Let us begin with the body. Some of them, to decorate it, even some women, draw lines and indelible figures on the most visible parts of their bodies."[63] The characterization of the practice as part of Montagnais "style" undermines the earlier assertion that the Montagnais were concerned only with survival, as do the verbs *orner* (adorn) and *embellir* (decorate) that are used to describe it. The passage goes on to give detailed descriptions of other Montagnais fashions, such as anointing and greasing the face and body with aromatic and colourful ointments, hairstyles meant to contain long and unruly locks, piercing of body parts, and jewellery including bracelets and anklets.

A second, shorter omitted passage describes ornaments that were sometimes added to robes. Wrote Le Jeune, "The richest and most magnificent sometimes attach two bands of decorative beads around their robes. These bands are here as highly prized as are those great braids from Milan, or rather golden braids."[64] By indicating that ornaments added to robes could serve as symbols of social status and wealth among the Amerindians, and explicitly comparing the preferred style to European fashions, the deleted passage moves the discussion of clothing from the realm of protection from the elements to those of aesthetic choices and social status. Remarkably, the brief passage ends by undermining its own point, saying that the author had not actually seen such robes, and that they may be more common among the Huron. This apparent inconsistency could be one reason the passage was edited out prior to publication, but its initial inclusion in the manuscript suggests that Le Jeune was keen to attribute something other than strict utility to Montagnais clothing, despite the fact that the chapter opens with the claim that just the opposite was true. The presence of this perplexing passage in the manuscript also suggests that Le Jeune was eager to identify a cultural phenomenon that would be recognizable to French readers as fashion of the kind prized in France or Italy, even if he had to admit that the information was not particularly reliable.

Reading the two deleted passages in their original context makes it clear, then, that the chapter was edited in France to make the Montagnais appear simpler than Le Jeune had originally suggested they might be. As in the passage on Montagnais food in the same *Relation*, the different perspectives of missionaries in the field and their brethren in France might provide one explanation for these changes. Labouring to convert Amerindians, Jesuit missionaries were, as discussed in chapter five, on the lookout for similarities between European and Amerindian cultures that could be used to ease the way for the implantation of Christianity and that could reassure European readers of the humanity of the inhabitants of the New World. Jesuit editors in New France, on the other hand, may have preferred to emphasize the simplicity of the Amerindians – and therefore their distance from all things French and Catholic – in order to put the case for missionary intervention in the most urgent terms possible, in the hopes of attracting more material and political support for the Society's efforts.

The clues about how the *Relations* were edited for publication that are furnished by the 1616, 1633, and 1634 texts, as well as the cases where material clearly was added in Paris, indicate that Old World editors at least sometimes altered the Jesuits' accounts substantially. Indeed, a contemporary of the Jesuits, the Ursuline nun Marie de l'Incarnation, characterized such editorial intervention in terms that suggested it was the norm in a 1668 letter to her son in France. Wrote the missionary, "when they send copies of them from here, many things are cut out in France. Madame the Duchess of Sennessay, who does me the honor of writing to me every year, wrote to me last year of her displeasure at something that had been cut out, and she said something similar to me this year. M.C. who prints the relation, and who loves the Hospitalières here a lot, inserted therein on his own initiative a letter that the Superior had written to him, and that made a lot of noise in France."[65] Politically difficult topics, signs of missionary weakness, and clues that Amerindians were perhaps not so simple after all could be omitted after the manuscripts arrived in Paris. And the 1663 *Relation*, along with other cases in which contributors in Paris added material, confirms that editors did not regard the manuscripts as texts whose integrity as firsthand accounts had to be respected. This insight should give pause to scholars who have long relied on the published *Relations* for information about the early history of French America and Amerindian groups as they existed at the time of contact. The colony-centric movements of the texts traced earlier in this chapter make these changes all the more intriguing, since each edited text that made its way back to the Jesuits took its place in their library, a perch from which, as this chapter has argued, it could exercise influence over future texts in the series, much as letters from Europe also clearly shaped them.

In light of the changes made by editors in Europe, the colony-centric movement of the texts, and the missionaries' apparent attentiveness to feedback, it may be worthwhile for scholars to redouble their efforts to locate more early copies of the texts that might include material that was deleted prior to publication, or even original manuscripts. Detailed analysis of how the published texts differed from the manuscripts and how missionaries' writing choices may have been influenced by the consultation of edited versions of their texts will have to wait for the discovery of more early copies that could be compared to the printed *Relations*, should any yet survive. But our inability, for the present, to account for all of those changes, the motivations that produced them, and their influence on subsequent texts should not stop scholars from adjusting their understanding of the texts to account for the facts that each *Relation* was sent back to New France, that editorial intervention in Paris was at least sometimes more significant than previously believed, and that the Jesuit authors were attentive to the changes that Old World editors made to their texts. It is certainly true that the *Relations* were and continue to be received as a riveting account of Europeans' experience of the New World and a valuable source of information about New France and its Amerindian inhabitants. But as this chapter has argued, the texts were part of a more complex process through which information circulated between Worlds Old and New. The *Relations* do not merely reflect an effort, rooted in experience, to transmit to the home left behind information about a distant and poorly known place, biased and otherwise problematic though it may have been. Instead, the ethnographic "facts" in the Jesuit *Relations* must be regarded as the product of an ongoing discussion between readers at home on both sides of the Atlantic Ocean. This aspect of mission ethnography in the *Relations* adds another dimension to the point of view that this book has brought to bear on the Jesuit *Relations*. Not only do the efforts of missionaries to account in writing for Amerindian cultures reflect simultaneous efforts to learn from and make arguments to the inhabitants of both the New World and the Old; the very process through which the texts were produced and circulated gave European editors and authorities a chance to contribute directly to decisions concerning what to say, and how to say it, about the inhabitants of the New World.

Although this chapter has mostly served to undermine one of the fundamental claims of the Jesuit *Relations* to the status of ethnographic writing *avant la lettre* – their status as travel writing rooted in experience and intended to effect a rapprochement between traveller and those who stayed at home – it seems that their unorthodox circulation does not necessarily invalidate their status as travel writing, but may instead bring nuance to that genre. Strikingly, the Jesuit authors, who did not travel in the traditional circular sense, nonetheless produced texts that can be understood to conceptually resemble typical travel accounts. They undeniably communicated information about the New World and its inhabitants both to Europe in their own time and to posterity, while also, as this chapter has argued, furnishing an opportunity to their authors to reassess and renew their relationship with the home left behind, on the basis of feedback associated with the texts' circulation. The fact that this second function of travel writing is only possible in the case of the *Relations* thanks to the colony-centric movements of the texts points to a need, already heralded in some quarters, to question whether the traditionally presumed relationship between circular physical movement and travel writing is productive or needlessly limiting.[66]

In addition to bringing nuance to the status of the *Relations* as travel writing and to the limits of the genre itself, the reading offered here points to a potential response to the criticism that scholarship on travel writing often reproduces a Eurocentric point of view. Mary Louise Pratt, for example, has recently pointed out that "our scholarly analyses tend spontaneously to follow the traveler-author (as his reader does) and represent his discourse in our terms, as if we were looking over his shoulder, as readers and fellow travelers. 'This is how traveler X saw place Y.' The analyst follows the book that follows the trip."[67] Although work retracing the steps of traveller-writers incontestably has been of great value in distilling the precise contributions of travellers' tales to evolving Western knowledge about the outside world, it also risks perpetuating the colonial impulse to organize the world with Europe at its centre, with all other places and peoples interesting only for what could be extracted for Europe's benefit.[68] The example of the Jesuit *Relations* suggests that in at least some cases, travellers' tales could be understood to transmit information in more than one direction, allowing for readings of travel writing that privilege not what was learned in the exotic destination and then transported to Europe, but what was extracted from Europe for the benefit of the colony. To understand the Jesuit *Relations* this way is to decline to tag along on a Eurocentric voyage while reading the texts, and to see them and all of their contents as a reflection of an ongoing conversation between Jesuits on both sides of the Atlantic, rather than a traveller's earnest, if perhaps biased, perceptions of a foreign place.

The End(s) of
Jesuit Mission Ethnography

The story that this book has told about Jesuit mission ethnography began with the arrival of the missionaries in New France, and followed them through the fraught processes of learning to communicate with Amerindians, learning about their cultural beliefs and practices while attempting to teach them about Christianity, and then writing accounts of those experiences for readers in France. Although the priests remained in the New World and continued their mission until the end of the eighteenth century, even persevering after the suppression of the Society by papal order in 1773, the story of Jesuit mission ethnography ends, in one sense, with the unexpected cessation of publication of the annual *Relations* in 1673. The proximate cause of this abrupt end to the published series had nothing to do with the New France missionaries or their work, but was instead the result of a conflict between Church and Crown over what are often referred to as the "Chinese rites." The practice of Jesuit missionaries in a distant part of the world of adapting Catholicism to Chinese culture in the hopes of facilitating religious conversion had come under fire from the Society's detractors. Apparently hoping to prevent such controversies in the future, Pope Clement X forbade the publication of missionary reports without written permission from the Vatican's Sacred Congregation for the Propagation of the Faith. In a sign that the French Crown viewed the pope's move as usurpation of its own power, the Parlement of Paris specifically denied the Roman Congregation's authority in France. Continuing to publish the New France *Relations* in this political climate would have required defying either papal or royal authority. Not surprisingly, the Jesuits opted to discontinue the series rather than incur the wrath of the king or pope.[1] The *Relations* were a casualty of political circumstances, reminding us once again that Jesuit mission ethnography was not only a product of encounters in New France, but was also subject to the political and intellectual pressures of the Old World.[2]

Although the cessation of publication of the annual *Relations* may have brought an end to the Jesuits' ethnographic project as it has been traced in this book, the missionaries' influence on outsiders' perception of Amerindian cultures was not at an end at all, and in fact was just beginning. Indeed, as each of the preceding chapters has shown in engaging with the rich ethnohistorical literature that draws on the *Relations*, the Jesuits' texts are scholars' primary source of information on Iroquoian and Algonquian groups as they existed in the early decades of contact with Old World colonizers. And the proliferation of options for consulting the texts in recent decades certainly has cemented in place the missionaries' reputation as the single most authoritative voice on the colony and Amerindian cultures as they existed in the seventeenth century. For many decades after their original publication, the texts were available only in research libraries and private collections. It was not until 1858, when a complete modern edition was produced in Quebec, that the texts became more easily accessible to scholars and others curious about the colony and Amerindian cultures. The two twentieth-century editions cited in this book – Thwaites' *Jesuit Relations* and Campeau's *Monumenta Novae Franciae* – gave scholars unprecedented access to the texts in both French and English, as did new printings of older editions and the numerous collections of excerpts that have appeared in recent decades. And most recently, the availability online of the texts in both French and English, including both scanned images of the seventeenth-century originals and the contents of the Thwaites and Quebec editions, has made the Jesuits' ideas about Amerindian cultures more accessible and potentially influential than ever. Indeed, new scholarly books that draw on the *Relations* from a variety of theoretical points of view appear seemingly every year. Although once silenced, the Jesuits now speak perhaps louder than they ever have on the subjects of Amerindian cultures and the colonization of New France.[3]

That reality points to the importance of the broad questions taken up in this book: How did Jesuit missionaries perceive Amerindian cultures and represent them for the benefit of readers? How was that project related to and influenced by their simultaneous religious mission? And what are the consequences of ethnohistory's reliance on the *Relations*? One part of this book's answer to those questions is that the missionaries did indeed manage to collect and transmit Amerindian knowledge that is still recognizable as distinct from their own culture's practices and beliefs. The creation story discussed in chapter five, for example, resembles the more recently collected tales of groups related to the Montagnais at least as much as it resembles the stories in Genesis. Champlain's seventeenth-century description of cruel treatment of prisoners that is mentioned in chapter four confirms details found in the Jesuit *Relations*. And the rich linguistic materials produced by the Jesuits contain information on a language that was and continues to be distinct from French, as illustrated by the bilingual stop sign in Wendaké discussed at the end of chapter three. These and many other aspects of the Jesuits' texts discussed in the preceding chapters suggest that Jesuit mission ethnography – despite its limitations – did indeed record unique elements of Amerindian cultures and transmit them to posterity.

And yet, as each of the chapters of this book has also shown in various ways, the Jesuits spoke and continue to speak on behalf of their Amerindian cultural masters and religious students in ways that tended to erase rather than mark cultural differences, and to superimpose on Amerindian cultures lessons that would be politically useful or reassuring to readers at home in France. Indeed, Jesuit mission ethnography may best be understood as a kind of colonization, although not the material exploitation of Amerindians of which the Jesuits have sometimes been accused.[4] As this book has shown, Jesuit accounts of Amerindian cultures mirror broader European understandings of the inhabitants of the New World that date to Columbus, who saw them as "deficient in everything ... but paradoxically rich in everything the Spaniards were avidly searching for."[5] It was this double understanding of Amerindians that licensed their colonization by European powers, whether it was economic exploitation, the seizure of their land, or any of the other unsavoury elements of colonial history. This book has shown that a similar dynamic was at work in Jesuit mission ethnography. The "richness" of Amerindian languages, the resemblance of their creation myths to Genesis, and the imitation of Christ to be found in the suffering of torture victims were all signs of the potential of Amerindians to be converted and to truly embrace and understand Christianity. But at the same time, the "poverty" of their languages, the corruption by fables of their myths, and the astounding and in some cases instinctive cruelty of Amerindian groups were signs of the deficiency of potential converts, justifying missionary intervention and framing it in the most urgent terms possible for readers at home in France. In the same way that the New World's material riches were carried back to Europe and fashioned into useful and prized products by Europeans who felt justified in extracting wealth from the continent by their own sense of superiority, the Jesuits shaped the raw material of Amerindian beliefs and practices into something useful to their European readers, and sent the colonized knowledge across the ocean in its new, written form, their religious certainty justifying their work.

The challenge that must be confronted by students of Amerindian cultures, then, is the extraction of information from a system of representation that does as much to obscure and alter it as it does to expose it. Although scholars bring a variety of theoretical understandings of colonial encounter to bear on the *Relations*, ethnohistorical uses of the texts often do not account for how the Jesuits' simultaneous roles as masters and students with regard to interlocutors on both sides of the ocean may have influenced their representations of Amerindian cultures. The preceding chapters of this book usually do not explicitly point out how failure to do so sometimes has led scholars to misread the *Relations*, but that has indeed sometimes been the result. It is worth citing at least one example here to show why it is important to read the texts as a record of two simultaneous missions instead of as earnest proto-ethnographic accounts, however biased they may be acknowledged to be. As mentioned in chapter four, the description in François-Joseph Le Mercier's 1637 *Relation* of the torture of an Iroquois captive named Joseph has become the standard account of Iroquoian torture. Scholars summarizing it or quoting from it have almost always edited out all references to the victim's conversion and steadfast Christian faith, as if the Jesuits' religious mission in this instance could be separated from their effort to record a distasteful Amerindian custom. Elisabeth Tooker, for example, high-lighted the captive's bravery in the face of brutal torment, citing his own words, as reported by Le Mercier: "My brothers, I am going to die; amuse yourselves boldly around me, – I fear neither tortures nor death." In the context of Tooker's version of Le Mercier's account – purged of all references to the victim's conversion – the speaker appears to be a defiant member of a rival Amerindian group facing his death with courage so as not to lose face in front of his enemies. Restored to its original context, however, the profession of courage comes after a priest assures the victim that the torment he will endure at the hands of his captors will be of short duration in comparison to the eternal pleasures that await him in heaven, and after the captive proclaims that he no longer fears death, now that he has been baptized.[6] Despite their different theoretical approaches, Bruce Trigger, Nathanial Knowles, and Peggy Reeves Sanday similarly treat the passage as a proto-ethnographic description of torture, without regard to the religious argument that it also contains, and therefore mistake a prized Christian convert who was reportedly emboldened by his faith for a typically stoic Amerindian.[7] Although bravery in the face of death may indeed have been considered a virtue in Amerindian cultures, it is odd to cite Le Mercier's text as evidence that such was the case, since the bravery displayed by Joseph is clearly linked to his newfound faith. It is only by thinking of the Jesuits as both masters and students – as proto-ethnographers and missionaries who furnished lessons to, and received them from, both Amerindians and Europeans – that the full significance of this passage and other descriptions of Amerindian cultures discussed in this book comes to light.

Even when details of cultural beliefs or customs appear to have survived unscathed in the *Relations*, editing out the religious commentary that surrounds them and ignoring their role as texts designed to garner support for the mission can only enhance the Jesuits' reputation as rigorous and meticulous students of culture – early participant-observers in the Malinowskian mold – obscuring the ways in which the Jesuit ethnographic and religious missions influenced each other. And the notion that Amerindian traditions could survive "unscathed" is itself problematic, since inherently variable oral knowledge and complex grammatical structures were standardized by the Jesuits, reduced to single versions that conformed to European expectations and then fixed in writing, whereas the traditions themselves might have never ceased evolving had they continued to be transmitted orally. Whether the subject was creation myths, torture, or unfamiliar languages, the New France Jesuits translated Amerindian oral knowledge into written form, making it conform to European expectations that knowledge could be fixed in writing and was invariable.[8] In both content and form, then, Jesuit mission ethnography was more the practice of redirecting information gleaned from Amerindians to the Jesuits' own ends than careful study and faithful transmission of lessons learned to European readers. Although the Jesuit ethnographic mission as traced in this book may have ended with the Jesuits being silenced, its afterlife has had a very different outcome. The missionaries' accounts of Amerindian cultures now are arguably more prominent and influential than at any time in the past. And, as this book has shown, it is the voices of their Amerindian interlocutors that have been silenced, or at least represented in such a way that they no longer can be distinguished easily from the voices of the Jesuit mission ethnographers.

NOTES

PREFACE

1 Anthropologist Orin Starn reported encountering similar interest in early anthropological works among indigenous groups in California. Starn, *Ishi's Brain*, 62.

2 See "Local Woman's Effort May Resurrect Classic Tlingit Reference."

3 See True, "Is It Time for a New Edition of the Jesuit *Relations* from New France?" Luca Codignola offers a good assessment of the weaknesses of the Thwaites edition relative to the Campeau edition, particularly with regard to the supplemental materials contained in each edition. See his article "The Battle is Over," recently reprinted as "Jesuit Writings according to R.G. Thwaites and Lucien Campeau, S.J.: How Do They Differ?" A third, less often cited edition is Augustin Côté's *Relations des Jésuites contenant ce qui s'est passé de plus remarquable dans les missions des pères de la Compagnie de Jésus dans la Nouvelle-France*. Côté's edition is exclusively in French and lacks the scholarly apparatus that is a particular strength of the Campeau edition. It is nonetheless the preferred alternative to the Thwaites edition for some francophone scholars. It was reprinted in six volumes in Montreal by Editions du Jour in 1972.

4 Melzer, *Colonizer or Colonized*, 4. Melzer's book can be taken as an example of the fruitful use of anachronistic concepts to make sense of seventeenth-century French texts and culture. For a cogent and extensive commentary on the value of anachronism in textual criticism, see Yves Citton, *Lire, Interpréter, Actualiser*.

5 On "Huron" and "Wendat," see Trigger's Preface to the Carleton Library Series Reprint of his book *The Children of Aataentsic*. In its modern use, "Innu" designates both Montagnais and Naskapi peoples. See Magocsi, *Encyclopedia of Canada's Peoples*, 36. On Iroquois/Nadouek, see Sioui, *Les Huron-Wendats*, 23–4.

6 For thoughtful remarks on the difficulties involved in selecting names for Amerindian groups in scholarship, see Sayre, *Les Sauvages Américains*, preface, and Franks, "In Search of the Savage *Sauvage*."

CHAPTER ONE

1 Russell, *The Sparrow*, prologue.

2 Ibid., 96.

3 The word "mission" can mean both the going forth of religious representatives to spread the faith and a political or diplomatic undertaking. The term also can designate a journey of discovery, especially, in our time, to outer space. See *Oxford English Dictionary*, s.v. "mission."

4 Although a world-wide network of Jesuit missionaries existed by the time the order arrived in New France in the seventeenth century, a plurality of the order's missionaries operated within Europe. "In 1653, it had a little less than 1,000 missionaries around the world, of whom the highest number (381) were in continental Europe and the lowest (9) in Scotland." Codignola, "Few, Uncooperative, and Ill-Informed?" 176. There has been a lot of recent historical scholarship on the various Jesuit missions around the world and in Europe that promises to aid scholars in better understanding how the order's global network functioned in the sixteenth, seventeenth, and eighteenth centuries, and could allow the questions that are posed here about a specific mission to be extended to other parts of the globe or to the entire Jesuit missionary enterprise. Such recent studies include Selwyn, *A Paradise Inhabited by Devils*; Van Der Cruysse, *Siam and the West*; Ross, *A Vision Betrayed*; Abé, *The Jesuit Mission to New France*; Deslandres, *Croire et faire croire*; and Zupanov, *Disputed Mission*. A good, brief survey of Jesuit mission work in Europe and around the world can be found in the introduction to Greer, *The Jesuit Relations*. For a general survey of Jesuit activities throughout North America, see Cushner, *Why Have You Come Here?* Bitterli's *Cultures in Conflict* offers a broad view of contact between European and non-European cultures throughout the world, including but not limited to Jesuit and other missions, making his book a useful tool for thinking about the Jesuit missions in a global context.

5 For more on the historical geography of Algonquian groups, see Beaulieu, *Convertir les fils de Caïn*, 21. On Huron territory, see Trigger, *The Children of Aataentsic*, 27–31, and Heidenreich, *Huronia: a History and Geography of the Huron Indians 1600–1650*. On the Iroquois League, see Snow, *The Iroquois*, 117–19; Trigger, *The Children of Aataentsic*, 98; and Parmenter, *The Edge of the Woods*. The term "Iroquoian" designates a language family including the Huron, the Iroquois, and various other groups. Trigger, *The Children of Aataentsic*, xliii.

6 Greer, *The Jesuit Relations*, 1. Francophone scholars have been no less quick to note the documentary value of the series. Wrote historian Alain Beaulieu, for example, "It is no longer necessary to insist on the interest of these *Relations* for the history of the beginnings of the colonization of New France. They constitute

by far the most important source of information on this period." Beaulieu, *Convertir les Fils de Caïn*, 19. Author's translation.

7 Sioui, *Les Hurons-Wendats: Une Civilisation Méconnue*, 8–9.

8 On Lafitau, see Campbell, *Wonder and Science*, chapter 9. The Jesuit historian Pierre de Charlevoix, in his 1744 *Histoire et Description Générale de la Nouvelle-France*, also praised the *Relations* as a unique source of information: "There is not even any other source on which one can draw to learn about the progress of religion among the savages, and to know these peoples of which they spoke." Charlevoix, *Histoire et Description Générale de la Nouvelle France*, vol. 2, XLVIII. Author's translation.

9 Russell, *The Sparrow*, 3. The priests who welcome Sandoz home in his troubled state, for example, explicitly compare him to New France Jesuit martyrs like Isaac Jogues, who, like Sandoz in Russell's sequel to *The Sparrow*, returned during a second mission to the people who had tortured him. The similarity between Sandoz and Jogues ends with their respective second visits to their tormentors. Unlike Jogues, Sandoz is not tortured and killed by those who harmed him during his first visit. See Russell, *Children of God*. Russell herself claimed to have chosen the Jesuits because "they have a long history of first contact with cultures other than their own." See "A conversation with Mary Doria Russell," appendix to *The Sparrow*.

10 Missionaries wrote reports for most of the years between 1611 and 1791, although they were published for only about forty years during the seventeenth century. Blackburn, *Harvest of Souls*, 4. The circumstances surrounding the beginning and end of the published series will be explained at later points in this book.

11 Loyola, *The Constitutions of the Society of Jesus*, 292.

12 Pouliot, *Etude sur les Relations des Jésuites*, 4.

13 Carayon's volume lists all mission texts in a single section, making it easy to gauge at a glance the scale and scope of Jesuit missionary publication around the time the New France *Relations* appeared. See Carayon, *Bibliographie Historique de la Compagnie de Jésus*.

14 Wroth, "The Jesuit Relations from New France," 112. As Joseph Donnelly, himself a Jesuit, has put it, "the forty-one little duodecimo vellum-bound volumes which alone can technically be called Jesuit *Relations* were not primarily designed as official reports of the superior of the Jesuit mission in New France to his provincial or to the Jesuit general. Beginning with Father Paul Le Jeune's *Relation* of 1632, these annual volumes were designed for public consumption." Donnelly, *Thwaites' Jesuit Relations: Errata and Addenda*, 1–2.

15 On the differences between French and English accounts of Amerindian cultures and Thoreau's preference for the French texts, see Sayre, *Les Sauvages Américains*, especially chapter 1. See also Melzer, *Colonizer or Colonized*, 75–8.

16 For reasons that are not entirely clear, the 1637 *Relation* was published in Rouen by Jean le Boullenger. Wroth speculates that a financial advantage could have led the Jesuit provincial to temporarily abandon the Parisian printer Cramoisy. In any case, the defection was short-lived, perhaps due to the multiple typographical errors that appeared in Boullenger's edition. The following year, Cramoisy resumed printing the *Relations*. For more on this question and on the popular success of the *Relations*, see Wroth, "The Jesuit Relations from New France," 138–43.

17 As Wroth observed, "the *Relations* were issued not in small editions for a fixed and limited group, and then forgotten in the usual manner of reports, but in comparatively large numbers for a public that awaited them eagerly and demanded from time to time reprintings of their matter. It is difficult to explain on any other ground the number and the complexity of the forms in which the great series was offered to the public." Wroth, "The Jesuit Relations from New France," 114. The various seventeenth-century reprints and distinct editions of the *Relations* are documented in McCoy, *The Jesuit Relations of Canada*. On pirated editions, see Pouliot, *Etude sur les Relations des Jésuites*, 24.

18 JR 10.7. "L'ancienne France brusle de très ardens désirs pour la nouvelle." MNF 3.307; JR 11.39. "en feu." MNF 3.524; JR 18.61. "une grande partie de la France." MNF 4.557.

19 Furetière, "Relation." Author's translation.

20 Melzer, *Colonizer or Colonized*, 76.

21 Van Den Abbeele, *Travel as Metaphor*, xx–xxi.

22 See, for example, Deffain, *Un Voyageur Français en Nouvelle-France au XVIIe Siècle*; Ouellet, ed., *Rhétorique et Conquête Missionnaire*; and Le Bras, *L'Amérindien dans les Relations du Père Paul*. Brébeuf also has occasionally been studied independently of other Jesuit missionary authors. See, for example, Le Bras, "Les *Relations* du Père Jean de Brébeuf en Huronie."

23 Codignola, "Few, Uncooperative, and Ill-Informed?" 181.

24 In a related vein, Gordon Sayre has pointed out that the way the *Relations* and similar French texts are packaged may inhibit their recognition as literary texts by foregrounding their status as official correspondence. Sayre, *Les Sauvages Américains*, 20.

25 On the composition of the 1641 *Relation*, see MNF 2.54–5. On the 1652 and 1653 *Relations,* see MNF 8.277 and 8.561, and on Le Jeune's role as a ghostwriter after his return to France, see Pouliot, "La Contribution de P. Paul Le Jeune aux *Relations des Jésuites* de 1650 à 1663." A useful appendix indicating who apparently assembled each of the texts can be found in Pioffet, *La Tentation de l'Epopée dans les Relations des Jésuites*.

26 An exception is the 1639 *Relation* composed by Le Jeune, who had recently been replaced as superior by Barthélemy Vimont. Despite no longer holding the post of superior, Le Jeune was credited on the frontispiece. MNF 4.262.

27 Wroth, "The Jesuit Relations from New France," 117–18.

28 Clifford, *The Predicament of Culture*, 28.

29 Marcus and Fischer, *Anthropology as Cultural Critique*, 24.

30 Parkman, *The Jesuits in North America in the Seventeenth Century*, vi.

31 See Tooker, *An Ethnography of the Huron Indians*, 5–6, 7. On "participant-observation" as a key concept in anthropology, see Clifford, "Introduction," 1.

32 Clifford, "Introduction," 15. In the work of salvage anthropologists, in contrast, "[c]ulture was construed as an ensemble of characteristic behaviors, ceremonies, and gestures susceptible to recording and explanation by a trained onlooker." Clifford, *The Predicament of Culture*, 31.

33 Clifford, *The Predicament of Culture*, 41. Recent scholarly contributions in cultural anthropology demonstrate that this concern for the relationship between anthropologists and the cultures they study has not waned in the decades since Clifford, Marcus, Fischer, and others brought it to the fore. Orin Starn's 2004 *Ishi's Brain*, for example, is as much an account of the author's personal history with and investigation of the story of America's so-called "last wild Indian" as it is a study of twentieth-century American identity politics, the history of anthropology, or any of the other subjects it takes up. Gananath Obeyesekere, at least as far as his rival Marshall Sahlins is concerned, went too far down this path in his 1992 *Apotheosis of Captain Cook* by "[p]retending as a fellow 'native' to speak on behalf of Hawaiian people against the calumny that they mistook Cook for their own God Lono" on the basis of his own Sri Lankan heritage. See Sahlins, *How "Natives" Think*, ix, and Obeyesekere, *The Apotheosis of Captain Cook*. As Starn noted, the shift away from neutrality as a guiding principle has not been universally embraced and its results sometimes are still questioned: "In the 1980s, the influence of postmodern theory introduced new doubts that anthropology could ever be more than a partial, subjective enterprise. It is still being debated even today whether anthropologists ought to embrace the ideal of neutrality or advocacy, and, for that matter, whether the study of other cultures should be conceived of as art, science, or something in between." Starn, *Ishi's Brain*, 140. It is nonetheless clear that late-twentieth-century theoretical work on the relationship between anthropologist and subject has left an enduring mark on the discipline.

34 Anthropologist Gananath Obeyesekere, for example, admonished that those drawing on colonial texts should be wary of "observational data collected by naive fieldworkers at a time when critical scholarship in ethnography was

virtually nonexistent. One must probe into the hidden agendas underlying the writing of these texts." Obeyesekere, *The Apotheosis of Captain Cook*, 66. Nathalie Zemon Davis has termed such attempts to account for those agendas as the "gaze strategy": "describing European attitudes and images of non-European peoples and showing them to be projections of European anxieties or elaborations from European categories of hierarchy or the pastoral." Davis, "Polarities, Hybridities: What Strategies for Decentring?" 21. Some scholars of Canadian history have been particularly interested in recent years in formulating strategies for understanding colonial contact in non-Eurocentric terms, a trend that is well illustrated by the collection of essays *Decentring the Renaissance*, in which Davis' essay appeared. In that volume, and in other recent, similar efforts, the colonial record is re-examined in order to "look not solely into the impact on Canada of people shaped by the European Renaissance and Early Modern periods, but to the impact of Canada on them." Warkentin and Podruchny, "Introduction: Other Land Existing," 7.

35 Clifford, *The Predicament of Culture*, 25. Credit for bringing attention to the relationship between cultures and ethnographic texts that describe them also must go to Clifford Geertz, who lamented that "[a]nthropologists have not always been as aware as they might be of this fact: that although culture exists in the trading post, the hill fort, or the sheep run, anthropology exists in the book, the article, the lecture, the museum display, or, sometimes nowadays, the film. To become aware of it is to realize that the line between mode of representation and substantive content is as undrawable in cultural analysis as it is in painting." Geertz, *The Interpretation of Cultures*, 16.

36 Delâge, *Bitter Feast*, 48.

37 Blackburn, *Harvest of Souls*, 11.

38 For a compelling portrait in this vein of one Iroquoian woman's negotiation of the challenges posed by French colonization and evangelization, see Allan Greer, *Mohawk Saint*.

39 See also Leavelle, *The Catholic Calumet*.

40 Chinard, *L'Amérique et le Rêve Exotique*, 125. Author's translation.

41 Melzer, "The Relation de Voyage: A Forgotten Genre of Seventeenth Century France," 50. See also Melzer, "The French *Relation* and its 'Hidden' Colonial History," 220–40, and Melzer, *Colonizer or Colonized*. For other recent examples in this vein, see Brazeau, *Writing a New France*; Grégoire, "Mais Comment Peut-on Etre Protestant en Nouvelle-France au 17e Siècle?"; True, "Retelling Genesis"; and McShea, *Cultivating Empire Through Print*.

42 On the scale of French travel writing in the seventeenth century, see Pioffet, "Présentation," 1. For examples of scholarly studies of the genre that draw on the Jesuit *Relations,* see Ouellet, *La Relation de Voyage en Amérique*; Pioffet, *La Ten-*

tation de l'Epopée dans les Relations des Jésuites; and Doiron, *L'Art de Voyager*. For a comprehensive study of the relationship between travel and French literature in the seventeenth century, including not only travel accounts but also other genres influenced by travel, see Requemora-Gros, *Voguer vers la Modernité*.

43 Sayre, *Les Sauvages Américains*, 121. See also Campbell, *Wonder and Science*, 45–6. Noted Sayre, "Exploration narrative depended on the veracity and autonomy of the eyewitness narrator, an empiricism that arose in the seventeenth-century philosophy of Francis Bacon and John Locke and the liberal individualism of the bourgeois public sphere. The travel narrator's empiricism is the same as that which supported the truth claims of the early English novel. In contrast to this individualism and innovation, ethnography arose from Europeans' sense of cultural universality and depended on long traditions of intellectual authority." Sayre, *Les Sauvages Américains*, 80.

44 In its fundamentally textual approach to the question of mission ethnography, this book has much in common with other recent interventions by scholars of literature who have, in recent years, turned their attention to the world outside of early modern France's borders, in the hopes of distilling lessons from its engagement with the outside world. To cite only a few examples, the present study is akin to Doris Garraway's *The Libertine Colony*, which casts a literary eye on texts written in the French Caribbean that normally are noted for their ethnographic qualities, and to Michèle Longino's work, which traces "the connections between the staging of cultural 'Other'ness and the construction of French collective identity." Longino, *Orientalism in French Classical Drama*, 9. Like Garraway's book, this study performs a close reading on texts that are mostly known for their ethnographic richness. Approaching ethnographic passages this way rather than attempting to extract data from them results, in the spirit of Longino's work, in an investigation of how public portrayals of the "Other" in seventeenth-century France both mirrored and shaped France's discussion of the implications of the existence and characteristics of distant and poorly known cultures. Stephen Greenblatt, Ellen Welch, Brian Brazeau, Sara Melzer, and others too numerous to name have also recently produced works in this burgeoning field, focusing on how various parts of the world shaped French literature, culture, and society in the seventeenth century.

CHAPTER TWO

1 Axtell, "Babel of Tongues," 15.
2 Axtell, *The Invasion Within*, 82.
3 Blackburn, *Harvest of Souls*, 101.
4 Beaulieu, *Convertir les Fils de Caïn*, 46. Author's translation.

5 Axtell, *The Invasion Within*, 36.

6 For more on the circumstances surrounding the Jesuits' arrival in New France, see Galland, *Pour la Gloire de Dieu et du Roi*, 82–93, as well as Blackburn, *Harvest of Souls*, chapter 2.

7 On the Recollets in New France and Champlain's role, see Galland, *Pour la Gloire de Dieu et du Roi*, 49–93.

8 For a concise treatment of the differences between Jesuit and Recollet methods and goals, see Galland, *Pour la Gloire de Dieu et du Roi*, 301–4. More details can be found in Goddard, "Two Kinds of Conversion ('Medieval' and 'Modern') among the Hurons of New France," and Goddard, "Converting the 'Sauvage.'" The first of these articles compares not only methods and goals, but also the two orders' differing understandings of the phenomenon of conversion. Many scholars have attributed these differences to the Jesuits' cultural relativism and the Recollets' cultural absolutism. In this vein, see Blackburn, *Harvest of Souls*, chapter 3 and conclusion, as well as Trigger, *The Children of Aataentsic*, especially 376–95 and 402–8. Drawing on the earlier example of Jesuit and Franciscan missions in Japan, Takao Abé recently has argued that the Recollets' preference for an assimilationist approach, including the use of the French language, was necessitated by circumstance in the earliest years of contact, and is better interpreted in continuity with the Jesuits' own efforts, rather than in contrast. See Abé, *The Jesuit Mission to New France*, chapter 3.

9 For detailed treatments of this period in New France's history, see Havard and Vidal, *Histoire de l'Amérique Française*, chapters 1 and 2, and Axtell, *The Invasion Within*, especially the section "Black Robes and Gray."

10 Scholars have traced the origin of the New France Jesuits' initial efforts to create closed communities of Christian converts to the Society's earlier missions elsewhere in the world, particularly in Paraguay and Japan. See Jetten, *Enclaves Amérindiennes*; Grégoire, "Les 'réductions' de Nouvelle-France"; and Abé, *The Jesuit Mission to New France*. For more on the utopian nature of Jesuit writing about New France, see True, "'Une Hiérusalem Bénite de Dieu,'" and Goddard, "Canada in Seventeenth-Century Jesuit Thought."

11 JR 7.271–3. "Je crains fort que le vice ne se glisse dans ces nouvelles peuplades. Si néantmoins ceux qui tiendront les resnes du gouvernement en main sont zélez pour la gloire de nostre bon Dieu, suivant les désirs et les intentions de Messieurs les directeurs et associez de la compagnie, il se dressera icy une Hiérusalem bénite de Dieu, composée de citoyens destinez pour le ciel. Il est bien aisé dans un pays nouveau, où les familles arrivent toutes disposées à recevoir les loix qu'on y establira, de bannir les méchantes coustumes de quelques endrois de l'ancienne France, et d'en introduire de meilleures." MNF 3.51.

12 Foucault, "Des Espaces Autres," 752–62, 760.

13 For more on this brief period of British control, see Nicholls, *A Fleeting Empire*.

14 See Galland, *Pour la Gloire de Dieu et du Roi*, chapter 2. For examples of the various reasons that have been cited for the exclusion of the Recollets, see Jouve, *Dictionnaire Biographique des Récollets Missionaires en Nouvelle-France*, xl; Lenhart, "Who Kept the Franciscan Recollets out of Canada?" 281; Jouve, "Le P Joseph Leclerc du Tremblay, Capuchin et les Missions de la Nouvelle France"; and Campeau, "Notre-Dame-Des-Anges," 95–105.

15 Sagard, *Histoire du Canada*, 1001–2. Author's translation. This same claim is made in a Recollet memo pleading their case to colonial authorities. See MNF 3.169.

16 Le Clercq, *First Establishment of the Faith in New France*, 1.321.

17 Lenhart, "Who Kept the Franciscan Recollets out of Canada?" 279. For more on Recollet expectations and preparations for a resumption of missionary activity in New France in the early 1630s, see Galland, *Pour la Gloire de Dieu et du Roi*, 110–13. Galland's analysis suggests that the effort to establish a bishopric in Canada may itself have hindered the Recollets' return, as it created diplomatic tension between Rome and the French Crown.

18 Trigger, *The Children of Aataentsic*, 403.

19 Axtell, *The Invasion Within*, 38; Galland, *Pour la Gloire de Dieu et du Roi*, 100–6.

20 JR 8.15. "Plus la puissance de nos François aura d'éclat en ces contrées et plus aisément feront-ils recevoir leur créance à ces barbares qui se mènent autant et plus par les sens que par la raison." MNF 3.64.

21 *Edict du Roy pour l'establissement de la Compagnie de la Nouvelle France*, 4–5. Author's translation. For more on the formation of the Compagnie de 100 Associés and its role in the early history of the colony, see Havard and Vidal, *Histoire de l'Amérique Française*, 86–92, and Galland, *Pour la Gloire de Dieu et du Roi*, chapter 2.

22 Loyola, *The Constitutions of the Society of Jesus*, 214.

23 Secular clergy "are engaged for the most part in pastoral work and … are not members of a religious institute. They are not bound by a vow of poverty or community life. But their celibacy, in the Latin Church, is under solemn oath and they promise obedience to a bishop as their immediate supervisor under the Pope." Harndon, *Modern Catholic Dictionary*, 496.

24 JR 1.161–3. Thwaites here renders "mal" as "trouble," a translation that is not necessarily incorrect in light of the meaning of the term in the seventeenth century, but that does not capture the moral connotations of the word. For lack of a perfect English synonym, the French term has here been added in brackets. "Le mal est qu'il ne les a peu instruire comme il eust désiré, faute de sçavoir la langue et d'avoir de quoy les entretenir. Car qui leur nourrit l'âme, faut quant et quant qu'il se délibère de sustenter leurs corps." MNF 1.140.

25 The word "mal," according to Furetière's *Dictionnaire Universel*, is "said figuratively in matters of morality of all that is contrary to virtue." Author's translation.

26 JR 4.211. "Chose estrange, il me promist sur l'heure qu'il me donneroit pendant
l'hyver tout le contentement que je pourrais désirer de luy. Or c'est icy où il faut
admirer une particulière providence de Dieu ... ce truchement n'avoit jamais
voulu communiquer à personne la cognoissance qu'il avoit de ce langage, non
pas mesme aux reverends Pères Récolects, qui depuis dix ans n'avoient cessé de
l'en importuner. Et cependant, à la première prière que je luy fis, me promist ce
que je vous ay dit et s'est acquité fidèlement de sa promesse pendant cet hyver."
MNF 2.147–8.

27 Le Jeune's repetition of the point can be found in MNF 2.418. Gabriel Sagard
acknowledged his failure to draw useful linguistic information from Marsolet
in his 1636 *Histoire du Canada*, 358–9. For Lalemant's description of his use of a
second interpreter, see MNF 2.148–9. Campeau speculates plausibly in a footnote
that the second interpreter in question was Etienne Brûlé.

28 JR 4.215. "Il suffit de dire qu'auparavant qu'il fust relevé de ceste maladie, pour
laquelle il n'attendoit que la mort, il nous asseura qu'il estoit entièrement à nostre
dévotion et que, s'il plaisoit à Dieu luy rendre la santé, l'hyver ne ce passeroit
jamais sans nous donner tout contentement; de quoy il s'est fort bien acquitté,
grâces à Dieu. Je me suis peut-estre estendu plus que de raison à racompter cecy;
mais je me plais tant à racompter les traits de la providence particulière de Dieu,
qu'il me semble que tout le monde y doit prendre plaisir. Et de fait, s'il s'en fust
retourné en France ceste année-là, nous estions pour n'avancer guère plus que les
reverends Pères Récolets en 10 ans. Dieu soit loué de tout." MNF 2.149–50.

29 Blackburn, *Harvest of Souls*, 30–1. Codignola, "Few, Uncooperative, and Ill-
Informed?" 176.

30 Rochemonteix, *Les Jésuites et la Nouvelle France au XVII Siècle*, vol 1, 187. Author's
translation. For an excellent account of the Recollets' fruitless efforts to return
to New France, see Galland, *Pour la Gloire de Dieu et du Roi*, 106–24. Lauson's
apparent invitation in 1633 is discussed on pages 108–10.

31 On arguments about the ownership of New France infrastructure, see MNF
3.170. Gabriel Sagard reprinted letters from royal and papal authorities supporting the Recollet cause. Sagard, *Histoire du Canada*. See also MNF 3.163.

32 Lenhart, "Who Kept the Franciscan Recollets out of Canada?" 285. Mendicant
orders like the Franciscans or Dominicans are "congregations of religious who
beg. In fact, they were founded as begging friars, but in the course of time the
emphasis was on poverty and frugality as a personal way of life and on the re-
fusal of fixed revenues for the communities. Even this last proved impracticable
if the members were to study and teach and preach ... They were intended to
be itinerant preachers, able to follow apostolic needs wherever they arose ...

They saw Jesus as living an itinerant life and identifying with the poorest, and they committed themselves in discipleship to do likewise." *The Modern Catholic Encyclopedia*, "Mendicant Order."

33 According to Lenhart, "the friars answered that they had worked side by side with the Jesuits in Canada for five years, and that harmony had always been maintained." "Who Kept the Franciscan Recollets out of Canada?" 285; see also Rochemonteix, *Les Jésuites et la Nouvelle-France au XVIIe Siècle*, vol. 1, 187.

34 Réveillaud, ed., *Histoire Chronologique de la Nouvelle France ou Canada*, 122. Author's translation. The editor of the 1888 first edition of this seventeenth-century text attributed it to the Recollet Sixte Le Tac, but scholars now dispute that attribution. See Galland, *Pour la Gloire de Dieu et du Roi*, 23–4.

35 At least one prominent modern scholar has concluded that the Recollet missionaries, perhaps naturally due to their shorter time in New France, produced fewer converts than the Jesuits. See Axtell, *The Invasion Within*, 20.

36 Réveillaud, ed., *Histoire Chronologique de la Nouvelle France ou Canada*, 122–3. Chrestien Le Clercq similarly emphasized that the Jesuits arrived in New France ten years after the Recollets, and asserted that they found themselves in the shadow of the already established and successful missionaries. Wrote Le Clercq, "One would have thought that the Jesuit Fathers, willing to sacrifice themselves for the country and begin their mission by so large a number of excellent men, would have been received with all possible gratitude, and even cheerfully; but, far from that, there was no one either of the chief men or of the settlers but showed a repugnance." Le Clercq, *First Establishment of the Faith in New France*, vol. 1, 237–8. Le Clercq went on to suggest that the reason for the Jesuits' cold reception was that their right to a presence in the colony was doubted, because they had received only oral permission from the king. Although they were able to stay due to Recollet generosity in providing shelter, their legitimacy was in doubt, the author suggested.

37 MNF 3.169. Author's translation. The document's original purpose is not made explicitly clear, but it appears to be addressed to Cardinal Richelieu, the head of the Compagnie de 100 Associés, which opposed the Recollets' efforts to return to New France. See Campeau, preface to the "Mémoire des Récollets demandant de Retourner au Canada," MNF 3.159. Sagard and Le Clercq made the same claim in their respective books.

38 For just one example of a modern repetition of the claim, see Jouve, "Le P Joseph," 133. Campeau refutes the claim in the introduction to MNF volume 2, and Galland concludes that the Jesuits were not invited by the Recollets, but rather invited themselves by exploiting the political opportunity afforded by Richelieu's efforts to form the Compagnie de 100 Associés. See Galland, *Pour la Gloire de Dieu et du Roi*, 85–7.

39 MNF 3.165. Author's translation.

40 Sagard, *Histoire du Canada*, 866.

41 On the return of the Recollets to New France, see Galland, *Pour la Gloire de Dieu et du Roi*, 139–75.

42 Réveillaud, ed., *Histoire Chronologique de la Nouvelle France*, 6. Author's translation.

43 Wrote Réveillaud, "He writes his book heated with the fire that smolders in his heart, and sometimes – when he touches on the risky subject of the Jesuits and their secret plot to supplant the Recollets – boiling with lava, quaking with the rumbling of poorly contained anger. He will tell his superior general to whom his book is first submitted, he will tell his brother Recollets in France, he will make the public know, for posterity, the services that the Recollets wanted to render in Canada and how they were prevented from doing so by the landmines that the Jesuits buried and exploded beneath their feet. He will tell … but he has already said too much. He spoke too loudly and too clearly; his book would cause a scandal." Réveillaud, ed., *Histoire Chronologique de la Nouvelle France*, ii–iii. Author's translation.

44 Rigault and Ouellet, "Relations des Jésuites," 640.

45 Wrote Rochemonteix, "the Jesuits of Québec sent them the desire that they had to see them again." Rochemonteix, *Les Jésuites et la Nouvelle-France au XVIIe Siècle d'Après Beaucoup de Documents Inédits*, 187. Author's translation.

46 Le Clercq, *First Establishment of the Faith in New France*, vol. 1, 344.

47 See MNF 2.295 and 3.514. The anonymous Recollet author of the *Histoire Chronologique de la Nouvelle France* claimed that Lalemant only wrote this letter "to better hide his game." Réveillaud, ed., *Histoire Chronologique de la Nouvelle France ou Canada*, 169–70. Author's translation.

48 The 16,000 figure comes from Axtell, *The Invasion Within*, 122. The results of the first five years of the mission are tallied in Beaulieu, *Convertir les Fils de Caïn*, 98–101.

49 Leahey, "Comment Peut un Muet Prescher l'Evangile?" 111.

50 JR 8.253–5. "Un sauvage luy répart: 'Va-t'en, on ne t'entend pas.' C'est une réponse que nous font parfois les sauvages, quand on les presse de faire une chose qui ne leur agrée pas. Il est vrai que nous ne parlons encore qu'en bégayant, mais néantmoins, quand nous leur disons quelque chose conforme à leurs désirs, jamais ils ne nous font ces reproches." MNF 3.201.

51 As Gray noted, citing the Jesuit *Relations*, "Perhaps because they perceived the language barrier as a defense against European cultural intrusion, Indian teachers proved impatient and uninterested. They would provide nothing 'unless their stomachs were first liberally crammed,' and 'being very impatient of even a short delay, would often be distracted and drawn away from one by earnest inquiry about any subject.'" Gray, *New World Babel*, 33–5.

52 JR 9.89–91. "S'il ne falloit que proposer en bégayant quelques véritez pour con-
    vaincre les sauvages plainement, ce seroit bientost fait; mais il faut intérroger et
    répondre, satisfaire aux demandes, obvier aux objections, disposer son auditeur.
    Bref, nos véritez, qui sont plus nouvelles à ces barbares que ne seroient les équa-
    tions de l'algèbre à qui ne pourrait compter jusqu'à dix, leur devroient presque
    faire oublier leur langue, quand nous en servons pour les leur expliquer, tant s'en
    faut que nous ayons peu sitost la nous rendre familière en de si hauts mystères.
    Et puis on demande d'où vient qu'on ait si peu avancé en la conversion de ces
    barbares. Les grandes affaires ne se font que dans un grand temps pour l'ordi-
    naire." MNF 3.236–7. Biard, writing before regular publication of the *Relations*
    began, had also cited deficient language skills as a reason for slow progress in
    converting the Micmacs with whom he lived. See Leahey, "Comment Peut un
    Muet Prescher l'Evangile?" 111.
53 According to Campeau, this dictionary was composed by priests Charles Lale-
    mant and Enémond Massé during their stint in New France from 1625 to 1629.
    MNF 2.408 (footnote).
54 JR 8.133. "Pour moy qui y fais leçon à nos François, si Dieu ne m'assiste extra-
    ordinairement, encor me faudra-t-il aller longtemps à l'escole des sauvages, telle
    est la fécondité de leur langue." MNF 3.108.
55 For much more on how France's educational ideal in the seventeenth century
    alienated students, and for a sustained argument that efforts to assimilate Amer-
    indians in New France followed a similar pattern, see Melzer, *Colonizer and
    Colonized*, chapter 6. A more general overview of Jesuit education can be found
    in Dainville, *L'Education des Jésuites*, and Hanzeli, *Missionary Linguistics in New
    France*, 33.
56 For a portrait of Pastedechouan's remarkable life, see Anderson, *The Betrayal of
    Faith*.
57 JR 5.111–13. The portion of this quote in brackets appears in Thwaites' translation
    as "so changeable was my master's way of teaching." It has been altered here to
    preserve the idea that the master's "variation" was due to his lack of familiar-
    ity with teaching. "Je me mets à travailler sans cesse. Je fay des conjugaisons,
    déclinaisons, quelque petite syntaxe, un dictionnaire, avec une peine incroyable;
    car il me falloit quelquefois demander vingt questions pour avoir la cognoissance
    d'un mot, tant mon maistre, peu duit à enseigner, variot. O que je suis obligé à
    ceux qui m'envoièrent l'an passé du pétum. Les sauvages l'aiment déréglément.
    A toutes les difficultez que je rencontrois, j'en donnois un bout à mon maistre,
    pour le rendre plus attentif." MNF 2.418.
58 As Edward G. Gray has pointed out, it seems that the missionaries truly were in
    a position of weakness in relation to Amerindian potential converts: "During the
    initial decades of the Jesuit mission, missionaries commonly lived within native
    communities, at great distances from European settlements, and almost entirely

at the mercy of the Indian flock for the basics of life. They were, in a certain sense, captives. Food, protection, shelter – for all these things they depended on the goodwill of the Indians." Gray, *New World Babel*, 31.

59 JR 9.89. "En effect, il faut parler pour estre entendu; c'est ce que nous ne pouvons encore faire qu'en enfans." MNF 3.236.

60 JR 12.173. "O quelle différence entre un homme qui parle et un enfant qui bégaie! Non, je ne croi pas que si on avoit la perfection de la langue, qu'on n'obtînt beaucoup sur ces peuples." MNF 3.654.

61 JR 13.11. "Nous tirons beaucoup d'avantage de ce petit exercice pour profiter en la langue; outre qu'enseignans les enfans, nous prenions l'occasion d'expliquer aux pères et aux mères quelques-uns de nos mystères, en quoy pour l'ordinaire nous usions de prévoyance. Au reste, les discours n'estoient pas bien longs. Il faut apprendre à mettre un pied devant l'autre avant que de marcher. Nous estions bien consolez de voir qu'on nous entendît et qu'un sauvage prist quelquefois la parole et répétast ce que nous avions dict." MNF 3.686.

62 Gray, *New World Babel*, 35.

63 Drawing on the work of François Mélançon, Galland makes a similar point about the timing of Sagard's dictionary and its role in the Recollets' ongoing effort to resume work in New France. See Galland, *Pour la Gloire de Dieu et du Roi*, 106–7.

64 Sagard, *Le Grand Voyage du Pays des Hurons*, 344. Author's translation. The standard translation of Sagard's *Grand Voyage*, published by the Champlain Society in 1939, does not include the dictionary, nor Sagard's introduction thereto.

65 Sagard, *Histoire du Canada*, 358–9. Author's translation.

66 Ibid., 363. Author's translation.

67 Axtell, *The Invasion Within*, 91.

68 Blackburn, *Harvest of Souls*, 123.

69 Axtell, *The Invasion Within*, 91.

70 Blackburn, *Harvest of Souls*, 123. See also Ouellet, "Pour une Poétique," 19–20.

71 Hanzeli, *Missionary Linguistics in New France*, 45.

72 Beaulieu, *Convertir les Fils de Cain*, 61, 65. Author's translation.

73 JR 14.125. "Premièrement, nous faisons des courses pour aller attaquer l'ennemy sur ses terres par ses propres armes, c'est-à-dire par la cognoissance des langues montagnèse, algonquine et hurone." MNF 4.77.

74 Hanzeli, *Missionary Linguistics in New France*, 50–1.

75 See, for example, O'Malley, *The First Jesuits*, 34.

76 JR 16.241. "car autant de barbares qui vous viennent voir, ce sont autant de maistres et d'escoliers qui nous vièrent trouver et vous délivrent de la peine de les aller chercher. Maistres, dis-je, pour l'usage de la langue; escoliers pour les affaires de leur salut et du christianisme." MNF 4.361. For another, similar example, see MNF 7.153.

CHAPTER THREE

1 JR 5.169. "Un de nos François qui a demeuré avec eux cet hyver passé nous a dit qu'il n'avoit mangé en deux jours qu'un petit bout de chandelle qu'il avoit porté par mesgarde dans sa pochette. Voilà peut-estre mon traitement pour l'hyver prochain. Car si je veux sçavoir la langue, il faut de nécessité suivre les sauvages. Je crains néantmoins que nostre famille accreue ne me retienne cette année, mais il y faut aller tost ou tard. J'y voudrais dèsjà estre, tant j'ay de mal au Coeur de voir ces pauvres âmes errantes sans aucun secours, faute de les entendre. On ne peut mourir qu'une fois, le plus tost n'est pas tousjours le pire." MNF 2.439.

2 MNF 2.649.

3 Many of these manuscripts are housed in the Fonds d'Archives du Séminaire de Québec at the Musée de la Civilisation. Others are scattered in various archives. For a list of known manuscripts and their locations, see Hanzeli, *Missionary Linguistics in New France*, appendix D.

4 Steckley, *Words of the Huron*, xiii.

5 Hanzeli, *Missionary Linguistics in New France*, 51, 100–1.

6 JR 14.11. "autant de pierres précieuses." MNF 3.768. Malinowski, *Argonauts of the Western Pacific*, 8, 14.

7 For examples of linguistic studies that rely on data collected by the Jesuits in seventeenth-century New France, see Hanzeli, *Missionary Linguistics in New France*; Steckley, *De Religione* and *Words of the Huron*; and Lagarde, *Le Verbe Huron*.

8 JR 5.115. "d'une mesme oeconomie." MNF 2.419.

9 The group that is today known to scholars as the Laurentian Iroquois no longer inhabited the St. Lawrence River valley by the time the Jesuits and their contemporaries arrived in the seventeenth century, having given way at some point in the intervening century to Algonquian groups. Parmenter, *The Edge of the Woods*, 14. Linguistic and archaeological evidence indicates that they were related to but distinct from other Iroquoian groups in northeastern North America. Snow, *The Iroquois*, 49. The fate of the Laurentians has long been a mystery, but as Jon Parmenter recently observed, "evidence suggests that the Laurentian Iroquois were gradually dispersed by multiple adversaries rather than decimated in a one-time event traceable to a specific perpetrator." Parmenter, *The Edge of the Woods*, 15. For more on contact between the French and the Laurentian Iroquois and the dispersal of the latter, see pages 3–15 of Parmenter's book, as well as Trigger, *The Children of Aataentsic*, 177–83.

10 Cartier, *Relations*, 110–11. Author's translation.

11 Hanzeli, *Missionary Linguistics in New France*, 17.

12 Gabriel Sagard, *Le Grand Voyage du Pays des Hurons*, 344. Author's translation. On Sagard's dictionary, see Hanzeli, *Missionary Linguistics in New France*, 55–6,

and Chafe, "The Earliest European Encounters with Iroquoian Languages," 255–8.

13 Axtell, "Babel of Tongues," 31.

14 JR 5.113–15. "J'ay remarqué, dans l'estude de leur langue, qu'il y a un certain barragoin entre les François et les sauvages, qui n'est ny françois ny sauvage; et cependant, quand les François s'en servent, ils pensent parler sauvage, et les sauvages en l'usurpant croyent parler bon françois." MNF 2.419.

15 For more on these efforts, see Hanzeli, *Missionary Linguistics in New France*, 48–50. On gestures, see Gray, *New World Babel*, 37. On the use of images to convey Christianity in seventeenth-century New France, see Gagnon, *La Conversion par l'Image*.

16 MNF 3.50, JR 7.267. MNF 3.108, JR 8.131.

17 This chapter builds on a tradition of reading passages in the *Relations* that describe Amerindian languages and Jesuits' attempts to learn them with an eye to what they tell us about the colonial encounter and the questions posed by it. In this vein, Peter Dorsey has argued that the admiration that Jesuits expressed in the *Relations* for the languages they encountered was the motivation for their accommodation of certain elements of Amerindian religion, and that the link the missionaries drew between language and theology made them rigorous and culturally sensitive students of Amerindian life. See his article "Going to School with Savages." Margaret Leahey has examined the impact of the Jesuits' linguistic project on their published texts. See her articles "'Comment Peut un Muet Prescher l'Evangile?'" and "Iconic Discourse." See also Leahey's 1991 PhD dissertation *To Hear with My Eyes*. Historian Edward G. Gray's book *New World Babel* draws on the Jesuit *Relations*, among other sources, in tracing the emergence of the notion that linguistic differences could be attributed to differences in human character, and the implications of that idea for nation formation. This chapter shares the interest of these and other scholars in what passages in the *Relations* about Amerindian languages have to tell us aside from linguistic data. For a general survey of efforts to learn Huron in New France, see Schreyer, "Take Your Pen and Write."

18 As Hanzeli remarked, "The little we have seen published was too fragmentary to stimulate anyone, even in a linguistically more sophisticated age, to use these materials for comparative or general linguistic studies." Hanzeli, *Missionary Linguistics in New France*, 63.

19 Ibid., 101.

20 JR 10.55. "Finalement, nous nous occupasmes à reformer, ou plustost à ranger une grammaire. Je crains qu'il nous faille faire souvent de semblables réformes, car tous les jours nous allons descouvrans de nouveaux secrets en ceste science, ce qui nous empesche d'envoyer rien à imprimer pour le présent. Nous en sçavons,

grâces à Dieu, tantost suffisament, tant pour entendre que pour estre entendus, mais non encore pour mettre au jour." MNF 3.323. Brébeuf, who died in 1649, apparently did not manage to complete his grammar, nor his dictionary. See Chafe, "The Earliest European Encounters with Iroquoian Languages," 258.

21 Wrote Edward Gray, "Recollets and Jesuits produced grammars, dictionaries, prayer books, and catechisms in various indigenous languages. But, significantly, they were never able to do this on a large scale. Although Jesuits had asked for a printing press in 1665, the request was never granted." Gray, *New World Babel*, 33.

22 As Hanzeli has rightly observed, the Jesuits "were persuaded that their language learning was not inspired by a thirst for knowledge, but was rather a means of co-operating in the divine plan of salvation." Hanzeli, *Missionary Linguistics in New France*, 45.

23 JR 5.191."'Fides ex auditu'; la foy entre par l'aureille. Comment peut un muet prescher l'évangile?" MNF 2.447.

24 For a brief discussion of the importance and difficulty of language-learning and its place in the larger Jesuit religious project, see Grégoire, "'Pensez-Vous Venir à Bout de Renverser le Pays?'" See also Blackburn, *Harvest of Souls*, 88–9.

25 JR 7.275. The portion of this sentence in brackets apprears in Thwaites' original translation as "could accomplish much." It has here been altered to more closely follow the French original, and to preserve the idea that power, and not merely accomplishment, was the goal. "Quand vous leur parlez de nos véritez, ils vous écoutent paisiblement; mais au lieu de vous interroger sur ce sujet, ils se jettent incontinent sur les moyens de trouver de quoy vivre, monstrans leur estomach tousjours vuide et tousjours affamé. Que si on sçavoit haranguer comme eux et qu'on se trouvast en leurs assemblées, je croy qu'on y seroit bien puissant." MNF 3.52–3.

26 As Blackburn has noted, "In emulating these speech styles, the Jesuits appropriated the discursive mechanisms associated with authority in Aboriginal cultures in the Northcast [sic], where leaders cultivated and were expected to display considerable oratorical skills. The Jesuits did this in an effort to represent themselves as people who were also worthy of being heard." Blackburn, *Harvest of Souls*, 88–9. Normand Doiron has argued that the Jesuits projected classical ideals of eloquence on their would-be converts. See his articles "Génèse de l'Eloquence Sauvage" and "Rhétorique Jésuite de l'Eloquence Sauvage."

27 JR 5.195. "Secondement, qui sçauroit parfaitement leur langue, il seroit tout puissant parmy eux, ayant tant soit peu d'éloquence. Il n'y a lieu au monde où la rhétorique soit plus puissante qu'en Canadas. Et cependant, elle n'a point d'autre habit que celuy que la nature luy a baillé. Elle est toute nue et toute simple; et cependant, elle gouverne tous ces peuples. Car leur capitaine n'est esleu que pour sa langue et il est autant bien obéy qu'il l'a bien pendue. Il n'ont point d'autres

loix que sa parole." MNF 2.448. Le Jeune used a similar formulation, insisting on the power of Amerindian languages, in his very first *Relation*. See MNF 3.319.

28 JR 18.207. "Il n'y a coeur si dur que la Parole de Dieu n'amolisse à la longue. Un esprit rude et superbe me disoit, il y a quelque temps: 'Je me suis mocqué cent fois des discours du Père de Quen. J'ay résisté au Père Buteux, le voulant empescher de nous instruire. Pour toy, je ne te pouvais supporter. Je prenois plaisir de te quereller et quand je l'avois fait, je l'allois racompter par les cabanes comme une grande prouesse. Mais maintenant, vos paroles me semblent bonnes. Elles descendent petit à petit dans mon cœur. Je croy que mes oreilles se feront à les écouter." MNF 4.610.

29 Dorsey, "Going to School with Savages," 404, 416.

30 John 1:1–14. For examples of characterization of God as an "author" in the Bible and in the *Relations*, see Acts 3:15 and MNF 2.564, 3.574, and 7.421.

31 According to Jesuit scholar Walter J. Ong, "As a human being, with his human name, Jesus Christ is thus the Word whereby man addresses God the Father: *per Ipsum et cum Ipso et in Ipso*, the church prays, 'Through him and with him and in him.'" Ong, *The Presence of the Word*, 13.

32 For examples, see MNF 4.610, 5.708, 6.600, 6.649, and 7.329.

33 Dorsey, "Going to School with Savages," 404–5, 410.

34 Gen 11:6–7.

35 As Gray wrote on the subject, "Medieval and Renaissance writers generally assumed that in felling the Tower of Babel, God transformed the world from a place unified by a single language to one divided into seventy-two distinct mother tongues, scattered across the globe and correlating with seventy-two distinct nations. This deep and lasting reprimand brought with it the burden of reunifying humanity in the community of God through the universal language of prayer – an imperative that ... was very much central to the early modern Christian missionary impulse." Gray further observes that "language change is generally regarded as indicative of the inherent tension between the immutable process of historical adaptation and the social need to maintain some degree of linguistic familiarity ... It was, however, with the opposite conviction – that languages could be understood as corrupted descendents of a single, perfect, God-given tongue – that Christian missionaries came to the New World. And it was the struggle to reconcile that conviction with vexing barriers to oral and written communication that occupied those missionaries almost without end." Gray, *New World Babel*, 21–7. Although perhaps affected by what Gray called the "corrosive effects of historical change," Amerindian languages were, as far as the New France Jesuits were concerned, complex and highly ordered tongues to be admired, not disdained as degenerated forms of a pre-Babel universal language. Although New France Jesuits were generally consistent in their appreciation

of Amerindian languages as divine media, it is worth noting that competing ideas sometimes were expressed by Jesuits elsewhere about what it meant to speak in the languages of unconverted peoples. Julien Maunoir, a Jesuit missionary in Brittany in the seventeenth century, hesitated to learn the dialect of his would-be converts, fearing that doing so would corrupt his own soul, at least according to his biographer, the Jesuit Antoine Boschet. For more on the fear of harming themselves by learning too much about the languages and cultures of the unconverted that some Frenchmen, including Jesuits, expressed in the seventeenth century, see Melzer, *Colonizer or Colonized*, 115–18, and Boschet, *Le parfait missionnaire*.

36 Elliott, *The Old World and the New*, 8. As Paul Hazard wrote in his classic study of early modern European thought, "It is perfectly correct to say that all the fundamental concepts, such as Property, Freedom, Justice and so on, were brought under discussion again as a result of the conditions in which they were seen to operate in far off countries." Hazard, *The European Mind*, 10.

37 See, for example, Kupperman, ed., *America in European Consciousness*, and Arciniegas, *America in Europe: A History of the New World in Reverse*.

38 It must be admitted that this argument glosses over the not insignificant doctrinal and political differences that existed within Europe, especially during the seventeenth century after decades of religious strife in France. One could no doubt fruitfully examine the differences between Protestant and Catholic reactions to Amerindian cultures, or the differences across political boundaries. And yet, it is surely also true that the differences between religious and political factions in Europe were trivial in comparison to the differences between European and Amerindian cultures. Whether Catholic or Protestant, Europeans shared a common scripture and basic understanding of the origin of the world and man's place in it. Although it is somewhat simplistic to talk about the intellectual and political concerns of Christian Europe, it is nonetheless true that the example of the Amerindian Other would have been surprising and troubling to Europeans of all stripes. For more on this, see Greenblatt, *Marvelous Possessions*, 8–9.

39 Jaenen, "The Image of New France," 62. For more on the Catholic Church's position on the possibility of converting Amerindians, see Codignola, "The Holy See and the Conversion of the Indians in French and British North America, 1486–1760."

40 Deslandres, *Croire et Faire Croire*, 20. Author's translation.

41 JR 5.115–17. "Je ne croy pas avoir ouy parler d'aucune langue qui procédast de mesme façon que celle-cy. Le Père Brébeuf m'asseure que celle des Hurons est d'une mesme oeconomie. Qu'on les appelle barbares tant qu'on voudra, leur langue est fort réglée. Je n'y suis pas encore grand maistre. J'en parleray quelque jour avec plus d'asseurance. Si je n'avois peur d'estre trop long, je mettrois icy une

grande et tout à fait estrange difference entre les langues d'Europe et celles-cy."
MNF 2.419–20.

42 JR 29.225–7. "Leurs compositions sont admirables et je puis dire que quand il n'y auroit point d'autre argument pour monstrer qu'il y a un Dieu que l'oeconomie des langues sauvages, cela suffiroit pour nous convaincre. Car il n'y a prudence ny industrie humaine qui puisse rassembler tant d'hommes pour leur faire tenir l'ordre qu'ils gardent dans leurs langues toutes différentes de celle d'Europe. C'est Dieu seul qui en maintient la conduite." MNF 6.631.

43 JR 10.117–23; MNF 3.343–5.

44 JR 5.115. "Je diray en passant que cette langue est fort pauvre et fort riche. Elle est pauvre, pour autant que n'ayans point de cognoissance de mille et mille choses qui sont en l'Europe, ils n'ont point de noms pour les signifier. Elle est riche, pource qu'ès choses dont ils ont cognoissance, elle est foeconde et grandement nombreuse." MNF 2.419.

45 JR 10.119. Thwaites translated "riche" as "copious." The translation has been here altered to improve its accuracy. "Cela est riche. Voicy qui ne l'est guères." MNF 3.343.

46 JR 7.21–3. "Tournons maintenant la médaille et faisons voir que cette langue regorge de richesses. Premièrement, je trouve une infinité de noms propres parmy eux, que je ne puis expliquer en nostre françois que par circumlocutions. Secondement, ils ont des verbes que je nomme absolus, dont ny les Grecs, ny les Latins, ny nous, ny les langues d'Europe dont je ne me suis enquis, n'ont rien de semblable. Par exemple, ce verbe 'nimitison' signifie absolument je mange, sans dire quoy. Car si vous déterminez la chose que vous mangez, il se faut servir d'un autre verbe. Tiercement, ils ont des verbes différents pour signifier l'action envers une chose animée et envers une chose inanimée, encore bien qu'ils conjoignent avec les choses animées quelques nombres des choses sans âme, comme le pétun, les pommes, etc. Donnons des exemples. Je vois un homme, 'niouapamaniriniou' je vois une pierre, 'niouabatenassini.' En grec, en latin et en françois, c'est un mesme verbe pour dire: je vois un homme, une pierre et toute autre chose." MNF 2.645–6.

47 It seems that Le Jeune was not entirely correct in his assertion that Montagnais required different verbs depending on the object described by the speaker. As Hanzeli points out, the verbs the priest cites are "different verbs inasmuch as they represent different verb stems formed on the same verb root. The differences are created by gender markers and instrumental particles which are regularly added to the typical Algonquian verb root." Hanzeli, *Missionary Linguistics in New France*, 57.

48 JR 10.121. "Quant aux verbes, ce qui est de plus remarquable en leur langue est: 1. qu'ils en ont d'autres pour signifier les choses animées et d'autres pour celles

qui sont sans vie; 2. qu'ils varient leur temps en autant de façons que les Grecs."
MNF 3.344.

49 The Jesuits were not alone in making the assumption that unfamiliar languages
could be understood in terms of Old World languages: "Most seventeenth century language studies assume implicitly or explicitly the existence of a single
ideal grammar which reflected or was based on logical categories, the purest
manifestation of which was thought to be Latin." Hanzeli, *Missionary Linguistics
in New France*, 33.

50 JR 7.33. "la difficulté de ceste langue, qui n'est pas petite, comme on peut conjec-
turer de ce que j'ay dit, n'a pas esté un petit obstacle pour empescher une pauvre
mémoire comme la mienne d'aller bien loing." MNF 2.650.

51 Sagard, *Le Grand Voyage*, 347. Author's translation.

52 As Gray has pointed out, the difficulties that the Jesuits encountered cannot
be attributed solely to the Amerindian languages themselves: "While the Jesuits were inventive in their strategies for affecting souls, as linguists they actually tended to be rather rigid in their assumptions. When they complained
that native peoples lacked the words needed to convey Christian abstractions,
they were as much asserting seeming indigenous linguistic failures as they were
registering a profound intellectual dilemma of their own. Aside from the simple
fact that Jesuits were often dependent on Indians for both sustenance and translation, their intensive training in classical language and literature was almost
useless in North America. Indeed, little that they brought from Europe prepared
them to learn Native American languages." Gray, *New World Babel*, 41.

53 JR 7.21. "Tous les mots de piété, de dévotion, de vertu, tous les termes dont
on se sert pour expliquer les biens de l'autre vie, le langage des theólogiens, des
philosophes, des mathématiciens, des médecins, en un mot de tous les hommes
doctes, toutes les paroles qui concernent la police et le gouvernement d'une
ville, d'une province, d'un empire, tout ce qui touche la justice, la récompense
et le chastiment, les noms d'une infinité d'arts qui sont en nostre Europe, d'une
infinite de fleurs, d'arbres et de fruits, d'une infinité d'animaux, de mille et mille
inventions, de mille beautez et de mille richesses, tout cela ne se trouve point
dans la pensée, ny dans la bouche des sauvages, n'ayant ny vraye religion, ny connoissance des vertus, ny police, ny gouvernement, ny royaume, ny république,
ny sciences, ny rien de tout ce que je viens de dire. Et par consequent, toutes les
paroles, tous les termes, tous les mots et tous les noms qui touchent ce monde
de biens et de grandeurs doivent être défalquez de leur dictionnaire. Voilà une
grande disette." MNF 2.645.

54 JR 20.71. "Non seulement les mots leur manquent pour exprimer la saincteté
de nos mystères, mais mesme les paraboles et les discours plus familiers de Jésus
Christ leur sont inexplicables. Ils ne sçavent ce que c'est que sel, levain, chasteau,

perle, prison, grain de moutarde, tonneaux de vin, lampe, chandelier, flambeau. Ils n'ont aucune idée des royaumes, des roys et de leur majesté, non pas mesme de pasteurs, de troupeaux et de bergerie. En un mot, l'ignorance qu'ils ont des choses de la terre semble leur fermer le chemin du ciel." MNF 4.736–7.

55 For more examples and a discussion of the perceived deficiency of Amerindian languages, see Gray, *New World Babel*, 35–6.

56 JR 10.119–21. "Un nom relatif parmy eux enveloppe tousjours la signification d'une des trois personnes du pronom possessif, si bien qu'ils ne peuvent dire simplement: père, fils, maistre, valet, mais sont contraincts de dire l'un des trois: mon père, ton père, son père; quoy que j'aye traduit cy-devant en une oraison un de leurs noms par celuy du père, pour plus grande facilié. Suivant cela, nous nous trouvons empeschez de leur faire dire proprement en leur langue 'au nom du Père et du Fils et du Sainct-Esprit.' Jugeriez-vous à propos, en attendant mieux, de substituer au lieu: 'au nom de nostre Père et de son Fils et de leur Sainct-Esprit'? Certes, il semble que les trois personnes de la très saincte Trinité seroient suffisamment exprimées en ceste façon … Oserions-nous en user ainsi, jusqu'à ce que la langue huronne soit enrichie, ou l'esprit des Hurons ouvert à d'autres langues? Nous ne ferons rien sans conseil." MNF 3.343–4.

57 Torrance, *The Trinitarian Faith*, 10.

58 Gray, *New World Babel*, 36.

59 Indeed, it appears that Jesuits used a different translation later in the seventeenth century. In a text explaining the nature of Christianity that was composed in Huron in the late 1660s or 1670s, a different rendering is suggested, as John Steckley pointed out in the introduction to his translation of the text. "The Father is sa,[e]n, 'he has them (indefinite) as children'; the Son is honaen 'they (masculine plural) have him as child'; and the Holy Ghost is hoki data hoatato,eti 'he is a spirit, the very, he is the true one.'" This alternate translation is no less problematic than the first, as it similarly suggests a hierarchical relationship between the three figures and does not seem to adequately capture their unity. See Steckley, *De Religione*, 26. As Carole Blackburn has noted, "It is doubtful that this accommodation would have been either acceptable to the Jesuits' supporters or defensible if subjected to the scrutiny of their critics." Blackburn, *Harvest of Souls*, 7.

60 Lafitau, *Customs of the American Indians*, 2.264. For more on Lafitau's stint as a missionary and his text see Fenton, "Lafitau, Joseph-François."

61 JR 5.187–9. Thwaites translated the French word "bien" as "perfectly." It has here been corrected in brackets to more closely follow the French. "Je leur explique grossièrement le mystère de la saincte Trinité et de l'Incarnation. Et à tous bouts de champ je leur demande si je dis bien, s'ils entendent bien. Ils me respondent tous: 'Eoco, eoco, ninisitoutenan'; ouy, ouy, nous entendons. Je les

interroge par après s'il y a plusieurs Dieux et laquelle des trois personnes s'est fait homme. Je forge des mots approchans de leur langue, que je leur fais entendre. Nous commençons le catéchisme par ceste prière, après avoir fait le signe de la croix: 'Noukhimami Iesus, iagoua khistinohimaonitou khikhitouinacaié khiteritamouin. Ca cataouachichien Maria ouccaonia Iesu, ca cataouachichien Iospeh aiamihitouinan'; Mon Seigneur ou capitaine Jésus; enseignez-moy vos paroles et vostre volonté, O bonne Marie, mère de Dieu, ô bon Joseph, priez pour nous." MNF 2.445–6.

62 JR 12.7. "Ce n'est pas que le diable se communique à eux si sensiblement qu'il fait aux sorciers et aux magiciens d'Europe, mais nous n'avons point d'autre nom pour leur donner, veu mesmes qu'ils font quelques actions de vrays sorciers, comme de se faire mourir les uns les autres par sorts ou désirs et imprécations, par provocations du manitou, par des poisons qu'ils composent." MNF 3.600.

63 JR 7.21–3. "je trouve une infinité de noms propres parmy eux, que je ne puis expliquer en nostre françois que par circumlocutions." MNF 2.645.

64 JR 5.211. "Voilà à peu près la response de ce sauvage." MNF 2.455; JR 15.43. Thwaites rendered "quasi" as "about." "Nearly" has here been substituted for accuracy. "L'un d'eux parla quasi en ces termes." MNF 4.144; JR 16.117. "Il nous tint ces discours en meilleurs termes en sa langue que je ne les rapporte en la nostre." MNF 4.314; JR 22.149. "A cette harangue, plus éloquente en algonquin que je ne l'ay couchée en françois, Paul Atondo répartit encore plus élégamment en son langage." MNF 5.420.

65 Cf. Gray, *New World Babel*, 35: "Book learning, the knowledge of grammar and vocabulary, the use of Latin and Greek – all could assist in the learning of European languages. But missionaries found no such aids in America. The only means of acquiring these languages was use and rote memorization under the tutelage of the Indians themselves."

66 JR 5.113. "Il m'a fallu, avant que de sçavoir une langue, faire des livres pour l'apprendre; et quoy que je ne les tienne pas si corrects, si est-ce que maintenant, de l'heure que je parle, quand je compose quelque chose, je me fay bien entendre aux sauvages. Le tout gist à composer souvent, à apprendre quantité de mots, à me faire à leur accent, et mes occupations ne me le permettent pas. Je pensois m'en aller, cet hyver prochain, avec eux dans les bois; mais je prévoy qu'il me sera impossible, líe comme je suis. Si mon maistre ne m'eust pas quitté, dans peu de mois, j'aurois bien avancé." MNF 2.418.

67 Farrell, *Ratio Studiorum*, 15; Loyola, *Constitutions*, 191.

68 Hanzeli, *Missionary Linguistics in New France*, 43.

69 Ibid., 22–3.

70 JR 7.57. "En quatriesme lieu, se voulant récréer à mes dépens, il me faisoit par fois escrire en sa langue des choses sales, m'assurant qu'il n'y avoit rien de mauvais,

puis il me faisoit prononcer ces impudences, que je n'entendois pas, devant les sauvages." MNF 2.660.

71 JR 8.131–3. "Premièrement, nous nous sommes employez en l'estude de la langue, qui à cause de la diversité de ses mots composez est quasi infinie. On ne peut néantmoins rien faire sans cet estude. Tous les François qui sont icy s'y sont ardemment portez, ramenant l'ancien usage d'escrire sur des escorces de bouleau, faute du papier." MNF 3.108.

72 JR 5.111–13. "J'en escrivay quelques mots l'an passé, que je qualifiois de mots de sauvages, le pensant ainsi. Par exemple, le mot d''Ania', dont j'ai encore fait mention cy-dessus, est un mot barbare. Les sauvages s'en servent à tout bout de champ, parlant aux François, et les François parlant aux sauvages; et tous s'en servent pour dire: mon frère; mais en vrai sauvage de Montagnaits: 'Nichtais', c'est-à-dire mon frère aisné, 'Nichim', mon cadet. Le mot de 'sagamo' ne s'usurpe icy que par quelques-uns, pour dire capitaine. Le vray mot, c'est 'oukhimau'. Je croy que ce mot de 'sagamo' vient de l'Acadie. Il y en a quantité d'autres semblables. Au commencement qu'on entre en un pays, on escrit plusieurs choses, les pensant vrayes sur le rapport d'autruy. Le temps découvre la vérité." MNF 2.419.

73 MNF 2.649, JR 7.29–31, and MNF 3.343, JR 10.117.

74 According to Mignolo, "*Language* becomes then an object, with a grammar and vocabulary that you have and regulate. It also becomes the point of reference to measure and rank *languaging practices* that do not comply with the regulatory force of *language*." Delgado and Romero, "Local Histories and Global Designs: An Interview with Walter Mignolo," 16–17.

75 The last known speaker of the language died in Oklahoma in the mid-twentieth century. Steckley, *Words of the Huron*, xii.

76 Abley, "No One Alive Speaks Huron Fluently."

CHAPTER FOUR

1 Jaenen, "The Image of New France," 169. See also Jaenen, *Friend and Foe*, 120–52.

2 The account summarized here can be found in MNF 3.694–708.

3 JR 13.37–9. "Car c'est l'ordinaire que, lorsque quelque personne notable a perdu en guerre quelqu'un de ses parens, on luy fasse présent de quelque captif pris sur les ennemis, pour essuyer ses larmes et appaiser une partie de ses regrets." MNF 3.695.

4 Trigger, *The Children of Aataentsic*, 72; Brandão, *Your Fyre Shall Burn No More*, 41. The precise nature and motivation for Iroquoian warfare and associated capture and torture of enemies in the seventeenth century – commonly known as the "Beaver Wars" – is a broad debate that is beyond the scope of this chapter.

Some, such as anthropologist Roland Viau (*Enfants du Néant et Mangeurs des Ames*) and Daniel Richter (*The Ordeal of the Longhouse*), have argued that revenge against enemies was the primary purpose of Iroquoian warfare both before and after contact with Europeans. Others, such as George T. Hunt (*The Wars of the Iroquois*) and Harold Innis (*The Fur Trade in Canada*), have offered materialist analyses of Iroquoian warfare, examining how it may have been motivated by various forms of economic gain. Brandão's book *Your Fyre Shall Burn No More* focuses more on political and cultural, rather than economic, motivations for warfare. William J. Eccles approaches the topic from a similar perspective. See especially his articles "A Belated Review of Harold Adam Innis's *The Fur Trade in Canada*" and "The Fur Trade and Eighteenth-Century Imperialism" in his collection *Essays on New France*. Trigger provides a summary and critique of these various points of view in the preface to the Carleton Library Series reprint of his book *The Children of Aataentsic*, as well as the preface to the 1987 reprint. Trigger himself, however, has been reproached for what some scholars have seen as an at-times too economicist interpretation of these conflicts. This chapter does not seek to intervene in this longstanding debate, but rather to examine how the Jesuits represented Amerindian violence. A variety of sources on Amerindian violence are therefore used in an effort to balance the competing scholarly points of view on the topic without endorsing any of them in particular.

5 JR 13.41–3. Thwaites' translation here has been altered to improve its accuracy. He originally rendered "bourreaux" as "butchers," for which "torturers" has been substituted. "Tous ceux qui estoient autour de luy avec leur douceur estudiée et leurs belles paroles estoient autant de bourreaux, qui ne luy foisaient bon visage que pour le traitter par après avec plus de cruauté." MNF 3.696.

6 Knowles, "The Torture of Captives by the Indians of Eastern North America," 181, 190.

7 Ibid., 194.

8 Trigger, *The Children of Aataentsic*, 73–5, 441n45; Tooker, *An Ethnography of the Huron Indians*, 34–8; Sanday, *Divine Hunger: Cannibalism as a Cultural System*, 125–50.

9 Jaenen, "The Image of New France," 162. See also Jaenen, *Friend and Foe*, 17–18.

10 As Robert Berkhofer put it in his book on the subject, "Spaniards found the Indian wanting in a long list of attributes: letters, laws, government, clothing, arts, trade, agriculture, marriage, morals, metal goods, and above all religion. Judgments on these failures might be kind and sympathetic or harsh and hostile, but no one argued that the Indian was as good as the European in this early period." Berkhofer, *The White Man's Indian*, 10. See also Ouellet and Tremblay, "From the Good Savage to the Degenerate Indian," and Jaenen, "The Image of New France."

11 Berkhofer, *The White Man's Indian*, 11.

12 Ibid., 6–7.

13 Cited in Berkhofer, *The White Man's Indian*, 12. Las Casas, for his part, emphasized the gentle, virtuous, and obedient nature of the New World's inhabitants, painting them as ideal candidates for conversion: "Surely these people would be the most blessed in the world if only they worshipped the true God." Berkhofer, *The White Man's Indian*, 11.

14 Ibid., 13. According to Jaenen, "Most Frenchmen who showed any interest in America quickly became either indiophiles or indiophobes." Jaenen, *Friend and Foe*, 16.

15 Jaenen, *Friend and Foe*, 17.

16 Wrote Jaenen of Montaigne, "His essay, '*Des Cannibales*,' unmistakably indicated Montaigne's belief in the myth of a Golden Age metamorphosed into that of the *bon sauvage,* and his acceptance of the relativity of customs and mores, which were to his mind grounded ultimately in human opinions and prejudices." Jaenen, *Friend and Foe*, 147. Although he admitted that cruelty toward prisoners was perhaps "against reason," Montaigne, in contrast to many other thinkers of his time, apparently was not willing to count Amerindians incapable of rational thought on those grounds. See Montaigne, *Les Essais*, book 1, 202–17.

17 For a brief treatment of the arrival in France of Tupinamba boys from Brazil and the reaction of French spectators, see Melzer, *Colonizer or Colonized*, chapter 4 (especially pages 91–4). For more details on Amerindians who were transported to France by explorers and the spectacles they sometimes appeared in, see Jaenen, *Friend and Foe*, 12–15.

18 JR 6.229. "Pour l'esprit des sauvages, il est de bonne trempe. Je croy que les âmes sont toutes de mesme estoc et qu'elles ne different point substantiallement. C'est pourquoy ces barbares, ayans un corps bien fait et les organes bien rangez et bien disposez, leur esprit doit opérer avec facilité." MNF 2.596.

19 For Berkhofer, the Hurons' place in the eighteenth-century noble savage myth "must be ascribed to the voluminous *Relations* of the Jesuits. Published annually from 1632 to 1674 and sporadically before and after those years, the *Relations* from Canadian missions often provided flattering descriptions of Native Americans and their ways of life in order to gain contributions for missionary work from the faithful and to prove points against their Jansenist and atheistic opponents." Berkhofer, *The White Man's Indian*, 74. As Michèle Duchet has pointed out, negative portrayals of the Iroquois and contrasting favourable depictions of the Huron survived in French literature well into the eighteenth century, with the Huron coming to serve as a public face of the Enlightenment "Noble Savage" myth, and the Iroquois representing all that was frightening about Amerindians. Wrote Duchet: "Lahontan's Adario is not just any 'savage,' but a Huron … 'a

Machiavelli born in the woods … the most intrepid, the most firm, and the most enlightened savage found in northern America.' Also a Huron is Delisle's *Arlequin Sauvage*, and Voltaire's *Ingénu*, one of the spiritual sons of Adario, is half Huron. But Maubert de Gouvest's *Igli* is Iroquois, and probably not out of a simple concern for variety, but because the Iroquois, fierce enemies of the French, illustrate better than any other nation the latent hostility of the savage world." Duchet, *Anthropologie et Histoire au Siècle des Lumières*, 31–2. Author's translation. To Duchet's list of favourable Enlightenment depictions of the Huron, one could add Jean-François Marmontel's 1768 comedy-ballet *Le Huron*, in which the title character is described thus: "He is valiant, honest; he thinks nobly, the shadow of a lie injures him." Marmontel, *Le Huron*, 40. Author's translation.

20 For a concise discussion of Recollet attitudes toward Amerindians, see Axtell, *The Invasion Within*, 49–53.

21 Hennepin, *A New Discovery of a Vast Country in America*, vol 2, 616. Chrestien Le Clercq similarly claimed that Amerindians were "cut off from intercourse, living in the Indian way, incompatible with real Christianity, giving no signs of religion but the chant of hymns and prayers, or some exterior and very equivocal ceremonies." Le Clercq, *First Establishment of the Faith in New France,* vol. 1, 256.

22 Wrote Lahontan, "The Recollets brand the Savages for stupid, gross and rustick Persons, uncapable of Thought or Reflection: But the Jesuits give them other sort of Language, for they intitle them to good Sense, to a tenacious Memory, and to a quick Apprehension season'd with a solid Judgement. The former allege that 'tis to no purpose to preach the Gospel to a sort of People that have less Knowledge than the Brutes. On the other hand the latter (I mean the Jesuits) give it out, that these Savages take Pleasure in hearing the Word of God, and readily apprehend the meaning of the scriptures. In the meantime, 'tis no difficult matter to point to the Reasons that influence the one and the other to such Allegations; the Mystery is easily unravell'd by those who know that these two Orders [do not get along very well] in Canada." Lahontan, *New Voyages to North America*, vol 2, 413. This translation has been corrected to better align with the original French, and to remove the odd expression "cannot set their horses together," which appeared between the brackets at the end of the passage.

23 Le Clercq, *First Establishment of the Faith in New France*, vol. 1, 401.

24 Réveillaud, ed., *Histoire Chronologique de la Nouvelle France*, 4. Author's translation.

25 Healy, "The French Jesuits and the Idea of the Noble Savage," 149.

26 Blackburn, *Harvest of Souls*, 63–4. Le Bras, *L'Amérindien dans les Relations du Père Paul Lejeune*, 35. Ouellet and Tremblay, "From the Good Savage to the Degenerate Indian," 162.

27 JR 13.43. "Vostre Révérence eust eu de la consolation de voir avec quelle attention il escouta ce discours. Il y prist tant de plaisir et le comprist si bien qu'il le
répéta en peu de mots et tesmoigna un grand plaisir d'aller au ciel." MNF 3.696.

28 See MNF 3.397–9 and JR 13.45–7. For Joseph's three affirmations of his faith, see
MNF 3.699, 3.701, and 3.706; for uses of Joseph's newly given Christian name,
see MNF 3.699, 3.700, 3.701, etc; for an example of his description as "our new
Christian," see MNF 3.705.

29 Farrell, *The Jesuit Ratio Studiorum*, 30.

30 JR 18.87. "Bref, ce pauvre peuple se vient rendre à Jésus-Christ de jour en jour."
MNF 4.566–7. Farrell, *The Jesuit Ratio Studiorum*, 17. For more on the Jesuit
tradition of pedagogical theatre, see McCabe, *An Introduction to the Jesuit Theatre*, especially 11–18, and Paschoud, "Puissance de l'image et efficacité de la
representation."

31 On Jesus' entanglement with Pontius Pilate and the crown of thorns, see chapter 27 of the Gospel of Matthew in the Bible. Mark, Luke, and John contain
similar accounts; for Joseph's similar treatment, see MNF 3.695 and JR 13.39.
Pourcellaine, sometimes translated as "wampum," refers to the decorative shell
beads that apparently were traded among Amerindian groups at the time of
contact. See Sagard, *Grand Voyage du Pays des Hurons*, 229–30.

32 JR 13.71. "Néantmoins, une âme bien unie avec Dieu eust eu là une belle occasion de méditer les mystères adorables de la passion de Nostre-Seigneur, dont
nous avions quelque image devant nos yeux." MNF 3.705.

33 Harrod, "Missionary Life World and Native Response: Jesuits in New France,"
183. As Carole Blackburn has pointed out, drawing on Harrod's argument, the
importance that Jesuit spirituality accorded to the imitation of Christ made martyrdom an especially desirable fate for a Jesuit missionary. Blackburn, *Harvest of
Souls*, 66. Frank Lestringant made a similar point with regard to the travails of
martyred French Jesuits in his influential literary study of cannibalism: "Cannibalism may well have been part of a vengeance ritual, but to the Jesuit histori-
ographer it acquires perforce another meaning. It is one stage of a Passion, an
imitation of the sufferings of Christ on the Cross." Lestringant, *Cannibals*, 134.

34 See, for just two examples, Viau, *Enfants du Néant et Mangeurs des Ames*, 173–8,
and Jaenen, *Friend and Foe*, 141–5.

35 JR 9.67. "avec une constance digne d'étonnement." MNF 3.230.

36 JR 17.71. "Quelques sauvages ont rapporté, avec admiration et quelque espèce de
conviction des véritez que nous leurs preschons, qu'un peu devant qu'il receût
le dernier coup qui luy apporta la mort, il leva les yeux au ciel et s'escria avec
joye: 'Allons, donc, allons.' Comme s'il eust respondu à une voix qui l'invitoit.
Certes, il semble qu'il ne s'agissoit d'autre voyage que de celuy du ciel, où sans
distinction le captif, s'il le veut, a autant de droict et d'accez que celuy qui est en
liberté." MNF 4.390.

37 Trigger, *The Children of Aataentsic*, 73.

38 JR 17.65. "ont fait paroistre tant de constance dans leur tourmens que nos barbares prirent résolution de ne plus souffrir qu'on baptisast ces pauvres infortu-
nez, réputans à malheur pour leur païs, quand ceux qu'ils tourmentent ne crient
point ou fort peu." MNF 4.388.

39 JR 30.243. "Jamais, au rapport d'une personne qui le veid dans ses souffrances,
il ne jetta aucun cry ny ne donna jamais aucun signe d'un cœur abattu. Il levoit
les yeux au ciel du milieu de ses flammes, regardant fixement le lieu où son âme
aspiroit?" MNF 7.78–9.

40 In addition to the examples cited above, the intersection of torture and religious
conversion can be found in MNF 4.401, 5.179, 6.174, 7.77–9, etc.

41 JR 33.97–9. "Nous ne désirons pas ny les souffrances, ny les malheurs à nos
chrestiens, mais toutefois je ne puis m'empescher de bénir Dieu dans ceux qui
leur arrivent, l'expérience m'ayant fait reconnoistre que jamais leur foy n'est plus
vive, ny leur cœur jamais plus à Dieu qu'au temps qu'envisageant les choses d'un
œil trop humain, nous avons plus de crainte et plus de compassion pour eux.
Je n'en ay veu aucun de ceux qui sont tombez entre les mains de l'ennemy et
se sont sauvez par après, qui ne m'ayent avoué que dans le plus fort de leur mal
ils n'y eussent esprouvé un courage plus chrestien, une consolation plus douce
et un recours à Dieu plus entier qu'ils n'avoient ressenty toute leur vie passée et
que mesme ils n'en ressentoient après leur délivrance. Ainsi nous ne sçavons que
désirer à nos Chrestiens et à nous-mesme; et quelques grandes pertes que puisse
recevoir cette église nous en bénirons Dieu, voyans à l'œil qu'il en tire sa gloire
plus avantageusement que nous n'eussions osé l'espérer par aucune autre voye."
MNF 7.379–80.

42 JR 46.85. "Qui croiroit que les tourmens du feu, qui jettent souvent dans le
desespoir, et qui font quelquefois brèche à la constance des meilleurs chrestiens,
ouvrent le chemin du ciel à des Iroquois et que ces feux soient les moiens les plus
certains, 'quibus certissime liberantur quicumque liberantur'? Ils sont si certains,
que nous n'avons presque point veu brûler d'Iroquois, que nous ne l'aions jugé
dans le chemin du paradis, et nous n'avons jugé aucun d'eux estre certainement
dans le chemin du paradis, que nous ne l'aions veu passer par ce supplice." MNF
9.498.

43 Champlain, *The Voyages*, vol. 1, 214–15.

44 JR 13.47–9. "Une bonne troupe de sauvages, qui estoient là présens, non seulement ne l'interrompoient point, mais mesme l'escoutèrent avec beaucoup
d'attention, où il prist sujet de les entretenir sur la bonté de Dieu, qui ayme
universellement tous les hommes, les Iroquois aussi bien que les Hurons, les cap-
tifs aussi bien que ceux qui sont en liberté, les pauvres et les misérables à l'esgal
des riches, pourveu qu'ils croyent en luy et gardent ses saincts commandemens.
Que c'est un grand avantage d'avoir la langue en maniment, d'estre aymé de ces

peuples et en credit parmy eux. Vous eussiez dit que tout ce monde se fust assemblé, non pour passer le temps autour du prisonnier, mais pour entendre la parole de Dieu. Je ne pense pas que les véritez chrestiennes ayent esté jamais preschées dans ce pays en une occasion si favorable, car il y en avoit quasi là de toutes les nations qui parlent la langue huronne." MNF 3.697–8.

45 MNF 3.705, JR 13.71.

46 JR 13.63. "Il falloit estre là pour voir une vive image de l'enfer." MNF 3.702.

47 In Matthew 13:41–2, for example, hell is referred to as "the furnace of fire."

48 JR 13.63. "crioit comme une âme [damnée]." MNF 3.702. Campeau's edition mistakenly gives the end of this quote as "une âme darmée." The original Cramoisy edition confirms that "une âme damnée" is correct.

49 Blackburn, *Harvest of Souls*, 63.

50 JR 29.265. "Jamais on n'avoit entendu au milieu de ces cruautez de semblables harangues. On est arresté des menaces si estonnantes de ce nouveau prédicateur. 'Non, non, mes frères, adjouste-t-il, ne croyez pas que je veille arracher ce captif de vos mains, ny procurer sa liberté. Le temps de tout son bonheur est passé et maintenant qu'il brûle dans les flammes, la seule mort peut mettre fin à ses misères. Mes compassions sont pour vous-mesmes. Car je crains pour vous, infidèles, des malheurs mille fois plus terribles et des flammes plus dévorantes, à qui vostre mort donnera le commencement et qui jamais n'auront de fin.'" MNF 6.643.

51 Wrote Campbell of such scenes in Lafitau's text, "They force upon us the impression of the victim's subjectivity. We may repudiate that victimization, but if we do then we share the weaker sensations of the torturers and flesh eaters, who are also Americans, and at their most 'sauvage.' Either way we are sharing a virtual experience with American persons, rather than coolly observing a systematic pattern of lineage." Campbell, *Wonder and Science*, 304.

52 Jaenen, *Friend and Foe*, 121. In a similar vein, Blackburn points out that "[a]lthough Le Jeune associated it with savagery, this association belies the fact that in Europe as well as North America torture was never simply an expression of 'lawless rage,' such as would be associated with the absence of law and order; it was the result of premeditated and often carefully controlled technique – planned, regulated, sanctioned." Blackburn, *Harvest of Souls*, 63.

53 JR 13.75. "'Ouy dea, nous en faisons mourir, mais non pas avec ceste cruauté … le feu n'est que pour les crimes énormes et il n'y a qu'une personne à qui appartienne en chef ceste exécution. Et puis on ne les faict pas languir si longtemps. Souvent, on les estrangle auparavant et, pour l'ordinaire, on les jette tout d'un coup dans le feu, où ils sont incontinent estouffez et consommez.'" MNF 3.706.

54 JR 13.79–81. Thwaites translated "coustumes envieillies" as "customs grown old." The translation has here been corrected to improve its accuracy. "Des superstitions et des coustumes envieillies et authorisées par la suitte de tant de siècles ne

sont pas si aisées à abolir; souvent il arrive dans les meilleures villes de France qu'une troupe d'enfans, mettant à se battre à coups de fronde toute une ville, ses magistrats ont bien de la peine d'empescher ce désordre. Et qu'i pourroient profiter deux ou trois estrangers qui voudroient s'en mesler, sinon de se faire massacrer." MNF 3.707.

55 Eight missionaries who were tortured and killed during the Jesuits' tenure in New France were beatified in the twentieth century. This chapter focuses on Jesuit descriptions of torture of and by Amerindians, since the torture of priests had obvious and immediate religious significance. Drawing on the work of Guy Laflèche, Blackburn has argued that accounts of Jesuit missionaries' deaths are not necessarily accurate, but were "manipulated in order to achieve the impression of martyrdom." Blackburn, *Harvest of Souls*, 150n14, and 65. See also Laflèche, *Les Saints Martyrs Canadiens*. Perhaps because of their clear and specific religious significance, accounts of the torture and execution of Jesuits have not played the same role as accounts of Amerindian-on-Amerindian violence in the reconstruction of torture rituals by modern scholars. It is for this reason that such passages are not examined in this chapter, fascinating though they may be.

56 JR 30.229. Thwaites' original translation reads "chase after men," and has been corrected to preserve the notion present in the original that the Iroquois were hunting prey, not merely chasing enemies. "Incontinent après ces meurtres, dont nous n'avons eu connoissance qu'au printemps, ils se respandirent en divers endroits pour prendre, tuer et massacrer autant de François, d'Algonquins et de Hurons qu'ils pourroient. Suivons-les dans leurs courses et marquons les temps de leurs attaques et de leur chasse aux hommes." MNF 7.73–4. The apparent uptick in Iroquois violence during the decade in which Lalemant was writing has been attributed to various factors: tensions produced by trade, desire for revenge against enemies, mourning of relatives lost to epidemic disease, etc. For more on this longstanding debate, see the scholarly works listed in this chapter's fourth endnote.

57 JR 26.33. "Les ennemis mettent pied à terre avec leurs prisonniers, rompent tous les paquets où estoient les nécessitez de nos Pères, qui n'ont rien receu depuis trois ans, deschirent les lettres qu'on leur envoyait, partagent le but inesgalement et se jettent sur le corps de celuy qui fust tué, luy arrachent le cœur de la poitrine, luy enlevant la chevelure, luy coupent les lèvres et les parties les plus charnues des cuisses et des jambes, les font bouillir et les mangent en présence des prisonniers." MNF 6.126.

58 JR 30.259. "Elle avoit aussi ouy à son départ quelques jeunes gens qui, ne croyans pas qu'elle entendît leur langue, se demandoient l'un à l'autre quelle partie du corps ils trouveroient plus friande. L'un d'eux la regardant respondit que les pieds cuits sous la cendre estoient fort bons." MNF 7.83–4.

59 JR 10.229. The word "dish" has been substituted here for Thwaites' original translation of "mets" as "part," in order to more closely follow the original French. "quelques-uns ne goustent de ce mets, non plus que de tout le reste du corps, qu'avec beaucoup d'horreur. Il y en a qui mangent avec plaisir." MNF 3.376–7.

60 JR 5.31. Thwaites rendered the French word "catastrophe" as "horror," a translation that does not capture the meaning of the term, which designates not only a disaster, but also the final event in a tragedy. It has here been corrected to preserve the notion that the scene unfolding before the Jesuits had tragic resonance. "En fin, pour dernière catastrophe, ils les mangent et les dévorent quasi tout crus … Ils sont si enragez contre tout ce qui leur fait du mal qu'ils mangent les poux et toute autre vermine qu'ils trouvent sur eux, non pour aucun goust qu'ils y ayent, mais seulement, disent-ils, pour se vanger et pour manger ceux qui les mangent." MNF 2.305–6.

61 As Sara Melzer has recently pointed out, Claude d'Abbeville characterized the "assimilation" of Brazilian Tupinamba Amerindians as the transformation of wolves into lambs in his *Histoire de la Mission des Pères Capucins*. Melzer, *Colonizer or Colonized*, 94.

62 Blackburn, *Harvest of Souls*, 62. Le Bras, *L'Amérindien dans les Relations du Père Paul Lejeune*, 62.

63 Furetière, *Dictionnaire Universel*, s.v. "Loup." Author's translation.

64 Le Bras, *L'Amérindien dans les Relations du Père Paul Lejeune*, 62. Author's translation.

65 See, for example, Blackburn, *Harvest of Souls*, 62. For a concise examination of this metaphor as employed by various missionaries in New France, see Grégoire, "L'Iroquois est un Loup pour l'Homme."

66 Author's translation. The Jesuit authors sometimes varied the metaphor to include other violent big cats. Jérôme Lalemant's 1647 *Relation*, for example, referred to the Iroquois as "lions and leopards" in recounting the violent treatment of the missionary Isaac Jogues at their hands. MNF 7.99, 101.

67 JR 29.45–7. "Le dessein toutesfois principal de cette denomination est que cette mission soit assistée du crédit et faveur de ces sainctes et sacrées victimes qui ont l'honneur d'approcher de plus près l'Agneau et de le suivre partout." MNF 6.569. For a biblical example, see John 1:29.

68 Snow, *The Iroquois*, 119.

69 Trigger, *The Children of Aataentsic*, 645–7, 654–7. Brandão, *Your Fyre Shall Burn No More*, 35–6, 55–6, 98, 102–4.

70 JR 44.57. "changer ces loups et ces tygres en agneaux pour prendre leur place dans le bercail de Jésus-Christ." MNF 9.128.

71 JR 42.39–41. "Ces nations ne sont composées que de fourbes et toutefois il faut se confier à leur inconstance et s'abandonner à leur cruauté. Le Père Isaac Jogues fut

assommé de ces perfides lorsqu'ils luy témoignoient plus d'amour, mais puisque Jésus-Christ a envoyé ses apostres comme des agneaux entre des loups, pour faire d'un loup un agneau, nous ne devons pas craindre d'abandonner nos vies en semblables rencontres, pour mettre la paix et la foy, où la guerre et l'infidélité ont tousjours esté dans leur règne." MNF 8.836–7.

72 Brian Moore, *Black Robe*, author's note.

73 Bruce Beresford, *Black Robe*. This and other quotes from the film were transcribed by the author.

74 Sioui, *For an Amerindian Autohistory*, 56.

75 Particularly with regard to cannibalism, the question has been hotly debated in recent decades. William Arens touched off this debate in his much-discussed 1979 book *The Man-Eating Myth* by expressing doubt that any culture ever practiced ritualistic cannibalism. Arens argued that anthropologists had relied uncritically on accounts of such rituals, and had accepted their truth without adequate reflection. Arens, *The Man-Eating Myth*, 10. The book prompted a flurry of indignant responses. Some scholars argued that the evidence supporting the existence of ritual cannibalism was conclusive. See, for example, Abler, "Iroquois Cannibalism: Fact not Fiction." Other discussants blasted Arens for his argument, comparing it to Holocaust denial. For an examination of these charges, see Hulme, "Introduction: The Cannibal Scene," in *Cannibalism and the Colonial World*, 6–16. Largely lost in the dispute over the existence of ritual cannibalism was a not-meritless question that Arens posed in his book: was anthropology, as a discipline, being careful enough in its use of centuries-old writings by colonizers? The debate over whether ritual cannibalism ever existed seems to have been settled in the affirmative, but this chapter has sought, in part, to heed Arens' call for a more critical reading of colonial texts describing cannibalism and the violence that often preceded it.

CHAPTER FIVE

1 Gliozzi, *Adam et le Nouveau Monde*, 14. Author's translation.

2 Ibid., 27.

3 Wrote Eliade: "Myth narrates a sacred history; it relates an event that took place in primordial Time, the fabled time of the 'beginnings.' In other words, myth tells how, through the deeds of Supernatural Beings, a reality came into existence, be it the whole of reality, the Cosmos, or only a fragment of reality – an island, a species of plant, a particular kind of human behavior, an institution. Myth, then, is always an account of a 'creation'; it relates how something was produced, began to *be*." Eliade, *Myth and Reality*, 5–6.

4 Doiron, "Discours sur l'Origine des Amériquains," 48. Author's translation.

5 Jaenen, "The Image of New France," 62.

6 It is not possible, in the context of this chapter, to do justice to the full array of European theories about the origins of the Amerindians during the colonial period. Such theories, and the ideological and political forces behind them, varied widely. For an authoritative account of Europe's engagement with the question, see Gliozzi, *Adam et le Nouveau Monde*. Anglophone readers can find a good, but less exhaustive, summary in Huddleston, *Origins of the American Indians*.

7 Lescarbot, *Histoire de la Nouvelle-France*, I.24. Author's translation. Lescarbot's remarks on the origin of Amerindians are contained in chapter three of book one, entitled "Conjectures sur le peuplement des Indes Occidentales et consequemment de la Nouvelle-France comprise sous icelles," 19–28.

8 Lafitau, *Customs of the American Indians*, vol. 1, 79–80.

9 On La Peyrère, see Gliozzi, *Adam et le Nouveau Monde*, 437–47, and Jaenen, *Friend and Foe*, 21. On the power theological considerations had over the debate in Europe, see Huddleston, *Origins of the American Indians*, 11–12. It is worth noting that the question of the origins of the first Americans is still not definitively settled. Scientists long believed that the Americas were first populated about 12,000 years ago when Asians crossed Beringea – the Bering Land Bridge. Recent archaeological evidence, however, suggests that people may have been present in America before the bridge existed. See Switzer, "Evidence Shows Humans Were in America Earlier than Thought."

10 JR 11.151. "Nous luy accordasmes ce qu'il désiroit. Le soir donc, après avoir fait nos prières, au lieu de dormir, nous nous entretenions des articles de nostre créance, ce que nous faisions aussi pendant le jour, quand le temps nous le permettoit. Je luy expliquay la creation du ciel et de la terre, la cheute des anges rebelles, comme nostre premier père avoit esté créé." MNF 3.562.

11 JR 11.159. "Les hommes, luy disois-je, ne font rien de toutes ces choses et néantmoins elles paroissent tous les jours à nos yeux. Il faut donc qu'il y ait un autre principe plus puissant." MNF 3.565.

12 JR 21.251. "Seigneur Dieu enfin donc je te connois à la bonne heure maintenant je te connois; c'est toy qui as fait cette terre que voilà, et ce ciel que voilà; tu nous as fait nous autres qui sommes appellez hommes." MNF 5.210.

13 Jean de Brébeuf, "Doctrine Chrestienne du R.P. Ledesme de la compagnie de Jesus traduit en langage canadois par le R.P. Breboeuf de la mesme Compagnie." The text can also be found in MNF 2.238–57. Author's translation.

14 For more on the importance of naming and talking about God in the Jesuit project, see True, "Il faut parler pour estre entendu."

15 JR 13.219. "Outre cela, souvent, ils nous avoient advoué qu'ils nous prenoient pour des menteurs et ne croioient en façon du monde ce que nous enseignions, et que ce que nous disions n'estoit aucunement probable, qu'il n'y avoit aucune

apparence que nous eussions, eux et nous, un mesme Dieu, créateur de leur terre aussi bien que de la nostre, et que nous eussions tous pris naissance d'un mesme père. 'Comment, disoit un jour Sononkhiaconc; qui nous auroit amené en ce païs? Comment aurions-nous traversé tant de mers dans de petits canots d'escorce? Le moindre souffle nous auroit abysmez ou au moins serions-nous morts de faim au bout de quatre ou cinq jours. Et puis, si cela estoit, nous sçaurions faire des cousteaux et des habits aussi bien que vous autres." MNF 3.751–2.

16 JR 13.219. "Je perdrois trop de papier, si je voulois entreprendre de coucher icy toutes leurs extravagances." MNF 3.752.

17 On the Jesuits' treatment of a Huron myth in the Jesuit *Relations*, see True, "Retelling Genesis."

18 This summary is based on the two versions of the myth found in MNF 2.433–5 and 2.564–5. The story also is briefly mentioned in the seventeenth-century letters of the New France missionary Marie de l'Incarnation to her son in France. The Ursuline nun, however, seems to misattribute the tale to the Huron. The Huron, like other Iroquoian groups, had their own versions of the Earth Diver myth, featuring a female figure named Aataentsic, not Messou. See Marie de l'Incarnation, *Correspondance*, 916–17.

19 Dundes, "Earth-Diver: Creation of the Mythopoeic Male," 331; Thompson, *Motif Index of Folk Literature*, volume 1, 161–2.

20 For one example of a recently collected tale that may be related to the Montagnais' story about Messou, see Joe Kawapit's 1999 account at http://www.eastcree.org/cree/en/stories/text/maasu/.

21 Wrote Speck: "I have frequently asked narrators for the Earth Diver story, but have never found that it was known to any one in the Montagnais territory. Nor is it found among the Wabanaki. No sign of the tale has been discovered in northern New England or in eastern Canada, except for one reference in the Jesuit Relations, the authenticity of which may be doubted." Speck, "Montagnais and Naskapi Tales from the Labrador Peninsula," 2; Alexander, *The Mythology of All Races*, 38; MNF 2.93 (introduction).

22 Fontaine, *Croyances et Rituels Ches les Innus*, 22–3; Alexander, *The Mythology of All Races*, 20, 42; Bailey, *The Conflict of European and Eastern Algonquian Cultures*, 155; Cushner, *Why Have You Come Here?* 162; Anderson, *The Betrayal of Faith*, 13. Not all scholars have trusted Le Jeune, or other scholars who have cited Le Jeune's account. A good example of a more careful approach is historian Alain Beaulieu's 1990 book on Jesuit work among Algonquian peoples. He acknowledges the existence of the Messou story, but only as evidence of Le Jeune's ideas about Montagnais religion. He carefully avoids asserting that it actually represents the beliefs of the Montagnais. Beaulieu, *Convertir les Fils de Caïn*, 32.

23 JR 5.155. "Vous voyez qu'ils ont quelque tradition du déluge, quoy que meslée de fables, car voicy comme le monde se perdit, à ce qu'ils disent." MNF 2.434.

24 JR 6.157. The standard English version of the name of the famous flood survivor has been substituted here for Thwaites' original rendering, "Noë." "Pour
le Messou, ils tiennent qu'il a réparé le monde qui s'estoit perdu par le déluge
d'eau, d'où appert qu'ils ont quelque tradition de cette grande innondation uni-
verselle qui arriva du temps de Noé, mais ils ont rempli cette vérité de mille
fables impertinentes." MNF 2.564.

25 Mignolo, *The Darker Side of the Renaissance*, 3; see also Blackburn, *Harvest of
Souls*, 54–5, 109. The Vulgate was declared the only official, authentic version of
the Bible at the fourth session of the Council of Trent in 1546. It is therefore this
Bible, or more precisely a corrected version from the 1590s, that the Jesuits most
likely referred to. Although public access to scripture was generally through the
intermediary of a priest or iconography, it is true that early-seventeenth-century
Catholicism had a single standard version of scripture. For more, see Millet and
de Robert, *Culture Biblique*.

26 JR 11.153. "Que leur nation est provenue de ceste famille, que les premiers qui
sont venus en leur païs ne sçavoient ny lire ny escrire, voilà pourquoy leurs
enfans avoient demeuré dans la mesme ignorance; qu'ils avoient bien conservé la
mémoire de ce déluge, mais par une longue suitte d'années, ils avoient envelopé
ceste vérité dans mille fables; que nous ne pouvions estre trompez en ce point,
ayant la mesme créance que nos ancestres, puisque nous voyons leurs livres."
MNF 3.563.

27 Gen. 7:21–3.

28 Gen. 8:7.

29 Gen. 8:1–5.

30 Gen. 6:13–7:5.

31 JR 5.155. "Il entre dans l'eau pour les secourir, mais aussitost ce lac se desborde
et s'aggrandit si furieusement qu'il inonda et noya toute la terre. Le messou bien
estonné quitte la pensée de ses loups, pour songer à restablir le monde." MNF
2.434.

32 See MNF 2.565.

33 JR 6.159. "Voilà comme le Messou a tout restably." MNF 2.565.

34 Gen. 7:22.

35 MNF 2.403. Author's translation.

36 JR 6.29. "Mais il est tantost temps de m'aviser que je n'escry plus une lettre,
mais un livre, tant je suis long. Ce n'estoit point mon dessein de tant escrire.
Les feuillets se sont multipliés insensiblement et m'ont mis en tel point qu'il
fault que j'envoie ce brouillard pour ne pouvoir tirer et mettre au net ce que je
croirois debvoir estre présenté à Vostre Révérence. J'escriray une autre fois plus
précisément et plus asseurément." MNF 2.484.

37 As Jesuit scholar Léon Pouliot remarked of the 1634 *Relation*, "For the history of
the collection, this text is important: it tells us that the annual report no longer

was addressed only to the Provincial in Paris or only to Jesuits; in the thoughts even of its author, it was now in the public domain." Pouliot, *Etude sur les Relations des Jésuites*, 18. Author's translation.

38 For examples of references to the "Reverend Father" to whom the *Relations* were at least superficially addressed, see MNF 2.406, 485, 538, 740. For examples of "Your Reverence," see MNF 2.411, 578, 649, etc.

39 JR 7.251. "Relation de ce qui s'est passé en la Nouvelle-France en l'année 1635, envoyée au révérend Père Provincial de la Compagnie de Jésus en la Province de France, par le Père Paul Le Jeune de la mesme compagnie, Supérieur de la résidence de Québec." MNF 3.44.

40 JR 5.153. Thwaites translates "Leur cognoissance n'est que ténèbres" as "their knowledge is only as darkness." This rendering has been corrected to restore the suggestion present in the original that the Montagnais had some understanding of a higher power, albeit one that was not clearly defined or well understood. A shadow, after all, preserves at least the bare outline of the object that casts it. "Je confesse que les sauvages n'ont point de prières publiques et communes, ny aucun culte qu'ils rendent ordinairement à celuy qu'ils tiennent pour Dieu, et que leur cognoissance n'est que ténèbres. Mais on ne peut nier qu'ils ne recognoissent quelque nature supérieure à la nature de l'homme." MNF 2.433.

41 JR 5.153–5. "Ils disent qu'il y a un certain qu'ils nomment Atahocan, qui a tout fait. Parlant un jour de Dieu dans une cabane, ils me demandèrent que c'était que Dieu. Je leur dis que c'estoit celuy qui pouvoit tout et qui avoit fait le ciel et la terre. Ils commencèrent à se dire les uns aux autres: 'Atahocan, Atahocan; c'est Atahocan.'" MNF 2.433–4.

42 JR 5.157. "On voit par ces contes que les sauvages ont quelque idée d'un Dieu." MNF 2.434.

43 JR 5.155–7. "Ce seroit une longue fable de raconter comme il répara tout, comme il se vangea des monstres qui avoient pris ses chasseurs, se transformant en mille sorte d'animaux pour les surprendre. Bref, ce beau Réparateur, estant marié à une soury musquée, eut des enfans qui ont repeuplé le monde." MNF 2.434.

44 JR 6.159. "Je touchay l'an passé cette fable, mais désirant rassembler tout ce que je sçay de leur créance, j'ay usé de redittes." MNF 2.565.

45 JR 6.157. "J'ai interrogé là-dessus ce fameux sorcier et ce vieillard avec lesquels j'ay passé l'hiver. Ils m'ont respondu qu'ils ne sçavoient pas qui estoit le premier autheur du monde, que c'estoit peut-estre Atahocam, mais que cela n'estoit pas certain, qu'ils ne parloient d'Atahocam que comme on parle d'une chose si esloignée qu'on n'en peut tirer aucune asseurance." MNF 2.564. The variation in the spelling of "Atahocan" is present in the original texts. Except in quotations, this chapter uses Le Jeune's first spelling of the word ("Atahocan"), for the sake of consistency.

46 JR 6.157. "je raconte une fable; je dis un vieux conte fait à plaisir." MNF 2.464.

47 See, for example, Silvy, *Dictionnaire Montagnais-Français*.

48 Jauss, *Question and Answer*, 74–5. For much more, see pages 51–94 of Jauss' book.

49 Carter, *Creating Catholics*, 4.

50 The Baltimore Catechism was written in the late nineteenth century in an effort to standardize Catholic religious instruction in America. It was "the chief instrument for teaching Catholic doctrine to millions of lay people for more than 100 years ... In 1994, the more sophisticated *Catechism of the Catholic Church* finally replaced the Baltimore Catechism, although some conservative Catholics still use the Baltimore text on an unofficial basis." Flinn, "Baltimore Catechism," 83. On the rich history of French-language catechisms in Quebec, see the work of Raymond Brodeur, notably his book *Catéchisme et Identité Culturelle* and the edited volume *Les Catéchismes au Québec, 1702–1963*.

51 Farrell, *The Jesuit Ratio Studiorum*, 27–8; see also Loyola, *The Constitutions of the Society of Jesus*, 194n11.

52 JR 5.155. "Atahocan, Atahocan, c'est Atahocan!" MNF 2.434.

53 It is unfortunately unclear upon which version of the myth Cushner based his account. He cites Elisabeth Tooker's work as his source, but neither of the books mentioned appear to contain any mention of Atahocan and Messou. Cushner reports that the Montagnais believed that Atahocan had created the world, which would point to the 1633 version as his source. And yet, he uses the alternate spelling "Atahocam," a feature of the 1634 account. Cushner, *Why Have You Come Here?* 162.

54 Rothstein, "Adam and Eve in the Land of the Dinosaurs."

55 Associated Press, "Kentucky Creation Museum Opens to Thousands."

CHAPTER SIX

1 Wroth, "The *Jesuit Relations* from New France," 119. Clear evidence of the changes wrought at this stage can be found in volumes 57 and 58 of Thwaites' *Jesuit Relations*. The *Relation* for 1672–73, which was not published for nearly a century, is "given in its original form as prepared roughly by one of the fathers acting for the superior. By means of italics and brackets, the modern editor has indicated the omissions, transpositions, and connective sentences through which the finished *Relation* was formed by father Dablon, at that time superior of the Society in Canada. The notable feature of this officer's editing was the amount and character of the matter he removed from the document – weary, tedious pages of parochial detail. If the same proportion of omission was attained in the editing of the other *Relations*, one is moved to applaud the critical judgment of the superiors." Wroth, "The *Jesuit Relations* from New France," 118.

2 Wroth, "The *Jesuit Relations* from New France," 114; Pouliot, *Etude sur les Relations des Jésuites*, 24.

3 Fabian, *Time and the Other*, 87; cited in Sayre, *Les Sauvages Américains*, 99.

4 Clifford, *The Predicament of Culture*, 22, 41.

5 Campbell, *The Witness and the Other World*, 3. See also Carile, *Le Regard Entravé*, 29–30. Andrea Frisch has dissented from this view on the grounds that travellers claimed authority in a variety of ways beyond merely insisting on their presence and experience. See Frisch, *The Invention of the Eyewitness*, 49–53. Although this is certainly true, it does not necessarily mean that a traveller's different claim to authority stops modern ethnohistorians from recognizing his or her text as an experience-based account of Otherness and therefore a potential source of reliable ethnographic information.

6 For more on the relationship between travel writing and ethnography – both as practiced in colonial texts and the modern discipline – see Sayre, *Les Sauvages Américains*, chapter 3, especially 98–9.

7 Campbell, *The Witness and the Other World*, 6. See also Pioffet, "Présentation," 1–2.

8 Doiron, *L'Art de Voyager*, 74, 149–59.

9 Van Den Abbeele, *Travel as Metaphor*, xv–xviii; Clifford, *Routes*, 66.

10 Van Den Abbeele refers to such a point as an "oikos," Greek for "home." Van Den Abbeele, *Travel as Metaphor*, xvii–xviii. See also Doiron, *L'Art de Voyager*, 69, and "L'Art de Voyager," 85–6. The terms "journey," "voyage," and "travel" are used interchangeably in this chapter. They all are used to mean "travel" as defined here.

11 Van Den Abbeele, *Travel as Metaphor*, xix.

12 Harbsmeier, "Spontaneous Ethnographies," 219. For a detailed discussion of this and other *rituels du retour* that mark the traveller's reintegration into society, see Doiron, *L'Art de Voyager*, chapter 12.

13 For a concise but thorough description of the conceptual links between travel, writing about travel, and reading a travel account, see Montalbetti, *Le Voyage, le Monde, et la Bibliothèque*, especially 100–5.

14 Doiron, "L'Art de Voyager," 86. Author's translation. Doiron's book contains a useful list of texts that outlined expectations or norms for the genre in seventeenth-century France. See also Van Den Abbeele, *Travel as Metaphor*, xx–xxi.

15 Van Den Abbeele, *Travel as Metaphor*, xix; Campbell, *The Witness and the Other World*, 2–3.

16 JR 7.251. "Relation de ce qui s'est passé en la Nouvelle-France en l'année 1635, envoyée au révérend Père Provincial de la Compagnie de Jésus en la Province de France, par le Père Paul Le Jeune de la mesme compagnie, Supérieur de la résidence de Québec." MNF 3.44.

17 Pioffet, "Présentation," 1. See also Melzer, "Une 'Seconde France'?" 78, and Fur-etière's definition of "relation," cited in chapter one.

18 Doiron, "L'Art de Voyager," 85.

19 Pioffet, *La Tentation de l'Epopée*, 20. It should be recognized that Jesuit move-ments in the New World – Paul Le Jeune's 1634 adventure following a nomadic Montagnais band, for example – could perhaps be understood as travel in the sense outlined above. Accounting for the relationship between the *Relations* and the Jesuits' circular itineraries within the colony would be the work of a separate study.

20 JR 20.121–3. "J'espère qu'aussitost que je me seray acquitté de ma commission, Vostre Révérence me donnera mon passeport pour retourner en ce nouveau monde et mourir dans un nouveau païs ou parmy ces bons néophytes, qui m'ont ravy le cœur par leur piété et par leur devotion." MNF 5.62.

21 JR 7.225. "Je ne souhaitterois maintenant que cinq ou six de nos Pères en chaqu'une de ces nations et cependant je n'oserais les demander, quoyque pour un qu'on désire, il s'en présente dix tout prests de mourir dans ces travaux." MNF 2.736.

22 As one scholar has put it, "Those who volunteered to go to Canada knew that almost no Jesuits ever came back. A few stayed for their whole career, eventually dying of old age, but many others succumbed to sickness or suffered a violent death in one of the wars that shook much of the region during the seventeenth century." Laurent Dubois, "The *Jesuit Relations*," 52.

23 Blackburn, *Harvest of Souls*, 65.

24 MNF 6.56.

25 JR 11.39–41. "Prenant la plume en main pour donner commancement à la *Rela-tion* de ce qui s'est passé cette année en quelques endroits où nostre Compagnie fait sa demeure en la Nouvelle-France, mon esprit s'est quasi trouvé sans pensées, sinon bien confuses. Je me suis veu saisi d'un estonnement qui ne laissoit à mon âme qu'autant de forces qu'il en falloit pour jetter les yeux sur la grandeur de Dieu et pour adorer sa conduitte. Puis revenant à moy-mesme, je ruminois les différentes nouvelles qu'on m'escrivoit de votre Europe et de quelques endroits de nostre Amérique. J'apprenois par les yeux et par les oreilles comme la France estoit en feu pour nous et les païs plus hauts des sauvages n'estoient que glaces … Je cognoissois par un grand nombre de lettres que des personnes de condi-tion très relevée et d'une vertu très insigne combattoient pour nous au ciel et en la terre et on me faisoit voir, sur un bout d'escource ou de papier, que les démons estoient deschainez, s'opposans puissamment à nos desseins … Voilà les nouvelles que j'ay appris à la veue des vaisseaux venus de France et des canots d'escorce arrivez des Algonquins et des Hurons." MNF 3.524–5.

26 JR 16.225. "Mon dessein n'est pas de redire icy ce qui se peut trouver dans les précédentes Relations ou dans les autres livres qui ont dèsjà traicté de ce sujet,

mais seulement de suppléer au défaut de certaines circonstances sur lesquelles j'ay reconnu qu'on désiroit quelque satisfaction." MNF 4.353–4.

27 See MNF 7.711.

28 The relevant portion of the letter is reproduced in MNF 4.72–3.

29 For details on the publication of the two texts including their length, see Campeau's prefaces: MNF 3.520 and 4.73–4.

30 JR 14.123. "On est dèsjà si remply des façons de faire de nos sauvages et de nos petits travaux en leur endroit que j'appréhende le dégoust. C'est pourquoy je diray peu de beaucoup, omettant des chapitres entiers, de peur d'estre accusé de longueur." MNF 4.76–7.

31 JR 14.277. "Je croy que je n'ay point contrevenu à la resolution que j'avois prise d'estre court, puisque j'obmets quantité de choses de peur d'estre long." MNF 4.132.

32 André Beaulieu, *La Première Bibliothèque Canadienne*, 15. Scholars interested in this library will find a good account of the current state of scholarship on it in Biron, "Les livres que les missionaires de la Compagnie de Jésus ont apportés avec eux en Nouvelle-France," along with a comprehensive bibliography and some remarks on the use, provenance, and material characteristics of some of the library's known contents.

33 See Drolet, "La Bibliothèque du Collège des Jésuites"; Pariseau, *La Bibliothèque du Collège de Québec*; and Filion, "La Première Bibliothèque Canadienne."

34 Pouliot, *Etude sur les Relations des Jésuites*, 27, and Verreau, "La Bibliothèque du Collège des Jésuites de Québec," 356. Verreau and Pouliot claim that the library had all of the *Relations*, but regrettably do not state the grounds on which they reached this conclusion. Its truth, however, seems likely, as this chapter endeavours to show.

35 Pouliot, *Etude sur les Relations des Jésuites*, 30.

36 Drolet, "La Bibliothèque du Collège des Jésuites," 491.

37 Drolet, "Les Ouvrages de Médecine."

38 Drolet, "La Bibliothèque du Collège des Jésuites," 489; André Beaulieu, *La Première Bibliothèque Canadienne*, 17.

39 Donnelly, *Thwaites' Jesuit Relations: Errata and Addenda*, 2–3. MNF 2.136 (introduction).

40 Author's translation (Thwaites' edition does not account for this handwritten copy). "Si ces deux petites oraisons sont mises soubs la presse, je supplie l'imprimeur de prendre garde aux mots sauvages. Ceux qui estoient dans la Relation de l'an passé ont esté corrompus et remplis de fautes à l'impression." MNF 2.705.

41 For more on this temporary change of printers, see Wroth, "The *Jesuit Relations* from New France," 138–40.

42 JR 14.277. Thwaites' translation here has been altered to more accurately follow the original French. "J'auray cette consolation cette année que, disant peu,

il se glissera peu de fautes sous le rouleau de la presse. La *Relation* de l'année passée en est remplie. Il faut que j'en conte une, pour inviter l'imprimeur à prendre quelque jalousie de son ouvrage. Au chapitre 8, page 145, où il s'agist de quelque prise que j'eus avec un sorcier, au lieu de me servir d'exorcismes contre le diable, l'imprimeur me fait servir d'une espée. Voicy ce que j'avois couché dans l'original: 'En effet, j'avois dessein de me servir d'une espèce d'exorcisme'; l'imprimeur a mis: 'En effet, j'avois dessein de me servir d'une espée désormais.' Je vous confesse que ce beau rencontre m'a fait rire. Quand on parle de si loing, on ne fait pas si bien entendre ses pensées; l'escriture est une parole muette, qui se change aussi facilement qu'il est aisé de prendre un caractère pour un autre. On fait dire à un enfant ce qu'on veut, quand son père est absent." MNF 4.132.

43 Montalbetti, *Le Voyage, le Monde, et la Bibliothèque*, 53–64.

44 JR 27.139–41. "Nous ne parlerons point en particulier des diverses résidences ny des diverses missions de nostre Compagnie, de peur d'user de redites. Les choses qui se passent de nouveau ont tant de rapport avec celles qui ont dèsjà esté escrites que le danger du dégoust nous rendra succints de plus en plus. Si bien que nous ne toucherons en cette Relation que quelques sentimens et quelques actions des plus fervens chrestiens, sans spécifier s'ils sont de Montréal, de Sainct-Joseph ou de Tadoussac." MNF 6.328.

45 For more examples in the *Relations* of references to previous texts and/or a reluctance to repeat material already published, see MNF 4.558, 5.89, 6.328, and 6.636.

46 MNF 2.642, note 8; Pouliot, *Etude sur les Relations des Jésuites*, chapter 2; Greer, *The Jesuit Relations*, 14; Wroth, "The *Jesuit Relations* from New France," 118–19; Melzer, "The French *Relation*," 226. See also Donnelly, *Thwaites' Jesuit Relations: Errata and Addenda*, 3.

47 MNF 2.532.

48 MNF 2.135 (introduction). Author's translation.

49 Translation adapted from Thwaites' translation of the published *Relations*: JR 5.23. "Si tost qu'ils apperceurent nostre vaisseau, ils firent des feux, puis deux d'entre eux nous vindrent aborder dans un petit canot fait d'escorce d'arbres fort proprement. Le lendemain, il y en vint douze avec leur capitaine. Il me sembloit, les voiant entrer dans la chambre de nostre capitaine, où j'estois pour lors, que je voiois ces masques qui courrent à caresme prenant." MNF 2.285.

50 JR 5.23. "Si tost qu'ils apperceurent nostre vaisseau, ils firent des feux, puis deux d'entr'eux nous vindrent aborder dans un petit canot fait d'escorce fort proprement. Le lendemain, un sagamo, avec dix ou douze sauvages, nous vint voir. Il me sembloit, les voyant entrer dans la chambre de nostre capitaine, où j'estois pour lors, que je voyois ces masques qui courent en France à caresme prenant." MNF 2.303.

51 JR 48.152–3. "Comme l'on imprimoit cette Relation, il nous est tombé entre les mains le narré d'un voyage fait exprès par une personne de mérite, pour recon-

noistre le pays de la Nouvelle France, depuis l'entrée du Golphe Saint Laurent iusques à Montreal. Quelques personnes ont cru qu'il estoit à propos d'en faire un extrait, et de le communiquer au public dans cette Relation. Voicy ce qu'il en escrit." In this instance, both the translation and original French passage were drawn from Thwaites, since Campeau's edition regrettably ends with the 1661 *Relation.*

52 See MNF 8.724 and JR 41.199–201.

53 See Pouliot, "La Contribution de P. Paul Le Jeune aux *Relations des Jésuites* de 1650 à 1663." See also note 25 in chapter one.

54 See MNF 1.226–9. In an earlier analysis of Biard's 1616 *Relation* ("Autour de la Relation"), Campeau concluded that Biard himself was responsible for these changes to the *Relation*, and that they could be explained by the author's change of heart concerning criticism of the recently deceased Jean de Biencourt de Poutrincourt, the lieutenant governor of Acadia. Campeau revised his position on the basis of subsequently discovered materials, including the apparent deletion from chapter twenty-one and an annotated copy of the published *Relation* in which one of Biard's missionary colleagues attributed the truncations to maladroit *"compilateurs."* In addition, Campeau speculates that if Biard had made the deletions himself, he would have adjusted the surrounding text to re-establish the book's coherence. MNF 1.227.

55 JR 5.201. "Mais je le prie d'appliquer en particulier une seule goutte de celúy qu'il a beu pour ceux qui nous obligent tant, pour les associez de la Compagnie de cette Nouvelle-France, desquels Dieu se veut servir pour sa gloire, pour Vostre Révérence, pour toute sa province et pour tous ceux qui coopèrent au salut de tant de pauvre âmes esgarées. Une petite gouttelette de ce divin calice nous enrichera tous. Et puis que mes prières sont trop foibles pour obtenir un si grand bien, je supplie Vostre Révérence d'interposer les siennes et celles encore de tant d'âmes sainctes qui sont dessous sa charge. Mais passons outre." MNF 2.451.

56 JR 5.203. "Je remerciay le mieux qu'il me fut possible monsieur de Champlain de la charité qu'il avoit exercée envers nos Pères, qui a esté très grande, comme me témoignoit le Père Brébeuf." MNF 2.452.

57 Author's translation (Thwaites' edition includes this variant in a bibliographical note, but does not include a translation). "Il me vient quelquefois en pensée que ce grand homme, qui par son admirable sagesse, et non pareille conduite ez affaires s'est tant acquis de renommée sur la terre, se prépare une couronne de gloire très éclatante dans le ciel, pour le soing qu'il tesmoigne avoir en la conversion de tant d'âmes que l'infidélité perd en ces pays sauvages. J'en prie tous les jours affectueusement pour luy, et nostre compagnie, ayant par son moyen occasion de glorifier Dieu en cette si noble entreprise, luy en aura une obligation éternelle." MNF 2.452, footnote.

58 On each side of the debate over the relationship between the manuscript copy and published version of the 1634 *Relation*, see Laflèche, *Le Missionnaire, l'Apostat, le Sorcier*, 226, and MNF 2.532–4. Campeau builds a convincing case, summarized here, that the manuscript and the published *Relation* are independently produced copies of another version of the *Relation*, perhaps the original manuscript.

59 JR 6.277. "Or si toutes ces chasses ne donnent point – ce qui n'arrive que trop souvent pour eux – ils souffrent grandement." MNF 2.617.

60 Author's translation (Thwaites' edition of the 1634 *Relation* does not include material from the handwritten copy that was deleted prior to publication. Translations of this and other such passages therefore are based on Campeau's edition): "La première, à peine en pouvois-je manger, ce qu'aiant tesmoigné par mesgarde, ne sçachant pas que c'estoit leur nectar, je fus bien relevé de sentinelle, car on me dit que j'estois un superbe, que je n'avois point d'esprit, que je ne sçavois pas ce qui estoit bon, que c'estoit un festin de capitaine. Ce sont les caresses des sauvages. Il les faut recevoir comme ilz les donnent, sans se fascher." MNF 2.618.

61 JR 7.7–9. Thwaites' original translation renders "que de vivre et de manger" as "except that of eating and drinking." The passage has been corrected to more closely reflect the original French. "Ils ne pensent qu'à vivre; ils mangent pour ne point mourir; ils se couvrent pour bannir le froid, non pour paroistre. La grâce, la bienséance, la connoissance des arts, les sciences naturelles, et beaucoup moins les véritez surnaturelles, n'ont point encore de logis en cet hémisphère, du moins en ces contrées. Ce peuple ne croit pas qu'il y ait autre science au monde que de vivre et de manger. Voilà toute leur philosophie." MNF 2.637. For a detailed reading of Le Jeune's comments as reproduced by Thwaites, without the deleted material, see Melzer, *Colonizer or Colonized*, 162–5.

62 JR 7.9. "tout est bon, pourveu qu'il soit bien chaud. Ils sont couverts proprement quand ils le sont commodément." MNF 2.638.

63 Author's translation. "Mais considérons-les revestus et ornez à leur mode. Commençons par le corps. Quelques-un pour l'embellir, voire mesme des femmes, tirent en quelques parties les plus visibles de leurs corps des rayes et figures indélébiles." MNF 2.639.

64 Author's translation. "Les plus riches et les plus magnifiques attachent parfois deux bandes de matachias à l'entour de leurs robbes. Ces bandes sont icy autant prisées qu'en France ces grands passements de Milan, ou plustost que ces passements d'or." MNF 2.642.

65 Marie de l'Incarnation, *Correspondance*, 803. Author's translation.

66 See, for example, Ted Cachey, *Petrarch's Guide to the Holy Land*, introduction. Cachey argues that Petrarch's precise directions for pilgrims to the Holy Land – a voyage the author never made himself – signal a need to reconsider the distinction between accounts of real and imaginary travel.

67 Pratt, "Modernity, Mobility, and Ex-Coloniality," 18.

68 As Pratt has observed, "The *study* of travel writing operates along the same often colonial lines of power that generate the metropolitan travel and travel writing themselves ... The scholar's account is licensed to repeat the sequential centripetal-centrifugal movement that sends the metropolitan subject forth to know the world and brings him and sometimes her back to tell about it, the movement that performs Europe's self-creation and self-understanding as a planetary center, *the* planetary center." Pratt, Modernity, Mobility, and Excoloniality," 18. Emphasis in original. A revised version of Pratt's article appears in the 2008 second edition of her influential book *Imperial Eyes*, but regrettably does not include her insightful comments on the relationship between travel and travel scholarship. Christine Montalbetti has also traced the links between travel and travel criticism. See Montalbetti, *Le Voyage, le Monde, et la Bibliothèque*, especially pages 105–8.

CONCLUSION

1 As one scholar summarized, "A French book bearing the privilege of the Propaganda would have been refused the right of publication" by the French Crown. Wroth, "The *Jesuit Relations* from New France," 132. For more see Donnelly, *Thwaites' Jesuit Relations: Errata and Addenda*, 4–5.

2 This silencing of the Jesuits' voice from New France seems to have been acutely felt by readers in France. King Louis XIV of France himself reportedly expressed dismay at the discontinuation of the annual series through the intermediary of his confessor. In his nineteenth-century three-tome history of Jesuit activity in New France, Camille de Rochemonteix, himself a Jesuit, cited a seventeenth-century letter reportedly written by Father François de la Chaise, then royal confessor, to Jesuit official Gian Paolo Olivia, asking why publication of the annual New France *Relations* had ceased. Wrote the priest, "Now, we have a very Christian king ... who is very persuaded that the *Relations* will be everywhere very useful to French colonies; they are insistently requested by all those who deeply desire progress in our colonies, the propagation of the Faith and the French name." Rochemonteix, *Les Jésuites et la Nouvelle-France au XVIIe Siècle*, vol. I, LIV. Author's translation.

3 On the publication history of the *Relations*, see True, "Is It Time for a New Edition of the Jesuit Relations from New France?"; Donnelly, *Thwaites' Jesuit Relations: Errata and Addenda*, introduction; and Pouliot, *Etude sur les Relations des Jésuites*. More information on the various formats in which the texts today are available can be found in True, "The Jesuit Relations."

4 From the seventeenth century onward, the New France Jesuits have occasionally been suspected of focusing more on extraction of material wealth than on

converting Amerindians. In 1672, the Comte de Frontenac, governor of New France, icily declared that the Jesuits were more interested in converting beavers than souls, and George T. Hunt's influential 1940 book *The Wars of the Iroquois* labelled the priests mere "clerks of the fur trade." These accusations now appear to be generally specious. On the history of Jesuit involvement in commercial enterprises in New France as well as the history of perceptions thereof, see Trigger, "The Jesuits and the Fur Trade."

5 Ouellet and Tremblay, "From the Good Savage to the Degenerate Indian," 162. For a good discussion of these dualistic descriptions of Amerindians, see Berkhofer, *The White Man's Indian*.

6 See MNF 3.699.

7 Tooker, *An Ethnography of the Huron Indians*, 34–9; Trigger, *The Children of Aataentsic*, 441n45, 73; Knowles, "The Torture of Captives by the Indians of Eastern North America," 181–5; Sanday, *Divine Hunger*, 141–2.

8 As Walter Mignolo has pointed out, a similar principle is at work in studying indigenous languages and in writing down Amerindian oral knowledge: "When a situation such as this arises in which the act of writing the history of a community means both suppressing the possibility that community may be heard and not trusting the voice of the 'others,' we are witnessing a good example of the colonization of discursive genres (or types). The case seems to be similar to that of writing grammars. While in one case, grammars take the place of the native implicit organization of languages, writing histories takes the place of native explicit organization of past oral expression and nonalphabetic forms of writing. In the first case, an implicit knowledge is ignored; in the second, an explicit knowledge is being rewritten." Mignolo, *Local Histories / Global Designs*, 259.

WORKS CITED

Abé, Takao. *The Jesuit Mission to New France: A New Interpretation in Light of the Earlier Jesuit Experience in Japan.* Leiden, Netherlands: Brill, 2011.

Abler, Thomas S. "Iroquois Cannibalism: Fact Not Fiction." *Ethnohistory* 27, no. 4 (1980): 309–16.

Abley, Mark. "No One Alive Speaks Huron Fluently. Now the Hurons of Wendake Hope They Can Bring It Back from the Dead." *Montreal Gazette*, 13 June 1992.

Alexander, Hartley Burr. *North American: The Mythology of All Races.* Edited by Louis H. Gray. Boston: Marshall Jones Company, 1936.

Anderson, Emma. *The Betrayal of Faith: The Tragic Journey of a Colonial Native Convert.* Cambridge, MA: Harvard University Press, 2007.

Anderson, Karen. *Chain Her by One Foot: The Subjugation of Women in Seventeenth-Century New France.* London: Routledge, 1991.

Arciniegas, Germán. *America in Europe: A History of the New World in Reverse.* Translated by Gabriela Arciniegas and R. Victoria Arana. San Diego, CA: Harcourt Brace Jovanovich, 1986.

Arens, William. *The Man-Eating Myth: Anthropology and Anthropophagy.* New York: Oxford University Press, 1979.

Atkinson, Geoffroy. *Les Relations de Voyages du XVIIe Siècle et l'Evolution des Idées; Contribution à l'Etude de la Formation de l'Esprit du XVIIIe Siècle.* Paris: Champion, 1924.

Axtell, James. "Babel of Tongues: Communicating with the Indians in Eastern North America." In *The Language Encounter in the Americas, 1492–1800*, edited by Norman Fiering and Edward G. Gray. New York: Berghahn Books, 2000.

– *The Invasion Within: The Contest of Cultures in Colonial North America.* New York: Oxford University Press, 1985.

Bailey, Alfred G. *The Conflict of European and Eastern Algonquian Cultures, 1504–1700.* 2nd ed. Toronto: University of Toronto Press, 1969.

Beaulieu, Alain. *Convertir les Fils de Caïn: Jésuites et Amérindiens Nomades en Nouvelle-France, 1632–1642.* Montreal, QC: Nuit Blanche Editeur, 1990.

Beaulieu, André. *La Première Bibliothèque Canadienne: La Bibliothèque des Jésuites de la Nouvelle France, 1632–1800 / The First Canadian Library: The Library of the Jesuit College of New France*. Ottawa: Bibliothèque Nationale du Canada, 1972.

Beresford, Bruce, dir. *Black Robe*. Santa Monica, CA: Metro Goldwyn Mayer, 1991.

Berkhofer, Robert. *The White Man's Indian: Images of the American Indian from Columbus to the Present*. New York: Knopf, 1978.

Biron, Johanne. "Les Livres que les Missionaires de la Compagnie de Jésus Ont Apportés avec Eux en Nouvelle-France: Ecrire l'Histoire d'une Bibliothèque jésuite." In *De l'Orient à la Huronie: Du Récit de Pèlerinage au Texte Missionnaire*, edited by Guy Poirier, Marie-Christine Gomez-Géraud, and François Paré, 165–84. Quebec: Presses de l'Université Laval, 2011.

Bitterli, Urs. *Cultures in Conflict: Encounters Between European and Non-European Cultures, 1492–1800*. Translated by Ritchie Robertson. Cambridge: Polity Press, 1989.

Blackburn, Carole. *Harvest of Souls: The Jesuit Missions and Colonialism in North America, 1632–1650*. Montreal, QC: McGill-Queen's University Press, [2000] 2004.

Boschet, Antoine. *Le parfait missionnaire; Ou, la vie du R.P. Julien Maunoir, la compagnie de Jésus, missionnaire en Bretagne*. Paris: Jean Anisson, 1697.

Brandão, José. *'Your Fyre Shall Burn No More': Iroquois Policy toward New France and Its Native Allies to 1701*. Lincoln: University of Nebraska Press, 1997.

Brazeau, Brian. *Writing a New France, 1604–1632: Empire and Early Modern French Identity*. Farnham, UK: Ashgate, 2009.

Brébeuf, Jean de. "Doctrine Chrestienne du R.P. Ledesme de la Compagnie de Jesus Traduit en Langue Canadois par le R.P. Breboeuf de la Mesme Compagnie." *Les Voyages de la Nouvelle France Occidentale, Dicte Canada Faits par le Sr de Champlain*. Paris: Claude Collet, 1632.

Brodeur, Raymond. *Catéchisme et Identité Culturelle dans le Diocese de Québec de 1815*. Sainte-Foy, QC: Presses de l'Université Laval, 1998.

– ed. *Les Catéchismes au Québec 1702–1963*. Sainte-Foy, QC: Presses de l'Université Laval, 1990.

Cachey, Ted, ed. *Petrarch's Guide to the Holy Land*. Notre Dame, IN: University of Notre Dame Press, 2002.

Campbell, Mary Baine. *Wonder and Science: Imagining Worlds in Early Modern Europe*. Ithaca, NY: Cornell University Press, 1999.

– *The Witness and the Other World: Exotic European Travel Writing, 400–1600*. Ithaca, NY: Cornell University Press, 1988.

Campeau, Lucien, ed. *Monumenta Novae Franciae*. 9 vols. Rome: Monumenta Hist. Soc. Jesu, 1967–2003.

– "Notre-Dame-Des-Anges." *Lettres du Bas-Canada* 8 (1954): 95–105.

– "Autour de la relation du P. Pierre Biard." *Revue de l'Histoire de l'Amérique Française* 6, no. 4 (1953): 517–35.

Carayon, Auguste. *Bibliographie Historique de la Compagnie de Jésus: Ou Catalogue des Ouvrages Relatifs à L'histoire des Jésuites Depuis Leur Origine Jusqu'à Nos Jours* (1846). Geneva, Switzerland: Slatkine Reprints, [1846] 1970.

Carile, Paolo. *Le Regard Entravé: Littérature et Anthropologie dans les Premiers Textes sur la Nouvelle France*. Sillery, QC: Septentrion, [1987] 2000.

Carter, Karen E. *Creating Catholics: Catechism and Primary Education in Early Modern France*. Notre Dame, IN: University of Notre Dame Press, 2011.

Cartier, Jacques. *Relations*. Edited by Michel Bideaux. Montreal, QC: Presses de l'Université de Montréal, 1986.

Chafe, Wallace. "The Earliest European Encounters with Iroquoian Languages." In *Decentring the Renaissance: Canada and Europe in Multidisciplinary Perspective 1500–1700*, edited by Germaine Warkentin and Carolyn Podruchny, 252–61. Toronto: University of Toronto Press, 2001.

Champlain, Samuel de. *The Voyages and Exploration of Samuel de Champlain*. Translated by Annie Nettleton Bourne. New York: Allerton Book Company, 1922.

– *Les Voyages de la Nouvelle France Occidentale, Dicte Canada Faits par le Sieur de Champlain*. Paris: Claude Collet, 1632.

Charlevoix, Pierre de. *Histoire et Description Générale de la Nouvelle France Avec le Journal Historique d'un Voyage Fait par Ordre du Roi dans l'Amérique Septentionale*. 3 vols. Paris: Pierre-François Giffert, 1774.

Chinard, Gilbert. *L'Amérique et le Rêve Exotique dans la Littérature Française au XVIIe et XVIIIe Siècle*. Paris: Hachette, 1913.

Citton, Yves. *Lire, Interpréter, Actualiser: Pourquoi les Etudes Littéraires?* Paris: Amsterdam, 2007.

Clifford, James. *The Predicament of Culture: Twentieth-Century Ethnography, Literature and Art*. Cambridge, MA: Harvard University Press, 1998.

– *Routes: Travel and Translation in the Late 20th Century*. Cambridge, MA: Harvard University Press, 1997.

– "Introduction." In *Writing Culture: The Poetics and Politics of Ethnography*, edited by James Clifford and George Marcus, 1–26. Berkeley, CA: University of California Press, 1986.

Codignola, Luca. "Jesuit Writings According to R.G. Thwaites and Lucien Campeau, SJ: How Do They Differ?" In *Little Do We Know: History and Historians of the North Atlantic, 1492–2010*, edited by Matteo Binasco. Cagliari,

Italy: Istituto di Storia dell'Europa Mediterranea del Consiglio Nazionale delle Ricerche, 2011.

— "Few, Uncooperative, and Ill-Informed? The Roman Catholic Clergy in French and British North America, 1610–1658." In *Decentring the Renaissance: Canada and Europe in Multidisciplinary Perspective, 1500–1700*, edited by Germaine Warkentin and Carolyn Podruchny, 173–85. Toronto: University of Toronto Press, 2004.

— "The Battle Is Over: Campeau's Monumenta vs. Thwaites's Jesuit Relations, 1602–1650." *European Review of Native American Studies* 10, no. 2 (1996): 3–10.

— "The Holy See and the Conversion of the Indians in French and British North America, 1486–1760." In *America in European Consciousness, 1493–1750*, edited by Karen Ordahl Kupperman, 195–242. Chapel Hill, NC, and London: The University of North Carolina Press for the Institute of Early American History and Culture, 1995.

Cushner, Nicholas P. *Why Have You Come Here?: The Jesuits and the First Evangelization of Native America*. Oxford, UK: Oxford University Press, 2006.

Dainville, François de. *L'Education des Jésuites (XVIIe–XVIIIe Siècles)*. Paris: Editions de Minuit, 1978.

Deffain, Dominique. *Un Voyageur Français en Nouvelle-France au XVIIe Siècle: Etude Littéraire des Relations du Père Paul Lejeune (1632–1641)*. Tübingen, Germany: Max Niemeyer Verlag, 1995.

Delâge, Denys. *Bitter Feast: Amerindians and Europeans in Northeastern North America 1600–1664*. Translated by Jane Brierly. Vancouver: University of British Columbia Press, 1993.

Delgado, L. Elena, and Rolando J. Romero. "Local Histories and Global Designs: An Interview with Walter Mignolo." *Discourse* 22, no. 3 (2000): 7–33.

Deslandres, Dominique. *Croire et Faire Croire: Les Missions Françaises au XVIIe Siècle*. Paris: Fayard, 2003.

Doiron, Normand. *L'Art de Voyager: Le Déplacement à l'Epoque Classique*. Sainte-Foy, QC: Presses de l'Université Laval, 1995.

— "Discours sur l'Origine des Amériquains." In *Figures de l'Indien*, edited by Gilles Thérien, 46–60. Montreal, QC: Typo, 1995.

— "Genèse de l'Eloquence Sauvage: La Renaissance Française de Tacite." In *La Recherche Littéraire: Objets et Méthodes*, edited by Claude Vachon and Claude Duchet, 173–82. Montreal, QC: XYZ Editeur, 1993.

— "Rhétorique Jésuite de l'Eloquence Sauvage au XVIIe Siècle: Les Relations de Paul Lejeune (1632–1642)." *XVIIe Siècle* 173 (1991): 375–402.

— "L'Art de Voyager: Pour une Définition du Récit de Voyage à l'Epoque Classique." *Poétique* 73 (1988): 83–108.

Donnelly, Joseph P., S.J. *Thwaites' Jesuit Relations: Errata and Addenda*. Chicago: Loyola University Press, 1967.

Dorsey, Peter. "Going to School with Savages: Authorship and Authority among the Jesuits of New France." *The William and Mary Quarterly* 55, no. 3 (1998): 399–420.

Drolet, Antonio. "La Bibliothèque du Collège des Jésuites." *Revue de l'Histoire de l'Amérique Française* 14, no. 4 (1961): 487–544.

– "Les Ouvrages de Médecine à la Residence des Jésuites de Québec 1632–1798." *Laval Médical* 22 (1957): 688–99.

Dubois, Laurent M. "The *Jesuit Relations*." In *A New Literary History of America*, edited by Greil Marcus and Werner Sollers, 50–4. Cambridge, MA: The Belknap Press of Harvard University Press, 2009.

Duchet, Michèle. *Anthropologie et Histoire au Siècle des Lumières*. Paris: Albin Michel, [1971] 1995.

Dundes, Alan. "Earth-Diver: Creation of the Mythopoeic Male." In *The Meaning of Folklore: The Analytical Essays of Alan Dundes*, edited by Simon J. Logan Bronner, 325–42. Logan, UT: Utah State University Press, 2007.

Eccles, W.J. *The French in North America, 1500–1783*. Markham, ON: Fitzhenry and Whiteside, 1998.

Edict du Roy Pour L'establissement de la Compagnie de la Nouvelle France Avec l'Arrest de Verification de la Cour de Parlement de Paris. Paris: Cramoisy, 1657.

Eliade, Mircea. *Myth and Reality*. Translated by Willard R. Trask. New York: Harper and Row, 1963.

Elliott, J.H. *The Old World and the New 1492–1650*. Cambridge: Cambridge University Press, 1970.

Fabian, Johannes. *Time and the Other: How Anthropology Makes Its Object*. New York: Columbia University Press, 1983.

Farrell, Alan P., S.J. *The Jesuit Ratio Studiorum of 1599*. Washington, DC: Conference of Major Superiors of Jesuits, 1970.

Fenton, William N. "Lafitau, Joseph-François." In *Dictionary of Canadian Biography Online*. Accessed 25 August 2008. http://www.biographi.ca/en/bio/lafitau_joseph_francois_3E.html

Filion, Pierre-Emile. "La Première Bibliothèque Canadienne: Le Collège des Jésuites à Québec; Historique et Contribution à l'Inventaire du Fonds." In *Livre, Bibliothèque et Culture Québécoise: Mélanges Offerts à Edmond Desroches, SJ*, edited by Georges A. Chartrand, 273–98. Montreal, QC: ASTED, 1977.

Flinn, Frank K. *Encyclopedia of Catholicism*. New York: Facts on File, 2007.

Fontaine, Jean-Louis. *Croyances et Rituels Chez les Innus, 1603–1650*. Quebec: Les Editions GID, 2006.

Foucault, Michel. "Des Espaces Autres." In *Dits et Ecrits: 1954–1988*, 752–62. Paris: Gallimard, 1994.

Franks, C.E.S. "In Search of the Savage *Sauvage:* An Exploration of North America's Political Cultures." *American Review of Canadian Studies* 32, no. 4 (2002): 547–80.

Frisch, Andrea. *The Invention of the Eyewitness: Witnessing and Testimony in Early Modern France*. Chapel Hill, NC: University of North Carolina Press, 2004.

Furetière, Antoine. *Dictionnaire Universel, contenant généralement tous les mots françois tant vieux que modernes, et les termes de toutes les sciences et des arts*. The Hague and Rotterdam, Netherlands: A. et R. Leers, 1690.

Gagnon, François-Marc. *La Conversion par l'Image: Un Aspect de la Mission des Jésuites auprès des Indiens du Canada au XVIIe Siècle*. Montreal, QC: Les Editions Bellarmin, 1975.

Galland, Caroline. *Pour la Gloire de Dieu et du Roi: Les Récollets en Nouvelle-France au XVIIe et XVIIIe Siècles*. Paris: Cerf, 2012.

Garraway, Doris. *The Libertine Colony: Creolization in the Early French Caribbean*. Durham, NC: Duke University Press, 2005.

Geertz, Clifford. *The Interpretation of Cultures*. New York: Basic Books, 1973.

Gliozzi, Giuliano. *Adam et le Nouveau Monde: La Naissance de l'Anthropologie comme Idéologie Coloniale: Des Généalogies Bibliques aux Théories Raciales (1500–1700)*. Translated by Arlette Estève and Pascal Gabellone. Lecques, France: Théétète Editions, [1977] 2000.

Goddard, Peter. "Two Kinds of Conversion ('Medieval' and 'Modern') among the Hurons of New France." In *The Spiritual Conversion of the Americas*, edited by James Muldoon, 57–77. Gainesville, FL: University Press of Florida, 2004.

– "Canada in Seventeenth-Century Jesuit Thought: Backwater or Opportunity?" In *Decentring the Renaissance: Canada and Europe in Multidisciplinary Perspective, 1500–1700*, edited by Germaine Warkentin and Carolyn Podruchny, 186–99. Toronto: University of Toronto Press, 2001.

– "Converting the 'Sauvage': Jesuit and Montagnais in Seventeenth-Century New France." *The Catholic Historical Review* 84, no. 2 (1998): 219–39.

Gray, Edward G. *New World Babel: Languages and Nations in Early America*. Princeton, NJ: Princeton University Press, 1999.

Greenblatt, Stephen. *Marvelous Possessions: The Wonder of the New World*. Chicago: University of Chicago Press, 1991.

Greer, Allan. *Mohawk Saint: Catherine Tekawitha and the Jesuits*. New York: Oxford University Press, 2005.

– ed. *The Jesuit Relations: Natives and Missionaries in Seventeenth-Century North America*. Boston: Bedford/St. Martin's, 2000.

Grégoire, Vincent. "L'Iroquois est un Loup pour l'Homme, ou la Difficulté de 'Convertir les Loups en Agneaux' dans les Ecrits des Missionnaires de Nouvelle-France au Dix-septième Siècle." *Québec Studies* 54 (2012/2013): 17–30.

– "Mais Comment Peut-on Etre Protestant en Nouvelle-France au 17e Siècle?" *Seventeenth-Century French Studies* 31, no. 1 (2009): 46–58.

– "'Pensez-vous Venir à bout de Renverser le Pays': La Pratique d'Evangélisation en Nouvelle-France d'après les *Relations* des Jésuites." *XVIIe Siècle* 50, no. 4 (1998): 681–707.

– "Les 'Réductions' de Nouvelle-France: Une Illustration de la Pratique Missionnaire Jésuite." *XVIIe Siècle* 49, no. 3 (1997): 519–30.

Hanzeli, Victor E. *Missionary Linguistics in New France: A Study of Seventeenth- and Eighteenth-Century Descriptions of American Indian Languages.* The Hague, Netherlands: Mouton, 1969.

Harbsmeier, Michael. "Spontaneous Ethnographies: Towards a Social History of Travellers' Tales." *Studies in Travel Writing* 1 (1997): 216–38.

Harndon, John A., S.J. "Secular Clergy." *Modern Catholic Dictionary.* Garden City, NJ: Doubleday, 1980.

Harrod, Howard L. "Missionary Life World and Native Response: Jesuits in New France." *Studies in Religion* 13, no. 2 (1984): 170–92.

Havard, Gilles, and Cecile Vidal. *Histoire de l'Amérique Française.* Paris: Flammarion, [2003] 2006.

Hazard, Paul. *The European Mind, 1680–1715.* Translated by J. Lewis May. Cleveland, OH: World Publishing Co., 1963.

Healy, George. "The French Jesuits and the Idea of the Noble Savage." *The William and Mary Quarterly* 15, no. 2 (1958): 143–67.

Heidenreich, Conrad. *Huronia: A History and Geography of the Huron Indians 1600–1650.* Toronto: McLelland and Steward, 1971.

Hennepin, Louis. *A New Discovery of a Vast Country in America.* Edited by Reuben Gold Thwaites. Chicago: A.C. McClury and Company, 1903.

– *Nouveau Voyage d'Un Pays Plus Grand Que l'Europe: Avec les Reflections des Entreprises du Sieur de la Salle, sur les Mines de St. Barbe, et Enrichi de la Carte, de Figures Expressives, des Moeurs et Manières de Vivre des Sauvages du Nord et du Sud Avec Approbation et Dédié à Sa Majesté Guillaume III Roy de la Grande Bretagne.* Utrecht, Netherlands: A. Schouten, 1698.

Holy Bible with Apocryphal and Deuterocanonical Books, New Revised Standard Version. New York: American Bible Society, 1989.

Huddleston, Lee Aldridge. *Origins of the American Indians: European Conceptions, 1492–1729.* Austin: University of Texas Press, 1967.

Hulme, Peter. "Introduction: The Cannibal Scene." In *Cannibalism and the Colonial World,* edited by Peter Hulme, Francis Barker, and Margaret Iversen, 1–38. Cambridge: Cambridge University Press, 1998.

Hunt, George T. *The Wars of the Iroquois: A Study in Intertribal Relations*. Madison: University of Wisconsin Press, 1940.

Innis, Harold A. *The Fur Trade in Canada: An Introduction to Canadian Economic History*. New Haven, CT: Yale University Press, 1930.

Jaenen, Cornelius J. "The Image of New France: Real and Imaginary." *Australian Journal of French Studies* 31, no. 2 (1994): 161–74.

– *Friend and Foe: Aspects of French-Amerindian Cultural Contact in the Sixteenth and Seventeenth Centuries*. New York: Columbia University Press, 1976.

Jauss, Hans Robert. *Question and Answer: Forms of Dialogic Understanding*. Translated by Michael Hays. Minneapolis, MN: University of Minnesota Press, 1989.

Jetten, Marc. *Enclaves Amérindiennes: "Les Réductions" du Canada 1637–1701*. Sillery, QC: Septentrion, 1994.

Jouve, Odoric. *Dictionnaire Biographique des Récollets Missionnaires en Nouvelle-France*. Saint-Laurent, QC: Bellarmin, 1996.

– "Le P Joseph Leclerc du Tremblay, Capuchin et les Missions de la Nouvelle France." *Bulletin des Recherches Historiques* 45, no. 5 (1939): 129–43, 164–77.

Kennedy, J.H. *Jesuit and Savage in New France*. New Haven, CT: Yale University Press, 1950.

"Kentucky Creation Museum Opens to Thousands." Associated Press, 29 May 2007.

Knowles, Nathanial. "The Torture of Captives by the Indians of Eastern North America." *Proceedings of the American Philosophical Society* 82, no. 2 (1940): 151–225.

Kupperman, Karen, ed. *America in European Consciousness 1493–1750*. Chapel Hill, NC: University of North Carolina Press, 1995.

Lafitau, Joseph-François. *Customs of the American Indians Compared with the Customs of Primitive Times*. Translated by William Fenton and Elizabeth Moore. Toronto: The Champlain Society, 1974.

– *Moeurs des Sauvages Ameriquains, Comparées aux Moeurs des Premiers Temps*. 2 vols. Paris: Chez Saugrain l'aîné, 1724.

Laflèche, Guy. *Les Saints Martyrs Canadiens: Histoire du Mythe*. Laval, QC: Singulier, 1988.

– ed. *Le Missionaire, l'Apostat, le Sorcier: Relation de 1634 de Paul Le Jeune*. By Paul Le Jeune. Montreal, QC: Presses de l'Université de Montréal, [1634] 1973.

Lagarde, Pierrette. *Le Verbe Huron: Etude Morphologique d'Après Une Description Grammaticale de la Seconde Moitié du Dix-septième Siècle*. Paris: L'Harmattan, 1980.

Lahontan, Baron de. *New Voyages to North America, Giving a Full Account of the Customs, Commerce, Religion, and Strange Opinions of the Savages of That*

Country. With Political Remarks Upon the Courts of Portugal and Denmark, and the Present State of the Commerce of Those Countries. London: H. Bonwicke, 1703.

– *Nouveaux Voyages de M. Le Baron de Lahontan dans l'Amérique Septentrionale.* The Hague, Netherlands: Les Frères L'Honoré, 1703.

Leavelle, Tracy Neal. *The Catholic Calumet: Colonial Conversions in French and Indian North America.* Philadelphia: University of Pennsylvania Press, 2012.

Le Bras, Yvon. "Les *Relations* du Père Jean de Brébeuf en Huronie: Ecriture Missionnaire et Ethnographie." In *De l'Orient à la Huronie: Du Récit de Pèlerinage au Texte Missionnaire*, edited by Guy Poirier, Marie-Christine Gomez, and François Paré, 139–48. Quebec: Presses de l'Université Laval, 2011.

– *L'Amérindien dans les Relations du Père Paul Lejeune (1632–1641).* Sainte-Foy, QC: Les Editions de la Huit, 1994.

Le Clercq, Chrestien. *First Establishment of the Faith in New France.* 2 vols. Translated by John Gilmary Shea. New York: John G. Shea, 1881.

Leahey, Margaret J. "Iconic Discourse: The Language of Images in Seventeenth-Century New France." In *The Language Encounter in the Americas, 1492–1800*, edited by Norman Fiering and Edward G. Gray, 102–18. New York: Berghahn Books, 2000.

– "'Comment Peut un Muet Prescher l'Evangile?': Jesuit Missionaries and the Native Languages of New France." *French Historical Studies* 19, no. 1 (1995): 105–31.

– "To Hear With My Eyes: The Native Language Acquisition Project in the *Jesuit Relations.*" PhD dissertation. Baltimore, MD: Johns Hopkins University, 1991.

Lenhart, John M. "Who Kept the Franciscan Recollets out of Canada?" *Franciscan Studies* 26, no. 3 (1945): 277–300.

Lescarbot, Marc. *Histoire de la Nouvelle-France.* Paris: Adrian Perier, 1617.

Lestringant, Frank. *Cannibals: The Discovery and Representation of the Cannibal from Columbus to Jules Verne.* Translated by Rosemary Morris. Berkeley, CA: University of California Press, 1997.

"Local Woman's Effort May Resurrect Classic Tlingit Reference." *Chilkat Valley News*, 24 January 2002.

Longino, Michèle. *Orientalism in French Classical Drama.* Cambridge: Cambridge University Press, 2002.

Loyola, Ignatius. *The Constitutions of the Society of Jesus.* Translated by George E. Ganss, S.J. St. Louis, MO: Institute of Jesuit Sources, 1970.

Magocsi, Paul R., ed. *Encyclopedia of Canada's Peoples.* Toronto: University of Toronto Press, 1999.

Malinowski, Bronislaw. *Argonauts of the Western Pacific*. Long Grove, IL: Waveland Press, [1922] 1984.

Marcus, George, and Michael Fischer. *Anthropology as Cultural Critique*. Chicago: University of Chicago Press, [1986] 1999.

Marie de l'Incarnation. *Correspondance*. Edited by Dom Guy Oury. Solesmes, France: Abbaye Saint-Pierre, 1971.

Marmontel, Jean François. *Le Huron: Comédie en Deux Actes et en Vers*. Paris: Merlin, 1772.

McCabe, William H. *An Introduction to the Jesuit Theatre*. Edited by Louis J. Oldani. St. Louis, MO: The Institute of Jesuit Sources, 1983.

McCoy, James C. *The Jesuit Relations of Canada, 1632–1673*. Paris: Arthur Rau, 1937.

McShea, Bronwen. *Cultivating Empire Through Print: The Jesuit Strategy for New France and the Parisian "Relations" of 1632–1673*. PhD dissertation. New Haven, CT: Yale University, 2011.

Melzer, Sara E. *Colonizer or Colonized: The Hidden Stories of Early Modern French Culture*. Philadelphia: University of Pennsylvania Press, 2012.

– "Une 'Seconde France'? Repenser le Paradigme 'Classique' à Partir de l'Histoire Oubliée de la Colonisation Française." In *La Littérature, le XVIIe Siècle et Nous: Dialogue Transatlantique*, edited by Hélène Merlin-Kajman, 75–84. Paris: Presses Sorbonne Nouvelle, 2008.

– "The Relation de Voyage: A Forgotten Genre of Seventeenth-Century France." In *Relations and Relationships in Seventeenth-Century French Literature: Actes du 36e Congrès de la* North American Society for Seventeenth-Century French Literature, edited by Jennifer Perlmutter, 33–52. Tübingen, Germany: Gunter Narr Verlag, 2006.

– "The French Relation and Its 'Hidden' Colonial History." In *A Companion to the Literature of Colonial America*, edited by Susan Castillo and Ivy Schweitzer, 220–40. Malden, MA: Blackwell, 2005.

Mignolo, Walter. *The Darker Side of the Renaissance: Literacy, Territoriality, and Colonization*. Ann Arbor, MI: University of Michigan Press, [1995] 2003.

– *Local Histories / Global Designs: Coloniality, Subaltern Knowledges, and Border Thinking*. Princeton, NJ: Princeton University Press, 2000.

Millet, Olivier, and Philippe de Robert. *Culture Biblique*. Paris: Presses Universitaires de France, 2001.

Modern Catholic Encyclopedia. Edited by Michael Glazier and Monika K. Hellwig. Collegeville, MN: Liturgical Press, 2004.

Montaigne, Michel de. *Les Essais*. Edited by Pierre Villey. 3 vols. Paris: PUF, 1999.

Montalbetti, Christine. *Le Voyage, le Monde, et la Bibliothèque*. Paris: PUF, 1997.

Moore, Brian. *Black Robe*. New York: Plume, [1985] 1997.

Nicholls, Andrew D. *A Fleeting Empire: Early Stuart Britain and the Merchant Adventurers to Canada*. Montreal, QC, and Kingston, ON: McGill-Queen's University Press, 2010.

O'Malley, John W. *The First Jesuits*. Cambridge, MA: Harvard University Press, 1993.

Obeyesekere, Gananath. *The Apotheosis of Captain Cook: European Mythmaking in the Pacific*. Princeton, NJ: Princeton University Press, 1992.

Ong, Walter J. *The Presence of the Word: Some Prolegomena for Cultural and Religious History*. Binghampton, NY: Global Publications / Binghampton University, [1967] 2000.

Ouellet, Réal. *La Relation de Voyage en Amérique (XVI–XVIIIe Siècles): Au Carrefour des Genres*. Quebec: Presses de l'Université Laval, 2010.

– "Pour une Poétique de la Relation de Voyage." In *Ecrire des Récits de Voyage (XVe–XVIIIe siècles): Esquisse d'une Poétique en Gestation*, edited by Marie-Christine Pioffet, 17–40. Quebec: Presses de l'Université Laval, 2008.

– ed. *Rhétorique et Conquête Missionnaire: Le Jésuite Paul Lejeune*. Sillery, QC: Septentrion, 1993.

Ouellet, Réal, and Mylène Tremblay. "From the Good Savage to the Degenerate Indian." In *Decentring the Renaissance: Canada and Europe in Multidisciplinary Perspective*, edited by Germaine Warkentin and Carolyn Podruchny, 159–70. Toronto: University of Toronto Press, 2001.

Pagden, Anthony. *The Fall of Natural Man: The American Indian and the Origins of Comparative Ethnology*. Cambridge: Cambridge University Press, 1982.

Pariseau, Claude. *La Bibliothèque du Collège de Québec*. Montreal, QC: McGill Graduate School of Library Science, 1972.

Parkman, Francis. *The Jesuits in North America in the Seventeenth Century*. Boston: Little, Brown and Company, [1867] 1901.

Parmenter, Jon. *The Edge of the Woods: Iroquoia, 1534–1701*. East Lansing, MI: Michigan State University Press, 2010.

Paschoud, Adrien. "Puissance de l'Image et Efficacité de la Représentation: Le Theater d'Edification dans les Missions Jésuites d'Amérique Méridionale (XVIe–XVIIIe Siècles)." *The Irish Journal of French Studies* 4 (2004): 5–15.

Pioffet, Marie-Christine. "Présentation." In *Ecrire des Récits de Voyage (XVe–XVIIIe siècles): Esquisse d'une Poétique en Gestation*, edited by Marie-Christine Pioffet, 1–16. Quebec: Presses de l'Université Laval, 2008.

– *La Tentation de l'Epopée dans les Relations des Jésuites*. Sillery, QC: Septentrion, 1997.

Pouliot, Léon, S.J. "La Contribution de P. Paul Le Jeune aux Relations des Jésuites de 1650 à 1663." *Bulletin des Recherches Historiques* 68, no. 1 (1966): 49–53; 68, no. 2 (1966): 77–85; 68, no. 3 (1966): 131–5.

– *Etude sur les Relations des Jésuites de la Nouvelle-France (1632–1672)*. Paris: Des-clée de Brouwer, 1940.

Pratt, Mary Louise. *Imperial Eyes: Travel Writing and Transculturation*. London: Routledge, [1992] 2008.

– "Modernity, Mobility, and Excoloniality." In *Seuils et Traverses: Actes du Colloque de Brest*, vol. 1, edited by Jean-Yves Le Disez, 13–30. Brest, France: Centre du Recherche Bretonne et Celtique, 2002.

Relations des Jésuites Contenant Ce Qui S'est Passé de Plus Remarquable dans les Missions des Pères de la Compagnie de Jésus dans la Nouvelle-France. 3 vols. Quebec: A. Côté, 1858.

Requemora-Gros, Sylvie. *Voguer vers la Modernité: Le Voyage à Travers les Genres au XVIIe Siècle*. Paris: Presses de l'Université Paris-Sorbonne, 2012.

Réveillaud, Eugène, ed. *Histoire Chronologique de la Nouvelle France ou Canada Depuis Sa Découverte (Mil Cinq Cents Quatre) Jusques en l'An Mil Six Cents Trente Deux*. Montreal, QC: Elysée, [1888] 1975.

Richter, Daniel K. *The Ordeal of the Longhouse: The Peoples of the Iroquois League in the Era of European Colonization*. Chapel Hill, NC: University of North Carolina Press for the Institute of Early American History and Culture, 1992.

Rigault, Claude, and Réal Ouellet. "Relations des Jésuites." In *Dictionnaire des Oeuvres Littéraires du Québec*, edited by Maurice Lemire, 637–48. Montreal, QC: Fides, 1980.

Rochemonteix, Camille de. *Les Jésuites et la Nouvelle-France au XVIIe Siècle d'Après Beaucoup de Documents Inédits*. 3 vols. Paris: Letouzey et Ané, 1895.

Ross, Andrew C. *A Vision Betrayed: The Jesuits in Japan and China 1542–1742*. Maryknoll, NY: Orbis Books, 1994.

Rothstein, Edward. "Adam and Eve in the Land of the Dinosaurs." *The New York Times*, 24 May 2007.

Russell, Mary Doria. *Children of God*. New York: Villard, 1998.

– *The Sparrow*. New York: Fawcett Columbine, 1996.

Sagard, Gabriel. *Histoire du Canada et Voyages Que Les Frères Mineurs Recollects Y Ont Faicts Pour la Conversion des Infidelles*. Paris: Claude Sonnius, 1636.

– *Le Grand Voyage du Pays des Hurons, Suivi du Dictionnaire de la Langue Huronne*. Edited by Jack Warwick. Montreal, QC: Presses de l'Université de Montréal, [1632] 1998.

Sahlins, Marshall. *How "Natives" Think: About Captain Cook, For Example*. Chicago: University of Chicago Press, 1995.

Sanday, Peggy Reeves. *Divine Hunger: Cannibalism as a Cultural System*. Cambridge: Cambridge University Press, 1986.

Sayre, Gordon. *Les Sauvages Américains: Representations of Native Americans in French and English Colonial Literature*. Chapel Hill, NC: University of North Carolina Press, 1997.

Schreyer, Rüdiger. "Take Your Pen and Write: Learning Huron: A Documented Historical Sketch." In ... *And the Word Was God: Missionary Linguistics and Missionary Grammar*, edited by Even Hovdhaugen, 77–121. Münster, Germany: Nodus Publikationen, 1996.

Selwyn, Jennifer. *A Paradise Inhabited by Devils: The Jesuits' Civilizing Mission in Early Modern Naples*. Burlington, VT: Ashgate, 2004.

Silvy, Antoine. *Dictionnaire Montagnais-Français*. Edited by Lorenzo Angers, David E. Cooter, and Gérard E. McNulty. Montreal, QC: Presses de l'Université du Québec, 1974.

Sioui, Georges E. *Les Hurons-Wendats: Une Civilisation Méconnue*. Sainte-Foy, QC: Les Presses de l'Université Laval, [1994] 2004.

– *For an Amerindian Autohistory: An Essay on the Foundations of a Social Ethic*. Translated by Sheila Fischman. Montreal, QC: McGill-Queen's University Press, 1992.

Snow, Dean R. *The Iroquois*. Oxford, UK: Blackwell, 1994.

Speck, Frank G. "Montagnais and Naskapi Tales from the Labrador Peninsula." *The Journal of American Folklore* 38, no. 147 (1925): 1–32.

Starn, Orin. *Ishi's Brain: In Search of America's Last "Wild" Indian*. New York: Norton, [2004] 2005.

Steckley, John L. *Words of the Huron*. Waterloo, ON: Wilfred Laurier University Press, 2007.

– *De Religione: Telling the Seventeenth-Century Jesuit Story in Huron to the Iroquois*. Norman, OK: University of Oklahoma Press, 2004.

Switzer, John. "Evidence Shows Humans Were in America Earlier Than Thought." *Columbus Dispatch*, 27 March 2005.

Thompson, Stith. *Motif Index of Folk Literature: A Classification of Narrative Elements in Folktales, Ballads, Myths, Fables, Mediaeval Romances, Exempla, Fabliaux, Jest-books, and Local Legends*. 6 vols. Bloomington, IN: Indiana University Press, 1955.

Thwaites, Reuben Gold, ed. *The Jesuit Relations and Allied Documents: Travels and Explorations of the Jesuit Missionaries in New France 1610–1791*. 73 vols. Cleveland: Burrows Bros, 1896–1901.

Tooker, Elisabeth. *An Ethnography of the Huron Indians, 1615–1649*. Washington, DC: U.S. Government Printing Office, 1964.

Torrance, Thomas Forsyth. *The Trinitarian Faith*. London: T&T Clark, 1995.

Trigger, Bruce G. *The Children of Aataentsic: A History of the Huron People to 1660*. Montreal, QC: McGill-Queen's University Press, [1976] 2000.

– "The Jesuits and the Fur Trade," *Ethnohistory* 12, no. 1 (1965): 30–53.

True, Micah. "Is It Time for a New Edition of the Jesuit *Relations* from New France? Campeau vs. Thwaites." *Papers of the Bibliographical Society of Canada / Cahiers de la Société Bibliographique du Canada* 51, no. 2 (2014): 261–79.

– "Jesuit Relations." In *Oxford Bibliographies in American Literature*, edited by Jackson Bryer and Paul Lauter. New York: Oxford University Press, 2013.

– "'*Une Hierusalem Bénite de Dieu*': Utopia and Travel in the *Jesuit Relations* from New France." *Papers on French Seventeenth-Century Literature* 39, no. 76 (2012): 175–89.

– "Il Faut Parler Pour Estre Entendu: Talking about God in Wendat in Seventeenth-Century New France." *Cahiers du Dix-Septième* 12, no. 1 (2008): 17–36.

– "Retelling Genesis: The Jesuit Relations and the Wendat Creation Myth." *Papers on French Seventeenth-Century Literature* 34, no. 67 (2007): 465–84.

Van Den Abbeele, Georges. *Travel as Metaphor from Montaigne to Rousseau.* Minneapolis, MN: University of Minnesota Press, 1992.

Van Der Cruysse, Dirk. *Siam and the West, 1500–1700.* Translated by Michael Smithies. Chiang Mai, Thailand: Silkworm Books, 2002.

Verreau, H.A. "La Bibliothèque du Collège des Jésuites de Québec." *Bulletin des Recherches Historiques* 42, no. 6 (1936): 356–7.

Viau, Roland. *Enfants du Néant et Mangeurs des Ames: Guerre, Culture et Société en Iroquoisie Ancienne.* Montreal, QC: Boréal, 2000.

Warkentin, Germaine, and Carolyn Podruchny. "Introduction: Other Land Existing." In *Decentring the Renaissance: Canada and Europe in Multidisciplinary Perspective 1500–1700*, edited by Warkentin and Podruchny, 3–16. Toronto: University of Toronto Press, 2001.

White, Richard. *The Middle Ground: Indians, Empires, and Republics in the Great Lakes Region, 1650–1815.* Cambridge: Cambridge University Press, 1991.

Wroth, Lawrence. "The *Jesuit Relations* from New France." *The Papers of the Bibliographical Society of America* 30 (1936): 110–49.

Zemon-Davis, Nathalie. "Polarities, Hybridities: What Strategies for Decentring?" In *Decentring the Renaissance: Canada and Europe in Multidisciplinary Perspective 1500–1700*, edited by Germaine Warkentin and Carolyn Podruchny, 19–32. Toronto: University of Toronto Press, 2001.

Zupanov, Ines G. *Disputed Mission: Jesuit Experiments with Brahmanical Knowledge in Seventeenth-Century India.* New Delhi: Oxford University Press, 1999.

INDEX